Matters That Matter...

4,000 notable quotables and 900 relevant subject topics guaranteed to fertilize your mind and cultivate your life.

Compiled and Edited by
Daniel Taddeo

airleaf.com

ISBN: 1-60002-011-9

Library of Congress Catalog Card Number

Other books by Daniel Taddeo:
 Back to Basics
 Words of Wisdom
 Words of Wisdom, Too
 One Nation Without God
 Scripture Servings for Spiritual Strength
 Notable Quotables
To contact the author or place an order, write to:
 Back to Basics
 P.O. Box 30513
 Cleveland, OH 44130

CONTENTS

INTRODUCTION

The purpose of this book is to identify what eminent thinkers have to say about life and to help people better prepare themselves and their families to maximize their lives.

The 4,000 notable quotables that appear on these pages are far from exhaustive. However, they are, in my opinion, quotations that speak to the broadest scope of life with fewest words, from pre-birth to death and everything in between.

MATTERS THAT MATTER is an insightful and concise collection of quotes that focus on all the important aspects of living. It is through these priceless thoughts from an array of figures in history that the reader will come to terms with what truly matters in life.

It is my belief that the ten chapters with 900 relevant subject topics, arranged alphabetically, will truly fertilize your mind and cultivate your life to the fullest. "One of the greatest treasures is a collection of wise sayings and proverbs for sharpening the mind." -P. Toynbee, 1855-1932

A reasonable effort has been made to reference each quotation as to source or author. Those without a credit line are unknown to me at this time. Any omissions, upon notification, will be rectified in subsequent publications.

To all whose work, directly or indirectly, has contributed to making MATTERS THAT MATTER a reality, I express my sincere thanks and appreciation.

Daniel Taddeo

1.
AMERICA MATTERS

America

American youth attribute much more importance to arriving at drivers' license age than at voting age. *-Marshall McLuhan*

Americans have more timesaving devices and less time than any other group of people in the world. *-Duncan Caldwell*

As a great power, America has always seemed concerned with other peoples' welfare, especially in Europe. Twice in the 20th century, it saved the "Old World" from dictator and tyranny. *-Elie Wiesel, Nobel Prize in 1986*

Ask not what your country can do for you. Rather ask what you can do for your country. *-John F. Kennedy*

Blessed is the nation whose God is the Lord. *-Psalm 33:12*

Righteousness exalts a nation, but sin is a disgrace to any people. *-Proverbs 14:34*

The thing that impresses me most about America is the way the parents obey their children. *-Duke of Windsor*

Tyranny is always better organized than freedom. *-Charles Peguy, French Philosopher*

We've staked our future on our ability to follow the Ten Commandments with all our heart. *-James Madison*

Appeasement

No man can sit down and withhold his hands from the warfare against wrong and get peace from his acquiescence. *-Woodrow Wilson*

Authority

Authority is never without hate. *-Euripides 408 BC*

Lawful and settled authority is very seldom resisted when it is well employed. *-Samuel Johnson*

Brevity

There is too much speaking in the world, and almost all of it is too long. The Lord's Prayer, the Twenty-third Psalm, and Lincoln's Gettysburg Address are three great literary treasures that will last forever; no one of them is as long as three hundred words. With such striking illustrations of the power of brevity it is amazing that speakers never learn to be brief. *-Bruce Barton*

Budget

As quickly as you start spending federal money in large amounts, it looks like free money. *- Dwight D. Eisenhower*

In general, the art of government consists in taking as much money possible from one part of the citizens to give to the other. *-Voltaire*

Bureaucracy

The perfect bureaucrat everywhere is the man who manages to make no decisions and escape all responsibility. *-Brooks Atkinson*

Capitalism

The inherent vice of capitalism is the unequal sharing of blessings; the inherent virtue of socialism is the equal sharing of misery. *-Sir Winston Churchill*

Censorship

No government ought to be without censors; and where press is free, no one ever will. *-Thomas Jefferson*

Certainty

Every area of trouble gives out a ray of hope, and the one unchangeable certainty is that nothing is certain or unchangeable. *-John F. Kennedy*

Challenge

The challenge facing the Supreme Court of the United States today is whether the Constitution fits into the governing documents of other nations. *- Supreme Court Justice Stephen Breyer*

Change

Never doubt that a small group of thoughtful, committed citizens can change the world. Indeed, it is the only thing that ever has. *-Anthropologist, Margaret Mead*

Church

If this nation is going to remain free and strong, I think churches have an obligation to talk about issues. *-U.S. Representative Walter B. Jones of North Carolina*

The church must be reminded that it is not the master or the server of the state, but rather the conscience of the state. *-Martin Luther King Jr.*

Citizenship

Citizenship is one of the most crucial issues in our society today. *-Michael Schwartz, president of Cleveland State University*

The first requisite of a good citizen in this republic of ours is that he shall be able and willing to pull his weight. *-Theodore Roosevelt*

Civility

If we are to prevail as a free, self-governing people, we must first govern our tongues and our pens. Restoring civility to public discourse is not an option. It is a necessity. *-Edwin J. Feulner, President of Heritage Foundation*

Civilization

Civilization is a stream with banks. The stream is sometimes filled with blood from people killing, stealing, shouting, and doing the things historians usually record; while on the banks, unnoticed, people build homes, make love, raise children, sing songs, write poetry, and even whittle statues. The story of civilization is the story of what happened on the banks. *-Will Durant*

Communism

Communism works only in Heaven, where they don't need it, and in Hell, where they already have it. *-President Ronald Reagan*

Competence

The single most exciting thing you encounter in government is competence, because it is so rare. *-Daniel Patrick Moynihan*

Conduct

I believe that every right implies a responsibility; every opportunity, an obligation; every possession, a duty. *-John D. Rockefeller Jr.*

Conservation

The Nation behaves well if it treats the natural resources as assets which it must turn over to the next generation increased, and not impaired, in value. *-Theodore Roosevelt*

Conservative

The true conservative is the man who has a real concern for injustices and takes thought against the day of reckoning. -*Franklin Roosevelt*

Consistency

It is not best to swap horses while crossing the river. -*Abraham Lincoln*

Constitution

The Supreme Court is the greatest single threat to the Constitution. -*Senator James Eastland*

Constitution of the United States

"Separation of Church and State" is not constitutional- it is erroneous. The Founding Fathers never used the phrase. The First Amendment does say "Congress shall make no law respecting an establishment of religion, or prohibiting the free exercise thereof." -*Supreme Court Justice Antonin Scalia*

Crime

America's prison population is higher than any other country and continues to swell. One in every 138 U.S. residents is in prison or jail. In 2004, 61% of prison and jail inmates were racial or ethnic minorities. About 12.6% of all black men in their late 20's were in jail or prison, as were 3.6% of Hispanic men, and 1.7% of white men in that age group. -*Source: Department of Justice*

Crucial Moral Issues

It was an unelected court, answerable to no one, that legalized pornography, declared nude dancing, protected freedom of expression, expelled God and the Ten Commandments from the public schools, declared abortion and sodomy to be constitutional rights, outlawed the death penalty, and imposed the idiocy of forced busing for racial balance on entire cities. The legislature would have not dared vote for all this. -*Pat Buchanan*

Culture

Our culture has an insatiable appetite for new things. We don't need new beginnings nearly so much as we need to make sense of the old beginnings. -*Reverend Kelly Peters*

The culture we have does not make people feel good about themselves. And you have to be strong enough to say if the culture doesn't work, don't buy it. -*Morrie Schwartz*

Defense

Diplomacy and defense are not substitutes for one another. Either alone would fail. -*John F. Kennedy*

It is an unfortunate fact that we can secure peace only by preparing for war. -*John F. Kennedy*

It is not the armed forces which can protect our democracy. It is the moral strength of democracy which alone can give any meaning to the efforts of military security. -*Max Lerner*

To be prepared for war is one of the most effectual means of preserving peace. -*George Washington, 1790*

Democracy

A democracy is predicated on the idea that ordinary men and women are capable of governing themselves. -*Adolf Berle*

Democracy does not guarantee equality of conditions- it only guarantees equality of opportunity. - *Irving Kristol*

It has been said that democracy is the worst form of government except all the others that have been tried. - *Sir Winston Churchill*

It's a republic if you can keep it. -*Benjamin Franklin*

One of the evils of democracy is you have to put up with the man you elect whether you want him or not. -*Will Rogers*

Self-government requires qualities of self-denial and restraint. -*John F. Kennedy*

The real democratic American idea is not that every man shall be on a level with every other man, but that every man shall have liberty to be what God made him, without hindrance. -*Henry Ward Beecher*

There can be no daily democracy without daily citizenship. -*Ralph Nader*

Well-educated citizens should be capable of defending their own liberty or taking on the burden to defend the liberty of those who can't defend their own. -*Michael Schwartz, president of Cleveland State University*

Dictatorship

A society of sheep must in time beget a government of wolves. –*Edward R. Murrow*

Diplomacy

Diplomacy is the art of jumping into troubled waters without making a splash. -*Art Linkletter*

A diplomat is a person who can tell you to go to hell in such a way that you actually look forward to the trip. -*Caskie Stinnett*

Discipline

Discipline is freedom.

Discord

The unity of freedom has never relied on uniformity of opinion. -*John F. Kennedy*

Education

Religion, morality, and knowledge being necessary to good government and the happiness of mankind, schools and the means of education shall ever be encouraged. *-Article Three of the great Northwest ordinance of 1787*

Enemies

Enemies' promises were made to be broken. *-Aesop*

Enthusiasm

He too serves a certain purpose who only stands and cheers. *-Henry Adams*

Nothing great was ever achieved without enthusiasm. *-Ralph Waldo Emerson*

Equality

This isn't going to be a good country for any of us to live in until it's a good country for all of us to live in. *-Richard M. Nixon*

Era

The trouble with our age is that it is all signpost and no destination. *-Louis Kronenberger, 1954*

Evil

When you choose the lesser of two evils, always remember that it is still an evil. *-Max Lerner*

Faith

I believe with all my heart standing up for America means standing up for the God who has so blessed our land. We need God's help to guide our nation through stormy seas. But we can't expect Him to protect America in a crisis if we just leave Him over on the shelf in our day-to-day living. *- President Ronald Reagan*

The Founding Fathers believed that faith in God was the key to our being a good people and America's becoming a great nation. *-President Ronald Reagan*

False

The great masses of the people...will more easily fall victims to a big lie than a small one. *-Adolf Hitler*

Founded

It cannot be emphasized too strongly or too often that this great nation was founded, not by religionists, but by Christians; not on religions, but on the gospel of Jesus Christ. For this very reason peoples of other faiths have been afforded asylum, prosperity, and freedom of worship here. *-Patrick Henry*

Freedom

America will remain the land of the free so long as it is the home of the brave. *-Elmer Davis*

A train is free to travel only when it stays on the tracks. *-Editor*

Everyone is in favor of free speech. Hardly a day passes without it being extolled, but some peoples' idea of it is that they are free to say what they want but if anyone says anything back, that is an outrage. *-Sir Winston Churchill*

Freedom can't be bought for nothing. If you hold her precious, you must hold all else of little worth. *-Seneca, 100 AD*

Freedom is never license to do as we please, but only to do as we ought. *-Lord Acton*

Freedom is not this country's gift to the world; freedom is the almighty's gift to every man and woman in this world. *-President George W. Bush*

Freedom is the recognition that no single person, no single authority or government, has a monopoly on truth, but that every individual life is infinitely precious, that every one of us put on this world has been put here for a reason and has something to offer. -*President Ronald Reagan*

Freedom of speech means that you shall not do something to people either for the views they have, or the views the express, or the words they speak or write. -*Hugo Black*

I disapprove of what you say, but I will defend to the death your right to say it. -*Voltaire*

Free people are free to be wise and to be unwise. That's part of what freedom is. -*Donald Rumsfeld, Secretary of Defense*

If a nation values anything more than freedom, it will lose its freedom, and the irony of it is that if it is a comfort or money that it values more, it will lose that too. -*W. Somerset Maugham*

In the true sense freedom cannot be bestowed, it must be achieved. -*Franklin D. Roosevelt*

{On Ancient Athens}: In the end, more than freedom, they wanted security. They wanted a comfortable life, and they lost it all: security, comfort, and freedom. When the Athenians finally wanted not to give to society but for society to give to them, when the freedom they wished for most was freedom from responsibility then Athens ceased to be free and was never free again. -*Edward Gibbon*

The liberty of the individual must be thus far limited: he must not make himself a nuisance to other people. -*John Stuart*

Those who expect to reap the blessings of freedom must, like men, undergo the fatigue of supporting it. -*Thomas Paine, 1776*

The unity of freedom has never relied on uniformity of opinion. -*John F. Kennedy*

Those who deny freedom to others deserve it not for themselves. -*Abraham Lincoln*

Unrestrained freedom is anarchy. Restrained only by force and arms is despotism. Self-restrained is Republicanism. -*Edmund Fairfield, president of Hillsdale College (1848-1869)*

The difference between a river and a swamp is that a river is confined within banks, while a swamp is not...Because a river is confined, and channeled, it has life. It is a mighty, moving, living thing. Because a swamp has no restrictions, it becomes thin and stagnant...In our modern life we boast of freedom. We want life without restrictions and without confinement. Only we forget that such living becomes stagnant. -*Leonard Cochran*

Government

A government that is big enough to give you all you want is big enough to take it all away. -*Barry Goldwater*

Every time the government attempts to handle our affairs, it cost more and the results are worse than if we had handled them ourselves. -*Benjamin Constant*

If men were angels, no government would be necessary. -*Tony Snow*

I heartily accept the motto, "That government is best which governs least." - *Henry David Thoreau*

It is for men to choose whether they will govern themselves or be governed. - *Henry Ward Beecher*

It is the duty of all nations to acknowledge the providence of Almighty God, to obey His will, to be grateful for His benefits, and humbly implore His protection and favor. -*George Washington 1789*

Our best protection against bigger government in Washington is better government in the states. - *Dwight Eisenhower*

Our constitution was made only for a moral and religious people. It is wholly inadequate to the government of any other. *-John Adams*

Our government is a government of the people, by the people, and for the people. *-Abraham Lincoln*

The modern state no longer has anything but rights; it does not recognize duties anymore. *-George Bernanos 1955*

The responsibility of great states is to serve and not to dominate the world. *-Harry Truman 1945*

The state is the servant of the citizens and not his master. *-John F. Kennedy*

Too often individuals turn to the government for solutions that the government cannot provide without lessening our personal liberty. *- Matthew Abens*

Too often our Washington reflex is to discover a problem and then throw money at it, hoping it will somehow go away. *-Senator Kenneth B. Keating*

We have staked the whole of our political institutions upon the capacity of mankind for self-government, upon the capacity of each and all of us to govern ourselves, to control ourselves, to sustain ourselves according to the Ten Commandments of God. *-James Madison, Chief Architect of the Constitution*

Whenever you have an efficient government you have a dictatorship. *-Harry Truman*

History

History is filled with great civilizations that have come and gone. They all experienced moral decay from within. *-Editor*

The fight for freedom is an endless battle. Its victories are never final. Its defeats are never permanent. Each generation must defend its heritage, for each seeming conquest gives rise to new forces that will attempt to substitute fresh means of oppression for the old. There can be no peace in a world of life and growth. Every battle the fathers thought finished will have to be fought anew by their children if they wish to preserve and extend their freedom. -*Philip Van Doren Stern*

Honesty

To state the facts frankly is not to despair for the future does not indict the past. -*John F. Kennedy*

Honor

When there is a lack of honor in government, the morals of the whole people are poisoned. -*President Herbert Hoover*

What is honored in a country will be cultivated there. -*Plato*

Humor

In China we can criticize Darwin but not the government. In American you can criticize the government but not Darwin. -*A Chinese Scientist*

Income

In a free society, income is earned through pleasing and serving one's fellow man. -*Walter E. Williams, Ph.D., Professor, Author, and Syndicated Columnist*

Individuals

The things that are wrong with the country today are the sum total of all the things that are wrong with us as individuals. -*Charles W. Tobey*

Ingratitude

And having looked to government for bread, on the very first scarcity they will turn and bite the hand that fed them. -*Edmund Burke*

Judges

Today, we have an outrageous number of federal judges who do not respect the Constitution and its First Amendment guarantees of free speech and free worship. Instead, they are using their power to rewrite the laws, re-shape the Constitution, and effectively legislate from the bench. -*D. James Kennedy, Ph. D*

Labor

The truly American sentiment recognizes the dignity of labor and the fact that honor lies in honest toil. -*Grover Cleveland*

Laws

Morality cannot be legislated, but behavior can be regulated. Judicial decrees may not change the heart, but they can restrain the heartless. -*Martin Luther King Jr.*

Wherever law ends, tyranny begins. -*John Locke, 1690*

Laws too gentle are seldom obeyed; too severe, seldom executed. -*Benjamin Franklin*

The more laws, the less justice. -*German Proverb*

Lawyers

If there were no bad people there would be no good lawyers. -*Charles Dickens*

Leadership

He that would govern others, first should be the master of himself. -*Philip Massinger, 1624*

Our world creates a prison of fear that squelches the dignity, esteem, and creativity of people. One of the most important responsibilities of leaders at all levels is to drive out fear. -*Dr. W. Edwards Deming*

Liberty

If liberty means anything at all, it means the right to tell people what they do not want to hear. -*George Orwell*

I know not what course others may take, but as for me, give me liberty or give me death. -*Patrick Henry, 1775*

Let every nation know, whether it wishes us well or ill, that we shall pay any price, bear any burden, meet any hardship, support any friend, oppose any foe, in order to assure the survival and success of liberty. -*John F. Kennedy*

Liberty is always dangerous, but it is the safest thing we have. -*Reverend Harry Emerson Fosdick*

The independence and liberty you possess are the work of joint counsels and joint efforts, of common danger, suffering and successes. -*George Washington, 1776*

The shallow consider liberty a release from all laws, from every constraint. The wise see in it, on the contrary, the potent Law of Laws. -*Walt Whitman, 1881*

The thing they forget is that liberty and freedom and democracy are so very precious that you do not fight to win once and stop. -*Sergeant Alvin C. York*

The tree of liberty must be refreshed from time to time with the blood of patriots and tyrants. -*Thomas Jefferson*

Materialism

Materialism may do what a foreign invader could never hope to achieve. Materialism robs a nation of its spiritual strength. -*Billy Graham*

Melting Pot

America has been called a melting pot, but it seems better to call it a mosaic, for in it each nation, people, or race which has come to its shores has been privileged to keep its individuality, contributing at the same time its share to the unified pattern of a new nation. -*King Baudouin 1 of Belgium*

Minorities

No democracy can survive which does not accept as fundamental to its very existence the recognition of the rights of minorities. -*Franklin D. Roosevelt*

Money

In our culture we make heroes of the men who sit on top of a heap of money, and we pay attention not only to what they say in their field of competence, but to their wisdom on every other question in the world. -*Max Lerner*

We ought to change the legend on our money from "In God We Trust" to "In Money We Trust." Because, as a nation, we've got far more faith in money these days than we do in God. -*Arthur Hoppe*

Morality

History fails to record a single precedent in which nations subject to moral decay have not passed into political and economic decline. There has been either a spiritual awakening to overcome the moral lapse, or a progressive deterioration leading to ultimate national disaster. -*General Douglas MacArthur*

Of the twenty-two civilizations that have appeared in history, nineteen of them collapsed when they reached the moral state America is in today. – *Arnold J. Toynbee, Historian, 1975*

You can't have a national morality apart from religious principle. -*George Washington*

Nation

A nation can be no stronger abroad than she is at home. Only an America which practices what it preaches about equal rights and social justice will be respected by those whose choice affects our future. -*John F. Kennedy*

If a nation expects to be ignorant and free, it expects what never was and never will be. -*Thomas Jefferson*

A nation may be said to consists of its territory, its people, and its laws. The territory is the only part which is of certain durability. -*Abraham Lincoln*

Energy in a nation is like sap in a tree: it rises from the bottom up. -*Woodrow Wilson*

Optimism

I have been described as an undying optimist, always seeing a glass half f full when some see it as half empty. And, yes, it's true- I always see the sunny side of life. And that's not just because I've been blessed by achieving so many of my dreams. My optimism comes not just from my strong faith in God, but from my strong and enduring faith in our country. -*President Ronald Reagan*

Partisanship

A man doesn't save a century or a civilization, but a militant party wedded to a principle can. -*Adlai Stevenson*

Past

A nation that forgets its past can function no better than an individual with amnesia. -*David G. McCullough, award winning writer*

Patriot

Do not ever let anyone claim to be a true American patriot if they ever attempt to separate religion from politics. -*George Washington*

My country, right or wrong, is a thing no patriot would think of saying except in a desperate case. It is like saying, "My mother, drunk or sober!" - *G.K. Chesterton*

Patriotism

Love for one's country which is not part of one's love for humanity is not love, but idolatrous worship. -*Erich Fromm*

Patriotism is not enough. I must have no hatred or bitterness toward anyone. -*Edith Cavell*

Peace

If we are to live together in peace, we must come to know each other better. - *President Lyndon B. Johnson*

Peace can only be achieved from a position of strength. -*President Ronald Reagan*

Peace is a daily, a weekly, a monthly process, gradually changing opinions, slowly eroding old barriers, and quietly building new structures. -*John F. Kennedy*

Perfection

The pursuit of perfection prevents achievement of the satisfactory. -*George Will, Columnist*

Political Building

We've been assured in the sacred writings that unless the Lord builds the house, they labor in vain who build it. I firmly believe this, and I also believe that without His concurring aid, we shall not succeed in this political building. *-Benjamin Franklin, eldest member of the Constitutional convention*

Political Truth

There is no debate-free, royal road to truth, no prospect of perfect harmony, and no privileged class of individuals whose views are automatically to be trusted and whose dictates are absolutely to be followed. -*Neil Greenspan, Professor of Pathology at Case Western Reserve*

Politician

A politician can appear to have his nose to the grindstone while straddling a fence and keeping both ears to the ground.

How can you tell a politician is lying? His lips move.

Politician: a hot air balloon that talks. -*Johnny Hart*

The thing that gets under my skin more than anything else is that politicians have learned to never answer a question. They've learned to hide. -*Brian Lamb, C-Span*

There's a bit of the dictator even among the elected officials who use their powers for their own interests. -*Mort Walker*

Politics

If you ever injected truth into politics you have no politics. -*Will Rogers, 1949*

I looked up the word politics in the dictionary. It's actually a combination of two words; poli, which means many, and tics, which means bloodsuckers. -*Jay Leno, The Tonight Show*

I would remind you that extremism in defense of liberty is no vice. And let me remind you also that moderation in the pursuit of justice is no virtue. -*Barry Goldwater*.

Political Skill is the ability to foretell what is going to happen tomorrow, next week, next month, and next year and to have the ability afterwards to explain why it didn't happen. -*Sir Winston Churchill*

Politicians are people who, before election, promise a car in every garage. And after the election? They get busy putting up parking meters. -*John Cameron Swayze*

Politics is the art of preventing people from taking part in affairs which properly concern them. -*Paul Valery, 1943*

The friend of humanity cannot recognize a distinction between what is political and what is not. There is nothing that is not political. -*Thomas Mann, 1924*

The middle of the road is all the usable surface. The extremes, right and left, are in the gutters. -*Dwight D. Eisenhower*

The more you read and observe about this politics things you got to admit that each party is worse than the other. The one that's out always looks the best. -*Will Rogers, 1924*

Too bad that all people who know how to run the world are busy driving taxicabs and cutting hair. -*George Burns*

Under democracy one party always devotes its chief energies to trying to prove that the other party is unfit to rule and both commonly succeed, and are right. -*HL Mencken*

You cannot adopt politics as a profession and remain honest. -*Louis McHenry Howe*

What is morally wrong can never be politically right. -*Lord Shaftesbury*

I have the perfect simplified tax form for government. Why don't they just print our money with a return address on it? -*Bob Hope*

Standing in the middle of the road is very dangerous; you get knocked down by the traffic from both sides. -*Margaret Thatcher*

Popularity

The man with a host of friends who slaps on the back everybody he meets is regarded as a friend of nobody. *-Aristotle, 400 BC*

The more one pleases everybody, the less one pleases profoundly. *-Stendhal, 1822*

Poverty

Poverty has many roots, but the tap root is ignorance. *-President Lyndon B. Johnson*

Before the federal war on Poverty was launched, the illegitimacy rate in the 1950s was four percent, whereas today it is 35 percent. (68 percent amongs black Americans). *-Larry P. Arnn President, Hillsdale College*

Power

An honest man can feel no pleasure in the exercise of power over his fellow citizen. *-Thomas Jefferson*

Human nature being what it is, power is always abused. It is to the best interest of society, therefore, to see that no individual or group gets too much power or retains it too long. *-Waldo Lee McAtee*

No man is wise enough nor good enough to be trusted with unlimited power. *-Charles Caleb Colton*

Power tends to corrupt and absolute power corrupts absolutely. *-Lord Acton, 1887*

President

In America any boy may become President and I suppose it's just one of the risks he takes. *-Adlai Stevenson, 1952*

No easy problem ever comes to the President of the United States. If they are easy to solve, somebody else has solved them. *-Dwight D. Eisenhower*

Principle

The fate of America cannot depend on any one man. The greatness of America is grounded in principle and not on any single personality. *-Franklin D. Roosevelt*

We will not long survive as a nation unless and until we restore the moral and spiritual principles that made America great in the first place. *-Senator Jesse Helms*

Priority

The top priority of the federal government is the safety of this country. *-President Ronald Reagan*

Progress

If America forgets where she came from, if the people lose sight of what brought them along, if she listens to the deniers and mockers, then will begin the rot and dissolution. *-Carl Sandburg*

In times like these, it helps to recall that there have always been times like these. *-Paul Harvey*

Let's talk sense to the American people. Let's tell them the truth, that there are no gains without pains. *-Adlai Stevenson, 1952*

The best road to progress is freedoms' road. *-John F. Kennedy*

Public Office

When a man assumes a public trust he should consider himself as public property. *-Thomas Jefferson*

Public Opinion

With public sentiment, nothing can fail; without it, nothing can succeed. Consequently he who molds public sentiment goes deeper than he who enacts statutes or pronounces decisions. *-Abraham Lincoln*

Public Speaking

Speeches measured by the hour die with the hour. *-Thomas Jefferson*

Punishment

It is a cruelty to the innocent not to punish the guilty. *-Old Proverb*

Punishment is not for revenge, but to lessen crime and reform the criminal.- *Elizabeth Fry*

Rebellion

A little rebellion, now and then, is a good thing, and as necessary in the political world as storms in the physical. *-Thomas Jefferson*

Red Flags

The things that will destroy America are prosperity-at-any-price, safety-first instead of duty-first, the love of soft living, and the get-rich-quick theory of life. *-Theodore Roosevelt*

Reform

A nation without the means of reform is without means of survival. *-Edmund Burke*

There are a thousand hacking at the branches of evil to one who is striking at the root. *-Henry David Thoreau, 1854*

The men who have changed the universe have never accomplished it by changing officials but always by inspiring the people. *-Napoleon, 1804*

To give up the task of reforming society is to give up one's responsibility as a free man. -*Alan Paton*

Righteousness

For as the earth brings forth its bud, as the garden causes the things that are sown in it to spring forth, so the Lord God will cause righteousness and praise to spring forth before all the nations. -*Isaiah 61:11*

Rights

Government laws are needed to give us civil rights, and God is needed to make us civil. -*Ralph W. Sockman, Pastor*

Revolt

Not actual suffering but the hope of better things incite people to revolt. -*Eric Hoffer*

Save

In the United States whenever you hear the word "save," it is usually the beginning of an advertisement designed to make you spend money. -*Renee Pierre-Gosset*

Security

We hear of a silent generation, more concerned with security than integrity, with conforming than performing, with imitating than creating. -*Thomas J. Watson*

Self-Control

Freedom is not procured by a full enjoyment of what is desired, but by controlling the desire. -*Epictetus, 200 AD*

Selfish

We must especially beware of that small group of selfish men who would clip the wings of the American eagle in order to feather their own nests. -*Franklin D. Roosevelt*

Servitude

Freedom is indivisible, and when one man is enslaved, all are not free. -*John F. Kennedy*

No man is good enough to be another man's master. -*George Bernard Shaw*

Shame

The self-esteem movement declared war on shame decades ago. In trying to increase self-esteem, our society may have gone too far in the other direction. Maybe it's time to invite the useful aspects of shame back into our culture. -*Dr. Joyce Brothers*

Sin

The real trouble with our times is not the multiplication of sinners, it is the disappearance of sin. -*Etienne Gilson*

Society

A government that robs Peter to pay Paul can always depend upon the support of Paul. -*George Bernard Shaw*

Education is not an option or a privilege in society. It is the bedrock of democracy and the key to national and personal property. -*Alex Machaskee, President and Publisher of The Plain Dealer*

Society is no comfort to one not sociable. -*William Shakespeare*

What is not good for the hive is not good for the bee. -*Marcus Aurelius*

Yet we can maintain a free society only if we recognize that in a free society no one can win all the time. No one can have his own way all the time, and no one is right all the time. -*Richard M. Nixon*

You cannot build a better society without improving individuals. -*Madame Curie*

Speech

Every man has a right to utter what he thinks truth, and every other man has a right to knock him down for it. -*Samuel Johnson*

The recipe for a good speech contains some shortening.

Statesmanship

In statesmanship there are predicaments from which it is impossible to escape without some wrongdoing. -*Napoleon, 1804*

Strength

If we are strong, our character will speak for itself. If we are weak, words will be of no help. -*John F. Kennedy*

Suitability

The officer and the office, the doer and the thing done seldom fit so exactly that we can say they were almost made for each other. -*Sydney Smith, 1804*

Survival

Irrational barriers and ancient prejudices fall quickly when the question of survival itself is at stake. -*John F. Kennedy, 1959*

Talent

All of us do not have the same talents. But all of us should have the equal opportunity to develop our talents. -*John F. Kennedy*

Taxes

Taxes, after all, are the dues that we pay for the privileges of membership in an organized society. -*Franklin D. Roosevelt*

The income tax has made more liars out of the American people than golf has. -*Will Rogers, 1924*

The point to remember is that what the government gives it must first take away. -*John S. Coleman*

We contend that for a nation to try to tax itself into prosperity is like a man standing in a bucket and trying to lift himself by the handle. -*Sir Winston Churchill*

Togetherness

We have one country, one Constitution, and one future that binds us. And when we come together and work together, there is no limit to the greatness of America. -*President George W. Bush*

Tolerance

If we cannot end our difference, at least we can help make the world safe for diversity. -*John F. Kennedy*

Tradition

A love for tradition has never weakened a nation, indeed it has strengthened nations in their hour of peril; but the new view must come, the world must roll forward. -*Sir Winston Churchill, 1944*

Tragedy

To Americans, tragedy is wanting something very badly and not getting it. But many people have had to learn that perhaps the worst form of tragedy is wanting something badly, getting it, and finding it empty. -*Henry Kissinger*

Treaties

"Let us agree not to step on each others' feet" said the cock to the horse. -*English Proverb*

Let us never negotiate out of fear, but let us never fear to negotiate. -*John F. Kennedy*

Peace does not rest in charters and covenants alone. It lies in the hearts and minds of the people. -*John F. Kennedy*

Treaties are observed as long as they are in harmony with interests. -*Napoleon*

Treaties are like roses and young girls. They last while they last. -*Charles De Gaulle*

Tyranny

A police state finds it cannot command the grain to grow. -*John F. Kennedy*

The face of tyranny is always mild at first. -*Racine, 1669*

Unionism

It is one of the characteristics of a free and democratic modern nation that it have free and independent labor unions. -*Franklin D. Roosevelt, 1940*

Unionism seldom, if ever, uses such power as it has to insure better work; almost always it devotes a large part of that power to safeguarding bad work. -*HL Menchen, 1922*

Unity

A common danger unites even the bitterest enemies. -*Aristotle, 400 BC*

A single arrow is easily broken, but not ten in a bundle. -*Japanese Proverb*

Plurality which is not reduced to unity is confusion; unity which does not depend on plurality is tyranny. -*Pascal, 1670*

There are only two forces that unite men- fear and interest. -*Napoleon, 1804*

United we stand, divided we fall. -*Proverb*

We must all hang together, or assuredly we shall all hang separately. -*Benjamin Franklin, 1776*

Urban Life

Our national flower is the concrete cloverleaf. -*Lewis Mumford*

The higher the buildings, the lower the morals. -*Noel Coward*

Values

Great American values: the dignity of work, the warmth of family, the strength of neighborhood, and the nourishment of human freedom. -*President Ronald Reagan*

Today we are afraid of simple words like goodness and mercy and kindness. We don't believe in the good old words because we don't believe in the good values anymore. And that's why the world is sick. -*Lin Yutang*

Vice

Men are more easily governed through their vices than through their virtues. -*Napoleon, 1804*

Virtue

A general dissolution of the Principles and Manners will more surely overthrow the Liberties of America than the whole Force of the common enemy. While the people are virtuous they cannot be subdued; but when once they lose their virtue they will be ready to surrenders their liberties to the first external or internal invader…If virtue and knowledge are diffused among people, they will never be enslaved. This will be their great security. -*Samuel Adams, 1779*

Public virtue cannot exist in a nation without private, and public virtue is the only foundation of republics. -*John Adams, 1776*

While the people retain their virtue and vigilance, no administration, by any extreme of wickedness or folly, can very seriously injure the government in the short space of four years. -*Abraham Lincoln*

Vision

Where there is no vision, the people perish. -*Proverbs 29:18*

Voting

Bad officials are elected by good citizens who do not vote. -*George Jean Nathan*

Always vote for principle, though you may vote alone, and you may cherish the sweetest reflection that your vote is never lost. -*John Quincy Adams*

A vote is like a rifle: its usefulness depends upon the character of the user. -*Theodore Roosevelt*

I think most Americans care too little about voting. A lot of people, especially the middle class, they've got a little bit and they think they've got it all. I'm glad that the country has moved forward. I think it has a little bit further to go. -*Reverend Fred Shuttlesworth*

Just because you do not take an interest in politics doesn't mean politics won't take an interest in you. –*Pericles, 400 BC Statesman*

More men have been elected between sundown and sunup than ever were elected between sunup and sundown. -*Will Rogers, 1924*

Nobody will ever deprive the American people of the right to vote except the American people themselves- and the only way they can do that is by not voting. -*Franklin D. Roosevelt*

War

Battle: a method of untying with the teeth a political knot that would not yield to the tongue. -*Ambrose Bierce, 1881*

He who is the author of a war lets loose the whole contagion of Hell and opens a vein that bleeds a nation to death. -*Thomas Paine, 1776*

How different the new order would be if we could consult the veteran instead of the politician. -*Henry Miller*

I am not a pacifist because pacifism in this fallen world in which we live means that we desert the people who need our greatest help. -*Francis Schaeffer*

If a house is divided against itself, that house cannot stand. -*Mark 3:25*

I hate war as only a soldier who has lived it can, only as one who has seen its brutality, its futility, its stupidity. -*Dwight D. Eisenhower.*

In the final choice a soldier's pack it not so heavy a burden as a prisoner's claims. -*Dwight D. Eisenhower, 1953*

In war, the latest refinements of science are linked with the cruelties of the Stone Age. -*Sir Winston Churchill*

Laws are silent in time of war. -*Cicero, 52 BC*

Let him who does not know what a war is go to war. -*Spanish Proverb*

Mankind must put an end to war or war well put an end to mankind. -*John F. Kennedy*

Never trust a man who knows war only from books. -*Chinese Proverb*

Older men declare war. But it is youth that must fight and die. *-Herbert Hoover*

The belief in the possibility of a short decisive war appears to be one of the most ancient and dangerous human illusions. *-Robert Lynd*

The grim fact is that we prepare for war like precocious giants and for peace like retarded pygmies. *-Lester Pearson*

The way to prevent war is to bend every energy toward prevent it not to proceed by the dubious indirection of preparing for it. *-Max Lerner*

There never was a good war or a bad peace. *-Benjamin Franklin, 1773*

War is an ugly thing, but not the ugliest of things…A man who has nothing for which he is willing to fight- nothing he cares about more than his own safety- is a miserable creature who has no chance of being free, unless made and kept so by the exertions of better men than himself. *-John Stuart Mill*

War is cruelty, and you cannot refine it. *-William T. Sherman, 1875*

When elephants fight, the mousedeer between them is killed. *-Malay Proverb*

Without armaments peace cannot be kept; wars are waged not only to repel injustice but also to establish a firm peace. *-Martin Luther*

You may be obliged to wage war, but not to use poisoned arrows. *-Batasar Gracian, 1647*

The most disadvantaged peace is better than the most just war. *-Erasmus, 1500*

Water Supply

In the U.S., even though we've reduced consumption, we're still using far more water per persona than we need to, and it is being wasted in every sector of the economy. America could soon face a critical shortage. *-Peter H. Gleick, top expert on freshwater resources*

Wealth

Let not the nation count wealth as wealth; let it count righteousness as wealth. *–Confucius, 500 BC*

Work

Britain has invented a new missile. It's called the civil servant- it doesn't work and it can't be fired. *-General Sir Walter Walker*

Where there is no desire, there will be no industry. *-John Locke, 1693*

Worship

If you can go to church and worship- if you can study your Bible, read Christian magazines and literature, and listen to Christian radio- without fear of arrest, torture, or death, count your blessings- more than 3 billion people in our world do not enjoy that precious privilege. *-Reverend Greg R. Albrecht*

Zeal

The greatest dangers to liberty lurk in insidious encroachment by men of zeal, well-meaning but without understanding. *-Justice Louis Brandeis, 1928*

2.
BEHAVIOR MATTERS

Actions

Actions speak louder than words.

A field never gets plowed by turning it over in your mind.

Every action of yours, every thought, should be those of a man who expects to die before the day is out. -*Thomas A Kempis, 1400*

I am only one, but I am one. I cannot do everything, but I can do something. What I can do, I should do and, with the help of God, I will do! -*Everett Hale*

It doesn't matter how slowly you go as long as you do not stop. -*Confucius*

You can do anything in this world if you are prepared to take the consequences. -*W. Somerset Maugham*

What you do not want done to yourself, do not do to others. –*Confucius, 500 BC*

Advice

In giving advice seek to help, not to please your friend. -*Solon, 7 BC*

It is best to give advice in only two circumstances: when it is requested, and when it is a life-threatening situation. -*Andy Rooney*

Spend your time fixing the problem rather than finding someone to blame. -*Andrew A. Venable Jr., Public Library Director, Cleveland.*

Agreement

We are more inclined to hate one another for points on which we differ than to love one another for points on which we agree. -*Charles Caleb Colton*

Altitude

It's your attitude not your aptitude that determines your altitude. *-Zig Zigler, author*

Anger

It is easy to fly into a passion; anyone can do that, but to be angry with the right person to the right extent and at the right time and with the right object and in the right way- that is not easy, and it is not everyone who can do it. *-Aristotle, 4 BC*

Never answer an angry word with an angry word. It's always the second remark that starts the trouble.

Never go to bed mad. Stay up and fight.

"Venting" your anger doesn't work. Research shows that when people scream, swear, and throw things in a fury just become more enraged. *-Dianne Hales*

When angry, count to ten before you speak; if very angry, a hundred. *-Thomas Jefferson*

Appearance

Why not be oneself? That is the whole secret of a successful appearance. If one is a greyhound why try to look like a Pekinese? *-Edith Jitwell*

Apology

Apologize when you realize you are wrong. An apology never diminishes a person. It elevates him. *-Ann Landers*

Appreciation

Try to show appreciation in order to be appreciated; let him who desires affection to show affection. *-Baltasar Grecian, 1600*

Argue

It takes *you* to make an argument.

The best argument is that which seems merely an explanation. *-Dale Carnegie*

When you argue with a fool, chances are he is doing just the same.

Authority

Remind the people to be subject to rulers and authorities, to be obedient, to be ready to do whatever is good. *-Titus 3:1*

Beginning

Start where you are. You have now made the all-important beginning. *-Dr. Norman Vincent Peale*

You will never win if you never begin. *-Dr. Robert Schuller*

Best

Always do your best. What you plant now, you will harvest later. *-Og Mandino*

In all things do your best. The man who has done his best has done everything. The man who has done less than his best has done nothing. *- Charles M. Schwab*

People do their best in the situation they find themselves at that time. *-Editor*

You are doing your best only when you are trying to improve what you're doing.

Blame

No one is defeated until he starts blaming someone else. *-John Wooden, UCLA Coach*

People who blame are basically insecure, have low self-esteem, and do not really like themselves. *-Editor*

Boss

A good boss has to be honest, trustworthy, loyal, helpful, friendly, courteous, brave, clean, and reverent- just like a Boy Scout. *-Scott Cowan, President of Century Cyclops*

Brevity

Brevity charms, and better accomplishes the daily course; it makes up in manner, what it lacks in measure. The good, if short, is doubly good, and even the bad, if brief is not so bad. *-Baltasar Grecian*

Cause

He that hath the worse cause makes the most noise. *-Thomas Fuller, M.D.*

Try to leave the world a better place because you were here.

Censure

Before we censure a man for seeming what he is *not*, we should be sure that we know what he *is*. *-Thomas Caryle*

Change

Be not angry that you cannot make others as you wish them to be, since you cannot make yourself as you wish to be. *-Thomas A. Kempis*

Change the way you look at things and you will change the way you see things. -*Dr. Wayne Dyer*

If we try to create change in one's lifestyle we have to convince them that what we have to offer is far better than what they have at the present time. -*Laura Moore, Writer*

If we're hoping for someone to change, the best way to encourage change is through love. It's love that distinguish between the person and the behavior. -*Pastor Kelly Peters*

Consider how hard it is to change yourself and you'll understand what little chance you have trying to change others. -*Arnold Glasow*

You must be the change you want to see in the world. -*Mahatma Gandhi, 1900*

Challenged

Bless those who curse you. Think what they would say if they knew the truth. -*Mother Teresa*

If you want to walk on water, you've got to get out of the boat. -*John Ortberg, author*

Never let one be beaten down by persons or by events. -*Madame Curie*

Character

Good character is what we look for in others. It is what employers look for in us and most importantly, this is what God looks for in us. How we accomplish something should always have priority over what we accomplish. -*Editor*

Sow a thought, reap an act. Sow an act, reap a habit. Sow a habit, reap a character. Sow a character, reap a destiny. *Chinese proverb*

Cheer

The quickest way to cheer yourself is to cheer someone else.

Choice

When faced with a moral decision, ask yourself if you'd feel comfortable telling your parents or your children about your choice.

Common Sense

Do not squander favor. Great friends are for great occasions; so do not waste a great generosity upon a matter trivial, for that is to squander good will; let the holy anchor always be kept against the worst storm. -*Baltasar Grecian*

Never test the depth of the water with both feet.

One arrow does not bring down two birds. -*Turkish Proverb*

Compliment

Won't you come into the garden? I would like my roses to see you. -*Richard B. Sheridan*

Communication

You cannot write in the chimney with charcoal. -*Russian Proverb*

Commitment

Let us therefore make every effort to do what leads to peace and to mutual edification. -*Romans 14:19*

Conduct

An eye for an eye makes the whole world blind.

Be to his virtues very kind. Be to his faults a little blind.

Do all the good you can, by all the means you can, in all the ways you can, in all the places you can, at all the times you can. To all the people you can, as long as ever you can. -*John Wesley*

Do small things with great love. -*President George W. Bush*

Forbidden fruit makes many jams.

Let each of you look out not only for his own interest, but also for the interest of others. -*Philippians 2:4*

Let me do the thing that ought to be done, when it ought to be done, as it ought do be done, whether I like to do it or not.

Most of us spend the first six days of each week sowing wild oats; then we go to church on Sunday and pray for a crop failure. -*Fred Allen*

We cannot direct the wind, but we can adjust the sails. -*Proverb*

Conflict

Never wrestle with a pig. You both get all dirty, and the pig likes it.

Conformity

He who does anything because it is the custom, makes no choice. -*John Stuart*

Contention

For lack of wood the fire goes out, and where there is no whisperer contention ceases. -*Proverbs 26:20*

Contrary

We trifle with, make sport of, and despise those who are attached to us, and follow those that fly from us. -*William Haylitt, 1836*

Conversation

Conversation means being able to disagree and still continue the conversation. -*Dwight MacDonald*

Discretion in what is said is far better than eloquence. -*Baltasar Grecian*

Courage

A person of courage doesn't do what he wants to do- he does what he must do.

Courage is not the absence of fear. It's doing what it takes despite one's fear. - *Jack Canfield and Mark V. Hansen, authors*

Courage is the greatest of all virtues, because if you haven't courage, you may not have an opportunity to use any of the others. -*Samuel Johnson*

Correction

Correction does much, encouragement does more. -*Johann Wolfgang von Goethe*

Credit

It is amazing how much people can get done if they do not worry about who gets the credit. -*Sandra Swinney*

Criticism

I wonder how anyone can have the face to condemn others when he reflects upon his own thoughts. -*W. Somerset Maugham, 1938*

There is so much good in the worst of us, and so much bad in the best of us, that it behooves all of us not to talk about the rest of us. -*Robert Louis Stevenson*

When a man points a finger at someone else, he should remember that three of his fingers are pointing at himself.

Crowd

Do not follow the crowd in doing wrong. -*Exodus 23:2*

Debt

The borrower is servant to the lender.

Deception

He who digs a hole for another may fall in himself. -*Russian Proverb*

One deceit needs many others, and so the whole house is built in the air and must soon come to ground. -*Baltasar Grecian, 1600BC*

Decisions

Decisions do determine destiny. -*Mary Ann Mosack, executive director of Operation Leepsake*

Decline

The wolf loses his teeth, but not his inclinations. -*Spanish Proverb*

Deeds

The smallest deed is greater than the greatest intention.

Delay

Between saying and doing many a pair of shoes is worn out. *-Italian Proverb*

One of these days is none of these days. *-English Proverb*

Procrastination is the thief of time. *-Edward Young*

What may be done at any time will be done at no time. *-Thomas Fuller*

Destiny

As we are, so we do; and as we do, so is it done to us; we are the builders of our fortunes. *-Ralph Waldo Emerson*

What we seek we shall find; what we flee from flees from us. *-Ralph Waldo Emerson*

Development

Stretch your foot to the length of your blanket. *-Persian Proverb*

Differences

Acceptance and tolerance do not necessarily imply agreement and approval. *-Editor*

There is little difference in people, but that different makes a big difference. The little difference is attitude and the big difference is whether it is positive or negative. *-W. Clement Stone*

Dignity

The only kind of dignity which is genuine is that which is not diminished by the indifference of others. *-Dag Hammarskjold*

Disagree

We need not all agree, but if we disagree, let us not be disagreeable in our disagreements. -*Martin R. DeHaan*

Discipline

Do not consider painful what is good for you. -*Euripides, 431 BC*

He who requires much from himself and little from others will keep himself from being the object of resentment. –*Confucius, 500 BC*

Do It

Promptitude is the mother of fortune. He does much who leaves nothing for tomorrow. A magnificent motto: to make haste slowly. - *Baltasar Grecian, 1600*

One is daily annoyed by some little corner that needs clearing up, and when by accident one at last is stirred to do the needful, one wonders that one should have stood the annoyances so long when such a little effort would have done away with it. Moral: When in doubt, do it. -*Justice Oliver Wendell Holmes*

Effort

He that would have the fruit must climb the tree. -*Thomas Fuller*

Ego

The most dangerous height which I have ever climbed was Mount Ego. - *Robert Louis Stevenson*

The nice thing about egotists is that they don't talk about other people. - *Lucille S. Harper*

Encouragement

Never miss the opportunity to compliment or to say something encouraging to someone. *-Editor*

Endurance

Sorrow and silence are strong, and patient endurance is godlike. *-Henry Wadsworth Longfellow*

Enthusiasm

Enthusiastic leadership gets you a promotion when you least expect it.

Eloquence

True eloquence consists in saying all that should be said, and that only. *-La Rochefoucauld*

Enemies

Do not rejoice when your enemy falls, and let not your heart be glad when he stumbles. *-Proverbs 24:1*

If we could read the secret history of our enemies, we should find in each mans's life a sorrow and suffering enough to disarm all hostility. *-Henry Wadsworth Longfellow*

The best way to destroy an enemy is to make him a friend. *-Abraham Lincoln*

Enthusiastic

To get enthusiastic, learn more about the thing you are not enthusiastic about. *-David Joseph Schwartz, PhD*

Envy

Few men have the strength to honor a friend's success without envy. – *Aeschylus, 500 BC*

Man will do many things to get himself loved; he will do all things to get himself envied. -*Mark Twain*

Error

An error gracefully acknowledged is a victory won. -*Caroline Gascoigne*

It is one thing to show a man that he is in error, and another to put him in possession of the truth. -*John Locke*

We are more conscious that a person is in the wrong when the wrong concerns ourselves. -*Joseph Roux*

Example

Example is not the main thing in influencing others. It is the only thing! -*Dr. Albert Schweitzer*

What you do not want done to yourself, do not do to others. –*Confucius, 500 BC*

Exaggerate

We always weaken whatever we exaggerate. -*Jean Francois de Laharpe*

Excess

The archer that shoots over misses as much as he that falls short. -*Montaigne*

Excuses

Bad excuses are worse than none. -*Thomas Fuller, 1640*

Never let a problem become an excuse. -*Dr. Robert Schuller*

Often time excusing of a fault doth make the fault the worse by the excuse. -*William Shakespeare*

Experience

He who has once burnt his mouth always blows his soup. -*German Proverb*

Expectations

Just for today, I will not have any expectations about how I should be treated, and I will not compare myself with anyone else. I will just be glad that I am who I am.

Evil

Evil should never be our pleasure and, therefore, not our theme; the slanderer is forever despised; and he who speaks evil will always have to hear still greater. -*Baltasar Grecian, 1600*

Facts

Every man has a right to his opinion, but no man has a right to be wrong in his facts. -*Bernard M. Baruch*

Failure

Failure isn't falling down; it's staying down.

The faster you move on after failing the sooner you'll get to your next chance. -*Youbin Jung, 17*

The great question is not whether you have failed, but whether you are content with failure. -*Dr. Laurence J. Peter*

Faith

Feed your faith and doubt will starve to death!

Falsehood

A lie which is half a truth is ever the blackest of lies. *-Alfred, Lord Tennyson*

The cruelest lies are often told in silence. *-Robert Louis Stevenson*

Familiarity

Familiar acts are beautiful through love. *-Shelley*

Fanatic

A fanatic is one who can't change his mind and won't change the subject. *-Sir Winston Churchill*

Faults

Gladly we desire to make others perfect but we will not amend our own fault. *-Thomas A. Kempis*

When looking at faults, use a mirror, not a telescope. *-Yazid Ibrahim*

Whoever is aware of his own failing will not find faults with the failings of other men. *–Sa'di, 1200*

Fear

We fear the unknown: death, man, failure, betrayal, and lack. *-John Hagee, Pastor*

You will either conquer fear, or fear will conquer you.

Finish

Runners just do it. They run for the finish line even if someone else has reached it first.

Focus

Do you focus on what you have or what you don't have? *-Pastor Joel Osteen*

Don't cross the bridge until you get to it. *-Proverb*

Your goals decide your focus. *-Mike Murdock, Pastor*

Foolishness

But avoid foolish and ignorant disputes, knowing that they generate strife. *- 2 Timothy 2:23*

Forgetful

If you want to remember to take something with you when you leave, put your car keys on top of whatever it is. *-Editor*

Forgiveness

Forgive others as we want others to forgive us.

Always forgive your enemies; nothing annoys them so much. *-Oscar Wild*

To error is human, to forgive is divine. *-Alexander Pope*

Frankness

Straightforwardness without the rules of propriety becomes rudeness. *- Confucius, 500 BC*

Free

No man is really free who is afraid to speak the truth as he knows it, or who is too fearful to take a stand for that which he knows is right. *-Benjamin E. Mays*

Friends

Do a favor for a friend, and you'll feel like a new person. *-Norman Vincent Peale*

Friendship is really a matter of time…the time that you take when you care. *-Amanda Bradley*

Those are friends who make friends. *-Baltasar Grecian, 1600*

Fretting

Fretting springs from a determination to get our own way. *-Oswald Chambers*

Gain

More things have been gained by knack than by knock. *-Baltasar Grecian, 1600*

Gall

He has the gall of a shoplifter returning an item for a refund. *-W.I.E. Gates*

Gamble

The best throw of the dice is to throw them away. *-English Proverb*

Generosity

Good deeds are required to engender good will: do good and with both hands; be generous in speech and more generous in deed; love in order to be loved for true nobleness is the politic magic of the great. -*Baltasar Grecian, 1600*

Giving

A man there was and they called him mad; the more he gave the more he had. -*Bunyan*

Giving doesn't come easily to most people. Human nature leans much more toward getting. -*Editor*

It is well to give when asked, but it is better to give unasked, through understanding. -*Kahlil Gibran*

Things themselves do not remain, but their effects do. Therefore we should not be mean and calculating with what we have but give with a generous hand. -*John Chrysostom, 400*

To give and then not feel that one has given is the very best of all ways of giving. -*Max Beerbohm*

We give nothing so freely as advice. -*La Rochefoucauld*
When it comes to giving, some people stop at nothing.

Gossip

Whoever gossips to you will gossip of you. -*Spanish Proverb*

Gratitude

We seldom find people ungrateful so long as we are in a position to be beneficial. -*La Rochefoucauld*

Greatness

The greatest spirits are capable of the greatest vices as well as the greatest virtues. -*Descartes*

Greed

Greed's worst point is its ingratitude. -*Seneca*

He is better with a rake than a fork. -*English Proverb*

Watch out! Be on your guard against all kinds of greed; a man's life does not consist in the abundance of his possessions. -*Luke 12:15*

Grieve

Mourn with those who mourn. -*Romans 12:15*

Guilt

He declares himself guilty who justifies himself before accusation. -*Thomas Fuller, MD*

Suspicion always haunts the guilty mind; the thief doth fear each bush an officer. -*William Shakespeare*

Habit

Habit is overcome by habit. -*Thomas A. Kempis, 1400*

Handshake

I hate the giving of the hand unless the whole man accompanies it. -*Ralph Waldo Emerson*

Happiness

Responsible behavior creates a sense of inner harmony and contentment that generates happiness. -*Editor*

Haste

Do nothing hastily but catching of fleas. -*Thomas Fuller, MD*

Hurry, hurry has no blessing. -*Swahili Proverb*

Hate

The price of hating other human beings is loving oneself less. -*Eldridge Cleaver*

Hell

The national anthem of hell is 'I Did It My Way.' -*Peter Kreeft*

Helping

We live very close together. So, our prime purpose in this life is to help others. And if you can't help them, at least don't hurt them. -*Dalai Lama*

Even if it's a little thing, do something for those who have need of help, something for which you get no pay but the privilege of doing it. -*Albert Schweitzer*

Hope

He who fishes on catches one. -*French Proverb*

I've been given a chance to learn firsthand that it's the little things that matter. That every little bit of good you do helps, because it can compound and make a huge change in a person's life. It gives me hope. -*Natalie Portman, Actress*

Humanitarianism

It is better to light a candle than to curse darkness. -*Chinese Proverb*

Humility

If I only had a little humility, I'd be perfect. *-Ted Turner*

It is always the secure who are humble. *-G.K. Chesterton*

Idleness

Expect poison from standing water. *-William Blake*

Important

When you help others feel important, you help yourself feel important too. *-David Joseph Schwartz, PhD*

Impartiality

Neutrality is having the same weights and measures for each. *-Napoleon*

Indignation

Indignation is the seducer of thought. No man can think clearly when his fists are clenched. *-George Jean Nathan*

Industry

Mediocrity gets further with industry than superiority without it. *-Baltasar Grecian, 1600*

Initiative

While honey lies in every flower, no doubt, it takes a bee to get the honey out!

Injury

Forgetting of a wrong is a mild revenge. *-Thomas Fuller, MD*

Reject your sense of injury and the injury itself disappears. -*Marcus Aurelius, 200*

'Tis better to suffer wrong than do it. -*Thomas Fuller, MD*

Integrity

This above all: to thine own self be true, and it must follow, as the night the day, though canst not then be false to any man.-*William Shakespeare*

Judging

Do not judge, and you will never be mistaken. -*Rousseau*

Never judge from appearance. -*Proverb*

Remember: judge and be judged, be critical and be criticized, put down others and they will put you down. But love and be loved, be merciful and receive mercy, give and it will be given to you in abundance.

Judgment

He hath a good judgment that relieth not wholly on his own. -*Thomas Fuller, MD*

Kindness

Being kind is different from being nice. Being nice is when you say polite things like "please" and "thank you". You show kindness through actions. -*Courteney, 3rd grade*

Be kind. Everyone you meet is fighting a hard battle. -*John Watson*

Do unto others as you would have others do unto your children. -*Dr. Edwin Leap*

He who expects kindness should show kindness. -*Charles H. Spurgeon*

I shall pass through his world but once. Therefore, if there be any kindness I can show or any good thing I can do let me do it nor for I shall not pass this way again. -*Etienne de Grellet*

Kindness is a language which the deaf can hear and the blind can see.

Kindness is difficult to give away because it keeps coming back.

The kindest word in all the word is the unkind word, unsaid.

You can accomplish by kindness what you can not do by force. -*Publilius Syrus, 100 B.C.*

Laziness

Laziness travels so slowly that poverty soon overtakes him. -*Benjamin Franklin*

Leadership

What you cannot enforce do not command. -*Sophocles, 403 BC*

Lies

A little lie is like a little pregnancy: it doesn't take long before everyone knows. -*C.S. Lewis*

There are three kinds of lies: lies, damned lies, and statistics. -*Mark Twain*

Listening

A good listener is not only popular, but after awhile, he knows something.

Give every man thine ear, but few thy voice. -*William Shakespeare*

Love

Do not seek so much to be consoled, as to console; do not seek so much to be understood, as to understand; do not seek so much to be loved, as to love. -*St. Francis*

It is easier to give a cup of rice than to relieve the loneliness and pain of someone unloved in our own home. -*Mother Teresa*

Jesus said love one another. He didn't say love the whole world. -*Mother Teresa*

Let us not love with words or tongue but with actions and in truth. -*1 John 3:18*

Love me when I least deserve it, because that's when I really need it. -*Swedish Proverb*

Love is an attribute of God. To love others is evidence of a genuine faith. -*Kay Arthur, author*

Love sought is good, but given unsought is better. -*William Shakespeare*

Spread love everywhere you go. First of all in your own house... Let no one ever come to you without leaving better and happier. -*Mother Teresa*

We dare not let our love for others be conditioned by their behavior. -*Laine Rosin*

Making It

It never fails: everybody who really makes it does it by busting his ass. -*Alan Arkin*

Malice

He that scattereth thorns must not go barefoot. -*Thomas Fuller*

Materialism

He who trusts riches will fall, but the righteous will flourish like foliage. -*Proverbs 11:28*

Meddling

Don't scald your tongue in other people's broth. -*English Proverb*

Have you so much time to spare from your own affairs that you can attend to another man's with which you have no concern? -*Terence, 163 BC*

Miracle

True miracles are created by men when they use the courage and intelligence that God gave them. -*Jean Anouilh*

Misfortune

I never knew any man in my life who could not bear another's misfortunes perfectly like a Christian. -*Alexander Pope*

Mislead

A truth that's told with bad intent beats all the lies you can invent. -*William Blake*

Mistake

Measure thy cloth ten times, thou canst cut it but once. -*Russian Proverb*

Modesty

If you want people to think well of you, do not speak well of yourself. -*Blaise Pascal*

Moderation

Moderation is the silken string running through the pearl chain of all virtues.- *Joseph Hall*

Money

Never spend your money before you have it. *-Thomas Jefferson*

Motive

All that we do is done with an eye to something else. *-Aristotle, 400 BC*

It is the deed that matters, not the fame.

Mourning

The true way to mourn the dead is to take care of the living who belong to them. *-Edmund Burke*

Neighbor

Do not waste your time bothering about whether you love your neighbor; act as if you did...When you are behaving as if you love someone, you will presently come to love him. *-C.S. Lewis*

Occupation

The best career advice to the young is find out what you like doing best and get someone to pay you for doing it. *-Katherine Whiteborn*

Opposition

He that wrestles with us strengthens our nerves and sharpens our skills. Our antagonist is our helper. *-Edmund Burke, 1790*

Opportunity

It is possible to create light and sound and order within us, no matter what calamity may befall us in the outer world. -*Hellen Keller*

Optimist

An optimist is a person who makes the best of it when he gets the worst of it. -*Laurence J. Peter*

Others

We are better able to study our neighbors than ourselves, and their actions than our own. -*Aristotle, 400 BC*

Overcoming

It takes a strong man to swim against the current; any dead fish will float with it.

Pacifism

Non-violence is not a garment to be put on and off at will. Its seat is in the heart, and it must be an inseparable part of our being. -*Mahatma K. Ghandi, 1900*

Paranoid

Just because you're paranoid doesn't mean you're not being followed.

Passion

Only passions, great passions, can elevate the soul to great things. -*Denis Diderot*

Past/Future

The past cannot be changed, but the future is still in your power. *-Hugh White*

Patience

All men commend patience, although few are willing to practice it. *-Thomas A. Kempis*

Payment

He who pays the piper may call the tune. *-English Proverb*

Peace

Do everything possible to live in peace with everyone. *-Romans 12:18*

If you are not a peacemaker, at least do not be a troublemaker. *-Isaac from Syria*

Peer Pressure

Do not follow the crowd in doing wrong. *-Exodus 23:2*

People

I believe that there are two kinds of people in the world, "givers" and "takers." *-Karen McCarthy*

People do things that they know are wrong, but they think that the rules don't apply to them and that they can get away with it. *-Thomas Finley, PhD*

Performance

It is an immutable law in business that words are words, explanations are explanations, promises are promises- but only performance is reality. -*Harold S. Geneen, former Chairman, IT&T*

Persuasion

If the horn cannot be twisted, the ear can. -*Malay Proverb*

Perseverance

Most of the important things in the world have been accomplished by people who have kept on trying when there seemed to be no help at all. -*Dale Carnegie*

Perseverance can tip the scales from failure to success.

Press on. Nothing in the world can take the place of persistence. -*Ray A. Kroc, McDonald's Corporation*

'Tis a lesson you should heed, try, try again. If at first you don't succeed, try, try again. -*William Edward Hickson*

Throw your heart over the fence and the rest will follow. -*Norman Vincent Peale*

When you get to the end of your rope, tie a knot and hang on. -*Franklin D. Roosevelt*

Perspective

It's not what happens to you, it's what you do about it. -*W. Mitchell*

Power

All men having power ought to be distrusted to a certain degree. -*James Madison*

I often say of George Washington that he was one of the few in the whole history of the world who was not carried away by power. *-Robert Frost*

It is better to be the head of a mouse than the tail of a lion. *-Spanish Proverb*

Praise

Let another praise you, and not your own mouth; someone else, and not your own lips. *-Proverbs 27:2*

Praise is much more effective in bringing out the best in people than criticism. *-Editor*

The greatest form of praise is the sound of consecrated feet seeking out the lost and helpless. *-Billy Graham*

Polite

Anyone can be polite to a king. It takes a gentleman to be polite to a beggar.

Poor

What the poor need, even more than food and clothing and shelter (though they need these, too, desperately), is to be wanted. *-Mother Teresa*

Possible/Impossible

The difference between the impossible and the possible lies in a person's determination. *-Tommy Lasorda*

Poverty

Poverty often deprives a man of all spirit and virtue. *-Benjamin Franklin*

Poverty urges us to do and suffer anything that we may escape from it, and so leads us away from virtue. *-Horace Carmina*

The more is given the less people will work for themselves, and the less they work, the more their poverty will increase. -*Leo Tolstoy*

Potential

Treat people as if they were what they ought to be and you help them to become what they are capable of being. -*Johann W. Von Goethe*

Prejudice

A prejudiced person will almost certainly claim that he has sufficient warrant for his views. -*Gordon W. Allport*

Prejudice is a fragrant opinion without visible means of support. -*Amrbose Bierce*

It is never too late to give up your prejudices. -*Henry David Thoreau*

You can't hold a man down without staying down with him. -*Booker T. Washington*

Preparedness

For all your days prepare, and meet them all alike when you are the anvil, bear- when you are the hammer, strike. -*Edwin Markham*

We are all, it seems, saving ourselves for the Senior Prom. But many of us forget that somewhere along the way we must learn to dance. -*Alan Harrington*

Present

Real generosity toward the future lies in giving all to the present. -*Albert Camus*

Pretension

The frog tried to look as big as the elephant, and burst. -*African Proverb*

Pretend

We are what we pretend to be. -*Kurt Vonnegut, Jr., author*

Prepare

Prepare yourself in good fortune for the bad. Be expedient in the summer to make provision for the winter. -*Baltasar Grecian, 1600*

Pride

He was like a cock who though the sun had risen to hear him crow. -*George Eliot*

Pride is like a beard. It keeps growing. The solution? Shave it every day.

Principle

Moderation in temper is always a virtue; but moderation in principle is always a vice. -*Thomas Paine*

Procrastination

I'm going to stop putting things off starting tomorrow. Procrastination and worry are the twin thieves that will try to rob you of your brilliance- but even the smallest action will drive them from your camp. -*Gil Atkinson*

When your horse is on the brink of a precipice, it's too late to pull the reins. -*Chinese Proverb*

Most procrastinators jump from one task to the next and never finish anything. Make yourself complete one task before moving to another. -*Dr. Gail Saltz, Psychiatrist*

Procrastination is the fertilizer that makes your chores grow.

Twenty percent of Americans are considered "chronic procrastinators." Putting things off has more to do with emotional dramas we carry within us than laziness. *-Dr. Gail Saltz, Psychiatrist*

Promiscuity

Like the bee its sting, the promiscuous leave behind them in each encounter something of themselves by which they are made to suffer. *-Cyril Connolly*

Promises

Better break your word than do worse in keeping it. *-Thomas Fuller, MD 1732*

He who promises everything, promises nothing. *-Baltasar Grecian*

Make promises sparingly and keep them faithfully.

Vow not to make a promise you don't think you can keep. *-Ann Landers*

We promise much to avoid giving little. *-Vauvenargues, 1746*

Priorities

If unaware about your priorities, talk to someone with an incurable disease. *-Editor*

It's a good idea not to major in minor things. *-Anthony Robbins*

It's hard to overestimate the unimportance of most things.

We can always live on less when we have more to live for. *-S. Stephan McKenney*

Problem

The right angle from which to approach any problem is the try angle!

Profiteering

When a man sells eleven ounces for twelve, he makes a compact with the devil and sells himself for the value of an ounce. *-Henry Ward Beecher, 1887*

Prosperity/Adversity

Be moderate in prosperity, prudent in adversity. *-Periander, 585 BC*

Prudence

A prudent man does not make the goat his gardener. *-Hungarian Proverb*

If though canst not see the bottom, wade not. *-English Proverb*

Judgement is not upon all occasions required, but discretion always is. *-Lord Chesterfield, 1766*

The better part of valor is discretion. *-William Shakespeare*

Punctuality

Men count up the faults of those who keep them waiting. *-French Proverb*

Quarrel

You should either avoid quarrels altogether or else put an end to them as quickly as possible; otherwise, anger may grow into hatred, making a plank out of a splinter, and turn the soul into a murderer. *-St. Augustine*

Starting a quarrel is like breaching a damn, so drop the matter before a dispute breaks out. *-Proverbs 17:14*

Racism

Racism is not an excuse to not do the best you can. *-Arthur Ashe, Tennis Champion*

Regret

Regret is a waste of energy. You can't build on it; you can only wallow in it.

Remedy

It's a pity to shoot the pianist when the piano is out of tune. -*Rene Coty*

Required

Be able to speak to every man in his own language. -*Baltasar Grecian*

Responsibility

It is easy to dodge our responsibilities, but we cannot dodge the consequences of dodging our responsibilities. -*Lord Josiah Charles Stamp*

Resentment

Resentment always hurts you more than it does the person you resent. -*Rich Warren, Pastor*

Resentment is like taking poison and waiting for the other person to die. -*Malacky McCourt*

Revenge

A man that studieth revenge keeps his own wounds green which otherwise would heal and do well. -*Francis Bacon*

In taking revenge, a man is but even with his enemy; but in passing it over, he is superior. -*Francis Bacon*

No revenge is more honorable than the one not taken. -*Spanish Proverb*

Revenge is a dish that should be eaten cold. -*English Proverb*

Reward

The wicked man earns deceptive wages, but he who sows righteousness reaps a sure reward. -*Proverbs 11:18*

Ridicule

It is easier to ridicule than to commend. -*Thomas Fuller, 1640*

Secrets

He who tells his secrets to another makes himself his slave. -*Baltasar Grecian*

Self-Centered

They make the greatest show of what they have done, who have done the least; rest in accomplishment, and leave talk to others. -*Baltasar Grecian*

Self-Control

I think the first virtue is to restrain the tongue: he approaches nearest to God, who knows how to be silent, even though he is in the right. -*Cato*

The Godliest form of self-expression is self-control: maintaining an even keel through the turbulent sea of human life. -*Paul Crouch*

Self-Criticism

He who makes great demands upon himself is naturally inclined to make great demands on others. -*Andre Gide*

Selflessness

He that plants trees loves others besides himself. -*Old English Proverb*

Self-Righteousness

Why do you look at the speck in your brother's eye, and pay no attention to the beam that is in your own eye. -*Matthew 7:3*

Severity

I must be cruel, only to be kind. -*William Shakespeare*

Service

A favor well bestowed is almost as great an honor to him who confers it as to him who receives it. -*Richard Steele, 1711*

He merits no thanks that does a kindness for his own end. -*Thomas Fuller, 1640*

To oblige persons often costs little and helps much. -*Baltasar Grecian, 1647*

Shame

Better a red face than a black heart. -*Portuguese Proverb*

Blushing is the color of virtue. -*Diogenes The Cynic, 300*

Bad shame humiliates and makes you feel bad about the way you look or feel. -*Dr. Joyce Brothers*

Good shame can lead to self-discovery and growth and can nurture and protect. -*Dr. Joyce Brothers*

Silence

It is hard to be silent when you have nothing to say.

The silence often of pure innocence persuades when speaking fails. -*William Shakespeare*

Sin

A man does not sin by commission only, but often by omission. -*Marcus Aurelius, 200*

Anyone, then, who knows the good he ought to do and doesn't do it, sins. -*James 4:17*

Sin sees the bait but is blind to the hook.

Sincerity

Be as you would seem to be. -*Thomas Fuller, MD, 1732*

Slander

Folk whose own behavior is most ridiculous are always to the fore in slandering others. -*Moliere, 1664*

He that flings dirt at another dirtieth himself most. -*Thomas Fuller, MD 1732*

Smile

Smile, it is the key that fits the lock of everybody's heart. -*Anthony J. D'Angelo*

Smile when picking up the phone. The caller will hear it in your voice.

A smile is the universal language; speak it often.

Smoking

To cease smoking is the easiest thing I ever did. I ought to know because I've done it a thousand times. -*Mark Twain*

Soldiers

Theirs not to make reply, theirs not to reason why, theirs but to do or die. -*Alfred Lord Tennyson, 1854*

Sow/Reap

It is like the seed put in the soil- the more one sows, the greater the harvest. -*Orison Sivett Marden*

Remember this: whoever sows sparingly will also reap sparingly, and whoever sows bountifully will also reap bountifully. -*2 Corinthians 9:6*

Speaking

A fool gives full vent to his anger. -Proverbs 29:11

Before you say anything to anyone, ask yourself three things: Is it true? Is it kind? Is it necessary?

To speak ill of others is a dishonest way of praising ourselves; let us be above such transparent egotism…If you can't say good and encouraging things, say nothing. Nothing is often a good thing to say, and always a clever thing to say. -*Will Durant*

Spontaneity

We never do anything well till we cease to think about the manner of doing it. This is the reason why it is so difficult for any but natives to speak a language correctly or idiomatically. -*William Haylitt, 1839*

Stoicism

Let a man accept his destiny, no pity and no tears. -*Euripides, 414 BC*

Straight Talk

Say what you mean and mean what you say. -*Editor*

Strength

We all have enough strength to bear the misfortune of others. -*La Rochefoucauld*

Stupidity

Whenever a man does a thoroughly stupid thing it is always from the noblest motive. -*Oscar Wilde*

Success

Formula for success: under promise and over deliver. -*Tom Peters*

Success is to be measured not as much by the position that one has reaches in life as by the obstacles that one has overcome while trying to succeed. -*Booker T. Washington*

Sympathy

The comforter's head never aches. -*Italian Proverb*

Talk

Don't talk unless you can improve the silence. -*Vermont Proverb*

The more people try to impress you with how much they know, the less they know. -*Editor*

Temper

A tart temper never mellows with age, and a sharp tongue is the only edged tool that grows keener with constant use. -*Washington Irving*

When you are in the right you can afford to keep your temper, and when you are in the wrong, you cannot afford to lose it. -*Ghandi*

Temperance

Temperance is moderation in the things that are good and total abstinence from the things that are foul. -*Frances E. Willard*

Thankfulness

Give thanks in [not for] all circumstances. -*1 Thessalonians 5:18*

Threat

If you can't bite, don't show your teeth. -*Yiddish Proverb*

Timeliness

The time is always right to do what is right. -*Martin Luther King, Jr.*

A word spoken in the right moment- how good it is! -*Proverbs 15:23*

Truth

Those who feel it is okay to tell white lies soon go color blind.

Whoever is careless with the truth in small matters cannot be trusted with important matters. -*Albert Einstein*

View

It is easier to go down a hill than up, but the view is from the top.

Virtue

A timid question will always receive a confident answer. -*Lord Darling*

Search others for their virtues, thy self for thy vices. -*Benjamin Franklin*

Words/Deeds

A thousand words will not leave so deep an impression as one deed. -*Henrik Ibsen*

Work

I believe in the dignity of labor, whether with head or hand; that the world owes no man a living but that it owes every man an opportunity to make a living. -*John D. Rockefeller*

The best preparation for good work tomorrow is to do good work today. -*Elbert Hubbard*

Wrongdoing

A small demerit extinguishes a long service. -*Thomas Fuller, 1640*

You cannot do wrong without suffering wrong. -*Ralph Waldo Emerson*

Wrong/Right

The wrong shall fail, the right prevail. -*Henry W. Longfellow*

Yourself

Be yourself; an original is always worth more than a copy.

3.
EDUCATION MATTERS

Academies

They teach in academies far too many things, and far too much that is useless. -*Goethe*

Achievement

By their fruits you will know them. -*Matthew 7:20*

Achieving

All men who have achieved great things have been great dreamers. -*Orison Swett Marden*

Attitude

It is not the IQ but the I WILL which is important in education.

Books

A book is a mirror: if an ass peers into it, you can't expect an apostle to look out. -*Georg Christopher Lichtenberg*

Anyone who says "you can't judge a book by its cover" has never met the category buyer from Barnes & Noble. -*Terri Lonier*

A room without books is like a body without a soul. -*Cicero*

Even the most careful and expensive marketing plans cannot sell people a book they don't want to read. -*Michael Korda*

It is with books as with men- a very small number play a great part; the rest are lost in the multitude. -*Voltaire*

Many books can inform, but only the Bible can transform.

Of making many books there is no end, and much study wearies the body. -*Ecclesiastes 12:12*

Some books are to be tasted, others to be swallowed, and some few to be chewed and digested. -*Francis Bacon*

Some read to think- these are rare; some to write- these are common; and some read to talk- and these are the great majority. -*Charles Caleb Colton*

The Bible is unquestioningly the most important book in history. Two thousand years have passes since its last recorded words. Unlike other books, it has never dwindled down to the oblivion. -*Editor*

Character

Character is doing what is right when no one is looking. -*Buddy Watts, U.S. Representative*

Knowledge has outstripped character development, and the young today are given an education rather than an upbringing. -*Ilya Ehrenburg*

Civics

Civics education must help to shape character in young people. It's not just a class that students take for one hour a day. It must be a way of thinking about responsibilities and rights- especially the rights to life, liberty, and property. -*David Bobb, Hillsdale College*

Choice

When you have to make a choice and don't make it, that is in itself a choice. -*William James*

Columnist

A columnist is either in the heating or lighting business. You can heat things up or shed some new light. -*Thomas Friedman, New York Times Columnist*

Competition

A horse never runs so fast as when he has other horses to catch up and outpace. -*Ovid, 8 AD*

Comparing

Do your own work well, and then you will have something to be proud of. But don't compare yourself with others. -*Galatians 6:4*

Conduct

The true measure of a man is how he treats someone who can do him absolutely no good. -*Samuel Johnson*

Whatever you do, do it with all your might. -*Ecclesiastes 9:10*

Counted

Not everything that can be counted counts, and not everything that counts can be counted. -*Albert Einstein*

Critic

A critic is a man who creates nothing and thereby feels qualified to judge the work of creative men. -*Robert Heinlein, Writer*

Differences

Over the years, I had to learn to respect people with whom I have differences. I try to find common ground. -*Bill Faith, 2003 Ohioan of the Year*

Different

By nature all men are alike, but by education widely different. -*Chinese Proverb*

Direction

'Tis education that forms the common mind. Just as the twig is bent, the tree is inclined. -*Alexander Pope*

Discovery

Education is a progressive discovery of our own ignorance. -*Will Durant*

Education

Education is not an option or a privilege in this society. It is the bedrock of democracy and the key to national and personal prosperity. -*Alex Machaskee, President and Publisher of the Plain Dealer*

Highly educated young people are tutored, taught, and monitored in all respects of their lives, except the most important, which is character building. -*Tom Wolfe, Author*

Enlightenment

The task of a modern educator is not to cut down jungles, but to irrigate deserts. -*C.S. Lewis*

Experiences

He who neglects to drink of the spring of experience is likely to die of thirst in the desert of ignorance. -*Lina Po*

Experience/Travel

These are an education in themselves. *-Euripides, 426 BC*

Faults

When looking at faults, use a mirror, not a telescope. *-Yazid Ibrahim*

Fool

Only a fool tests the depth of the water with both feet. *-African Proverb*

Forgiveness

The weak can never forgive. Forgiveness is the attribute of the strong. *- Mahatma Ghandi*

Friend

Don't walk behind me, I may not lead. Don't walk in front of me, I may not follow. Just walk beside me and be my friend. *-Albert Camus*

Treat a friend as a person who may someday become your enemy; an enemy as a person who someday may become your friend. *-George Bernard Shaw*

Goal

The goal of education is the advancement of knowledge and the dissemination of truth.*-John F. Kennedy*

Imagine a school in which the goal for each child is not only to master areas of content knowledge and academic skills, but to understand how one learns so he or she can develop strategies to maximize performance in school and life beyond school. *-Katherine B. Howard*

Graduation

The truly graduated never graduate.

Higher Education

Know thyself-Socrates. Control yourself- Cicero. Give yourself- Christ. -*Walter T. Tatara*

Home

A growing body of evidence indicates that home-based education works-consistently, regularly, normally. -*Professor Simon J. Dablman*

On average, home-taught kids are brighter academically, more stable emotionally, more respectful to parents, more spiritually perceptive, more sociable, more bonded with siblings, and just generally happier than the average kid. -*Rick and Marilyn Boyer, 24 years of Home Schooling Experience*

Education, like neurosis, begins at home. -*Milton R. Sapirstein*

Honesty

Honesty without compassion is brutality.

Hypocracy

We ought to see far enough into a hypocrite to see even his sincerity. -*G.K. Chesterson*

Ignorance

He that knows little often repeats it. -*Thomas Fuller, MD, 1640*

Influence

Why not use your influence for something better than fame?   Be unforgettable. -*Regina Brett, Plain Dealer columnist*

Judging

Don't judge a man until you've walked a mile in his boots. -American Proverb

Judge a tree from its fruit- not from the leaves. -*Euripides, 400 BC*

Knowledge

Knowledge is of two kinds: we know a subject ourselves, or we know where we can find information upon it. -*Samuel Johnson*

The knowledge of the world is only to be acquired in the world, and not in a closet. -*Lord Chesterfield*

There is no subject so old that something new cannot be said about it. -*Dostoevsky*

Language

A child, when it begins to speak, learns what it is that it knows. -*John Hall Wheelock*

If language be not in accordance with the truth of things, affairs cannot be carried on to success. –*Confucius, 500 BC*

Life

The difference between an autobiography and an unauthorized biography is like the difference between an account of your life written by your mother and one written by your mother-in-law. -*Marilyn vos Savant*

Literature

The land of literature is a fairyland to those who view it at a distance; but like all landscapes, the charm fades on a nearer approach and the thorns and briars become visible. -*Washington Irving*

Means

The things taught in school are not an education but a means to an education. -*Ralph Waldo Emerson*

Mind

The direction of the mind is more important than its progress. -*Joseph Joubert*

Difficulties strengthen the mind, as well as labor does the body. *Seneca, 65 AD*

We should take care not to make the intellect our god; it has, of course, powerful muscles, but no personality. -*Albert Einstein, 1950*

Mistakes

A thousand mistakes are an education if you learn something from every one.

Movement

Anything in education that is labeled a "movement" should be avoided like the plague. -*Diane Ravitch*

News

Nowadays, truth is the greatest news. -*Thomas Fuller, MD 1732*

Opportunities

If you always do the best you can, opportunities will come your way. - *Susan Whitney, Office Director*

Plagiarism

If you steal from one another it's plagiarism; if you steal from many, it's research. -*Wilson Mizner*

Philosophy

Education is a multidirectional process that instills original thought and examination focusing on: ideas over people, self-reliance over dependency, reason over understanding, and creativity over rote memorization. The best education looks to the future and can be explained with plain language. -*Ralph Waldo Emerson, 1803-1882*

The philosophy of the schoolroom in one generation will be the philosophy of the government in the next. -*Abraham Lincoln*

Poetry

Poetry is the language in which man explores his own amazement. -*Christopher Fry*

Potential

Education is helping the child realize his potentialities. -*Erich Fromm*

Proverbs

A proverb is a short sentence with long experience.

In the proverbs, a drop of ink makes a thousand think. -*Bennet Cerf*

Proverbs give us quality, not quantity. An hour of reading proverbs is usually worth weeks, even months or years, of ordinary reading. Here is wisdom, not knowledge. -*Montaigne*

Proverbs introduce us to ourselves- to that bigger, grander man we never knew, beating beneath that dwarf of a man we always knew. That bigger man often haunts us until we express him. -*Ralph Waldo Emerson*

Quotations

It is a good thing for an uneducated [and educated] man to read books of quotations. -*Winston Churchill*

The wisdom of the wise and the experience of the ages are perpetuated by quotations. -*Benjamin Disraeli*

Fire your ambition and courage by studying the priceless advice of proverbs and wise sayings. They're the shortest road to wisdom you'll ever find. -*Alexander Graham Bell*

Reading

If the desire to read diminishes (television is seen as the culprit) so does one's ability to read. -*Norman Mailer, Author*

I have never known any distress that an hour's reading did not relieve. -*Montesquieu*

No man understands a deep book until he has seen and lived at least part of its contents. -*Ezra Pound*

Reading furnishes the mind only with materials of knowledge; it is thinking that makes what we read ours. -*John Locke, 1706*

To read without reflecting is like eating without digesting. -*Edmund Burke*

Respect

We must respect ourselves if we expect others to respect us.

Roots

The roots of education are bitter, but the fruit is sweet. -*Aristotle, 400 BC*

Scholars

The world's great men have not commonly been great scholars, nor its great scholars great men. -*Oliver Wendell Holmes, Sr.,1858*

Science

Science has always promised two things not necessarily related- an increase first in our powers, second in our happiness or wisdom, and we have come to realize that it is first and less important of the two promises which it has kept most abundantly. -*Joseph Wood Krutch*

Science can only ascertain what *is*, but not what *should* be, and outside of its domain value judgments of all kinds remain necessary. -*Albert Einstein*

School

In 1940, teachers were asked what they regarded as the three major problems in American schools. They identified the three major problems as littering, noise, and chewing gum. Teachers last year were asked what the three major problems in American schools were, and they defined them as rape, assault, and suicide. -*William Bennett, 1993*

Few parents realize how far their children have progressed by age six. Most seeds that determine behavior will have been planted. They have acquired two-thirds of their height. They will be one-third of the way toward being practically on their own. Some child experts say that by age six children learn over half of what they will ever know. Younger children (three of four boys and one of four girls) struggle in school because of age differences. For example, children must be five by September 30th to enroll in Kindergarten. Those born after this date must wait until the following year. This amounts to a one year age difference between the two extreme age groups, not taking into account the difference in maturity development. Children born in June,

July, August, and September would definitely benefit waiting until the following year. It is to the students' advantage to be one of the older rather than the younger members of the class, especially boys. *-Editor*

Schooling

I never let my schooling interfere with my education. *-Mark Twain*

Sculpture/Soul

What sculpture is to a block of marble, education is to the soul. *-Joseph Addison*

Self-Control

Prove that you can control yourself and you are an educated man; without this, all other education is good for nothing.

Self-Education

The object of education is to prepare the young to educate themselves throughout their lives. *-Robert Maynard Hutchins*

Self-Learning

They know enough who know how to learn. *-Henry Brooks Adams*

Simplicity

It is proof of high culture to say the greatest matters in the simplest way. *-Ralph Waldo Emerson, 1860*

Sleep

A full night's sleep is critical to enhancing learning. *-Matthew Walker, Harvard Medical School*

Students

All good students are the result of respect for teachers. We must put respect for teachers back in our society and back in our lives. -*Anthony Yen, Chinese immigrant and founder of Teacher's Day celebration*

Strength/Uniqueness

In a very troubled world, we have found our strength in our uniqueness. -*Di Anne McClenahan, Hillsdale College*

Study

All the end of study is to make you a good man and a useful citizen. -*John Adams, President*

Success

The ability to convert ideas to things is the secret of outward success. -*Henry Ward Beecher,1887*

Superiority/Inferiority

Superiority is a sure sign of inferiority. -*Editor*

Talent

Whether I'm a five-talent, two-talent, or one-talent person is not what counts in the long run…I must come to identify, cultivate, invest, prize, and enjoy the gifts that have been given to me. -*John Ortberg*

Talk

Do not let any unwholesome talk come out of your mouths, but only what is helpful for building others up according to their needs, that it may benefit those who listen. – *Henry Brooks Adams*

Teacher

A teacher affects eternity; he can never tell where his influence stops. *-Henry Brooks Adams*

I'm never going to be a movie star. But then, in all probability, Liz Taylor is never going to teach first and second grade. *-Mary J. Wilson, Elementary School Teacher*

In a completely rational society, the best of us would aspire to be teachers and the rest of us would have to settle for something less, because passing civilization along from one generation to the next ought to be the highest honor and highest responsibility anyone could have. *-Lee Iacocca*

Teaching

A man who knows a subject thoroughly, a man so soaked in it that he eats it, sleeps it, and reams it- this man can always teach it with success, no matter how little he knows of technical pedagogy. *-H.L. Mencken*

One good teacher in a lifetime may some times change a delinquent into a solid citizen. *-Philip Wylie*

Television

All television is educational television. The only question is, what is it teaching? *-Nicholas Johnson, Federal Communications Commission*

Thinking

The test of a truly educated man is what he is, and what he thinks, and what his mind absorbs or dreams, or creates when he is alone. *-Donald K. David*

Think before you speak; be slow to "correct" others, especially in objective matters. Instead, take a long, hard look at your own thinking. *-Marilyn vos Savant*

Time

Time has become the new money- the one nonrenewable resource; there's never enough for all we want to do. *-Janet H. Cho, Reporter*

Train

Train up a child in the way he should go; and when he is old, he will not depart from it. *-Proverbs 22:6*

Treasure

No one can ever take away your reputation or education. You can only give that away. *-John Ryan, Cleveland AFL-CIO*

Treat

Treat people as if they were what they ought to be and you can help them become what they are capable of being. *-Goethe*

Truth

Ideally, we should tell the truth because it is proper to do so, not because we fear being discovered and punished. Transforming our culture from vice to virtue will be a long battle that we must wage one kid at a time. It may take a generation. *-Michael Kirsh, Gastroenterologist, and father of two home-schooled children*

Understanding

Much learning does not teach understanding. *-Heraclitus*

To know a little less and to understand a little more; that, it seems to me, is our greatest need. *-James Ramsey Ullman*

Values

Understanding how values influence decision-making gives students the means to evaluate, not just blindly accept, information presented to them. -*Peg Yacobucci, Assistant Professor, Bowling Green State University*

Village

It takes a village to raise a child. -*African Proverb*

Vision

If I have seen further, it is by standing on the shoulders of giants. -*Bernard of Chartres*

Wisdom

A wise man hears one word and understands two. -*Yiddish Proverb*

It takes a wise man to recognize a wise man. -*Xenophanes, 600 BC*

The fool doth think he is wise, but the wise man knows himself to be a fool. -*Shakespeare, 1599*

Words

All words are pegs to hang ideas on. -*Henry Beecher, 1887*

Appreciative words are the most powerful forces for good on Earth. -*George W. Crane*

Words are like leaves; and where they most abound, much fruit of sense beneath is rarely found. -*Alexander Pope, 1711*

Words are like money; there is nothing so useless, unless in actual use. -*Uel Butler*

Do not use harmful words, but only helpful words, the kind that build up and provide what is needed, so that what you say will do good to those who hear you. *-Ephesians 4:29*

How forceful are right words! *-Job 6:25*

Words form the thread on which we string our experiences. *-Aldous Huxly, 1937*

Mark your words as a matter of caution; he too easy of speech, shortly falters and falls. *-Baltasar Grecian*

Words should be weighed and not counted. *-Yiddish Proverb*

Writing

A writer needs three things: experience, observation, and imagination. Any two of which, at times any one of which, can supply the lack of the others. *-William Faulkner*

If you would be a reader, read; if a writer, write. *-Epictetus, 200 AD*

In composing, as a general rule, run your pen through every other word you have written; you have no idea what vigor it will give your style. *-Sidney Smith, 1855*

Most people won't realize that writing is a craft. You have to take your apprenticeship in it like anything else. *-Katherine Anne Porter*

No one who cannot limit himself has ever been able to write. *-Nicolas Boileau, 1674*

Nothing goes by luck in composition. It allows for no tricks. The best you can write will be the best you are. *-Henry David Thoreau*

The pen is mightier than the sword. *-Bulwer-Lytton, 1838*

The secret of all good writing is sound judgement. *-Horace, 800 BC*

'Tis easy to write epigrams nicely, but to write a book is hard. -*Martial, 86 AD*

Try writing your own book. You will be totally surprised at how you view the next book you read! -*Editor*

Whatever sentence will bear to read twice, we may be sure was thought twice. -Henry David Thoreau

Writing comes more easily if you have something to say. -*Sholem Asch*

Writing is an exploration. You start from nothing and learn as you go. -*E.L. Doctorow*

You don't write because you want to say something; you write because you've got something to say. -*F. Scott Fitzgerald*

You must write for children the same way as you do for adults, only better. -*Maxim Gorky*

Your business as a writer is not to illustrate virtue but to show how a fellow may move toward it or away from it. -*Robert Penn Warren*

4.
FAMILY MATTERS

Accidents

Accidents will happen in the best regulated families. *-Charles Dickens*

Background

The most important factor in how well a child achieves is not how much the school spends to teach him. Rather, the student's family background is the greatest determinant of performance. *-James Coleman, Education Researcher*

Dinner

The National Center on Addiction and Substance Abuse (CASA) found that the more children eat dinner with their families, the less likely they are to use drugs, cigarettes, and alcohol. Also, studies link family dinners to good grades.

Spread the table and contention will cease. *-English Proverb*

Development

Childhood reveals tendencies. Youth develops personality. Maturity establishes character. *-Hubert van Zeller*

Family

Entire civilizations rise and fall on the strength of the family. *-Editor*

If anyone does not provide for his relatives, and especially for his immediate family, he has denied the faith and is worse than an unbeliever. *-1 Timothy 5:8*

Govern a family as you would cook a small fish: very gently. *-Chinese Proverb*

Happy families are all alike; every unhappy family is unhappy in its own way. *-Leo Tolstoy*

Human civilization is built from the bottom up, not the top down. The first brick of the foundation is individual human life, and the second brick is the family. *-Peter Sprigg, World Congress of Families*

The family is responsible for teaching lessons of independence, self-restraint, responsibility, and right conduct, which are essential to a free, democratic society. *-Barbara Da Foe Whitehead*

The family is the very foundation upon which society rests. It's the first and often the only place where children learn the right values to see them through adulthood, a place where they can be nurtured, loved, and accepted as God intended. *-Editor*

The most meaningful activities in the family are often those simple interactions that build lasting connections between generations. *-Dr. James Dobson*

The family is the nucleus of civilization. *-Will and Ariel Durant*

With the family influence gone, what I call vertical transmission of values from one generation to the next is gone, too. All you're left with is horizontal transmission of values through the influence of peers and other contemporary sources of information such as research studies, news media, and the entertainment-advertising industry. *-Robert S. Medelsohn, MD*

Family Pets

Keep in mind...to a dog you are family, to a cat you are staff.

Faults

There exists scarcely any man as accomplished, or so necessary to his own family, but he has some failing which will diminish their regrets at his loss. -*La Bruyere*

Fellowship

We are created for community, fashioned for fellowship, and formed for a family, and none of us can fulfill God's purposes by ourselves. -*Pastor Rick Warren*

Finance

Many families in financial difficult think that generating extra income, such as having the wife work, is the easiest and best way out of financial difficulties. That usually is not the case. Most problems are caused by overspending not insufficient income. In fact, more income will sometimes make a situation worse. As the total level of spending increases, so does the use of credit. -*Larry Burkett, Author*

Greed

A greedy man brings trouble to his family. -*Proverbs 15:27*

Home

If the home fails, the country is doomed. The breakdown of home life and influence will mark the breakdown of the nation's. -*Dr. Peter Marshall*

Obedience

If obedience is not rendered in the homes, we shall never have a whole city, country, principality, or kingdom well governed. For this order in the homes is the first rule; it is the source of all other rule and government. -*Martin Luther*

The basis of society, of any society, is a certain pride in obedience. When this pride no longer exists, the society collapses. *-E.M. Cioran*

Parents

We don't have choices about who our parents are and how they treated us, but we have a choice about whether we forgive our parents and heal ourselves. *-Bernie Siegel*

Prayer

The family that prays together, stays together is much more than a cliche! And when the family adds dimension of praying together in church, the truth becomes even stronger. *-Zig Zigler*

Priorities

If you would have a happy life, remember two things: in matters of principle, stand like a rock; in matters of taste, swim with the current. *-Thomas Jefferson*

Start/End

Other things may change us, but we start and end with family. *-Anthony Brandt*

MARRIAGE

Courtship

Choose your husband or wife with great care, as a friend as well as a lover, but having entered into matrimony, be willing to sacrifice any personal desires or possessions you have to make your marriage a success. -*Hervey Evans*

I flee who chases me, and chase who flees me. -*Ovid, 8 A.D.*

Keep your eyes wide open before marriage and half shut afterward. -*Benjamin Franklin*

Love is blind but marriage is a real eye-opener. -*Paula Deen*

Maidens! Why should you worry in choosing whom you shall marry? Choose whom you may; you will find you have got somebody else. -*John Hay, 1871*

Those marriages generally abound most with love and constancy that are preceded by a long courtship. The passion should strike root and gather strength before marriage be grafted on it. -*Joseph Addison*

A man falls in love through his eyes, a woman through her ears. -*Woodrow Wyatt*

Divorce

Alimony is like buying oats for a dead horse. -*Arthur Baer*

Because divorce has become so common, the whole world has downplayed the toll a divorce takes on kids. -*Gregory Keck, Psychologist*

Divorces fail as well as marriages. -*Editor*

Divorce is as difficult, or more so, for children to cope with than the death of a parent. -*Editor*

Divorce lingers forever with children. -*Gary Chapman*

Do not compare your mate with anyone else, for there is danger in becoming discontent by comparing your partner with others. -*Nick Holly*

Emotional divorce precedes actual divorce.

In divorce situations: a few are better off, a few are even worse off (especially financially), and the vast majority end up exchanging one set of problems for another. -*Editor*

It is very difficult and expensive to undo after you are married the things that your mother and father did to you while you were putting your first six birthdays behind you. -*Bureau of Social Hygiene Study*

Many marriages are destroyed each year in America by financial worries created by debt and poor money management. -*Larry Burkett, Author*

Many marriages today last about as long as those of a hundred years ago, only now they're terminated by divorce, not death. -*John W. Jacobs, MD, Therapist*

Only eight percent of marriages that began 50 or more years ago ended in divorce compared with today's forty percent divorce rate. -*Eva Kahana, Case Western Reserve University, Psychology Professor*

People wouldn't get divorced for such trivial reasons, if they didn't get married for such trivial reasons.

Second marriages have a higher failure rate than the first time down the aisle. -*Lyric Wallwork Winik*

There are four minds in the head of a divorced man who marries a divorced woman. -*Palestinian Talmund, 400 B.C.*

You can't escape marital stress the way you can other types of stress. Most people think marriage as a comfort zone and a place where you can relax, but when that is stressed, there is no safe haven. -*Professor Ann Marie Cans*

Husband & Wife

A good wife and health are a man's best wealth. *-Proverb*

An archeologist is the best husband any woman can have: the older he gets, the more interested he is in her. *-Agatha Christie*

An ideal wife is any woman who has an ideal husband. *-Booth Tarkington*

And let us consider how we may spur one another toward love and good deeds. *-Hebrews 10:24*

A perfect husband is one who doesn't expect a perfect wife (and vice versa). *-Editor*

A woman who has never seen her husband fishing doesn't know what a patient man she has married. *-Ed Howe*

Because marriage is a sacred institution and the foundation of society, it should not be re-defined by activist judges...I support a constitutional amendment to protect the institution of marriage. *-President George W. Bush*

Better to live on a corner of the roof than share a house with a quarrelsome wife [husband]. *-Proverbs 21:9*

Between a man and his wife nothing ought to rule but love. *-William Penn*

Blessed are the husband and wife who are as polite and courteous to one another as they are to their friends. Blessed are those mates who never speak loudly to one another, and who make their home a place "where seldom is a heard a discouraging word."

Disrespect for women has invariably been the surest sign of moral corruption. *-Baron Montesquieu, 1748*

Husbands and wives alike think that if they simply point out their spouses' bad points often enough, their partner will gladly comply, correct their faults, and again become the perfect angels they were when dating. It never works out that way. -*D. James Kennedy, Ph.D.*

If you educate a man you educate a person, but if you educate a woman you educate a family. -*Ruby Manikan*

In disagreements with loved ones, deal with the current situation. Don't bring up the past.

Joint undertakings stand a better chance when they benefit both sides. -*Euripides, 400 B.C.*

My wife said I never listen to her. At least I think that's what she said.

Please remember I am different from you (husband). I am like many women in that what I feel about something often speaks more clearly than what I think about it. -*Dice Fryling*

So husbands ought to love their own wives as their own bodies; he who loves his wife loves himself. -*Ephesians 5:28*

That we are what we are is due mostly to these two factors, mothers and fathers. -*Charlotte Perkins Gilman*

These impossible women [and men, Editor]! How they do get around us! The poet was right: can't live with them, or without them. -*Aristophanes, 411 B.C.*

When a wife or husband sins, neither is totally innocent. -*Italian Proverb*

Whether women are better than men I cannot say- but I can say they are certainly no worse. -*Golda Meir*

You can bear your own faults, and why not a fault in your wife? -*Benjamin Franklin*

Manhood: Husbands & Fathers

Masculinity ought to be defined in terms of relationships and taught in terms of the capacity to love and be loved. -*Joe Ehrmann, Football Coach*

Athletic ability, sexual conquest, and economic success are not the best measurements of manhood. -*Joe Ehrmann, Football Coach*

A father holds awesome power in the lives of his children, for good or ill. Families have understood that fact for centuries. -*Dr. James Dobson*

An angry father is most cruel toward himself. -*Publilius Syrus, 100 B.C.*

Children are likely to live up th what their fathers believe of them. -*Lady Bird Johnson*

Don't make a baby if you can't be a father. -*New York City Board of Education*

Fathers, do not provoke your children, lest they become discouraged. -*Colossians 3:21*

It behooves a father to be blameless if he expects a son to be. -*Homer, 1000 B.C.*

Greatness of name in the father often times overwhelms the son; they stand too near one another. The shadow kills the growth. -*Ben Johnson, 1640*

Husbands, love your wives and do not be harsh with them. -*Colossians 3:19*

Listen, my son, to your father's instruction and do not forsake your mother's teaching. -*Proverbs 1:8*

Male domination has had some very unfortunate effects. It has made the most intimate of human relations, that of marriage, one of master and slave, instead of one between equal partners. -*Bertrand Russell*

The most important thing a father can do for his children is to love their mother. -*Theodore Hesburgh*

There must always be a struggle between a father and son, while one aims at power and the other at independence. -*Samuel Johnson, 1763*

This is what a father ought to be about: helping his son to form the habit of doing right on his own initiative, rather than because he's afraid of some serious consequences. -*Terence, 160 B.C.*

You don't raise heroes, you raise sons. And if you treat them like sons, they'll turn out to be heroes, even if it's just in your own eyes. -*Walter Schierra, Sr., astronaut*

Marriage

A family based on marriage between a man and a woman was a pillar of society that justly had rights and duties specific to it. -*Pope John Paul II*

A girl who thinks that a man will treat her better after marriage than before is a fool. -*William Clarke Hall*

A man who marries a woman to educate her falls a victim to the same fallacy as the woman who marries a man to reform him. -*Elbert Hubbard*

A successful marriage requires falling in love many times, always with the same person. -*Mignon McLaughan*

Both marriage and death ought to be welcome; the one promises happiness, doubtless the other assures it. -*Mark Twain*

Components of a good marriage: mutual respect, genuine commitment, good communication, time and effort, spiritual unity. -*The Billy Graham Christian Worker's Handbook*

Concentrate on the biggest qualities in the person you want to love you. Put little things where they belong- in second place. -*David Joseph Schwartz, Ph.D.*

Couples can improve their relationship beyond belief if they can convince themselves that their partner, as a package, is equal to or greater than themselves. -*Editor*

Don't let your marriage run out of gas. Keep your tank full and pay attention to warning signals. -*Karen Porter*

Don't rest your laurels. Continue practicing the three T's: time together, talk, touch. -*Michele Weiner-Davis*

For a marriage to be peaceful the husband should be deaf and the wife blind. -*Spanish Proverb*

Gays and lesbians have a right to live as they choose, but they don't have the right to redefine marriage for our entire country. -*Matt Daniels, executive director of the Alliance for Marriage*

Give each other separate space and independence for other activities and friendships. No one can be all things to one. -*Editor*

God instituted marriage as the foundational building block of society. -*Dr. James Dobson*

Good things happen when we honor what marriage is; bad things happen when we dishonor it.

It is a fusion of two hearts- the union of two lives- the coming together of two tributaries, which after being joining in marriage, will flow in the same channel in the same direction...carrying the same burdens of responsibility and obligation. -*Peter Marshall, Pastor*

If you want to know how your girl will treat you after marriage, just listen to her talking to her little brother. -*Sam Levenson*

It is a matter of life and death for married people to interrupt each other's stories, for if they did not, they would burst. -*Logan Pearsall Smith*

It is not marriage that fails; it is people that fail. All that marriage does is to show them up. –*Reverend Harry Emerson Fosdick*

It is the peculiar quality of a fool to perceive the faults of others and to forget his own. -*Cicero*

It takes two halves coming together to make the ball bounce. -*Editor*

It seems to be our destiny never to love anything without seeking to alter it, and in altering it to make it other than what we first loved.

If you want to have a happier marriage, make the first move.

Let there be spaces in your togetherness. -*Kahlil Gibran*

Love built on beauty, soon as beauty, dies. - *John Donne*

Marriage is not an option. It is a precondition for social survival. -*Maggie Gallagher, National Review*

Married couples don't really know one another until they have eaten a bushel of salt together. -*Italian Proverb*

Marriages, like the people in them, are not perfect and take work. I believe you should always work toward these two goals: 1.) overcoming your own weakness; but 2.) allowing your spouse to have them. The goals may be unreachable, but if both husband and wife aim for them, they will become better people and avoid damaging their love relationship in the process. - *Marilyn vos Savant*

Most marriages recognize this paradox: Passion destroys passion; we want what puts an end to wanting what we want. -*John Fowles*

Neither sex, without some fertilization of the complementary characters of the other, is capable of the highest reaches of human behavior. -*H.L. Mencken*

Often the difference between a successful marriage and a mediocre one consists of leaving about three or four things a day unsaid. -*Harlan Miller*

Rarely marriages are wrecked on a big rock of adversity. It is on the smaller pebbles that they flounder. -*Velora Buscher*

Remember that the best relationship is one where your love for each other is greater than your need for each other.

Remember, all marriages have stormy periods. Seek professional help. Eighty-six percent of unhappy couples who stick it out report being much happier five years later. -*Linda Waite*

Show me one couple unhappy merely on account of their limited circumstances, and I will show you ten who are wretched from other causes. -*Samuel Taylor Coleridge*

Smile at each other, smile at your wife, smile at your husband, smile at your children, smile at each other- it doesn't matter who - and that will help you to grow up in greater love for each other. -*Mother Teresa*

Success in marriage does not come merely through finding the right mate, but through being the right mate. -*Barnett Brickner*

That is why a man will leave his father and mother and will be united with his wife, and they will become one flesh. -*Genesis 2:24*

The key to a good marriage is voluntary submission on the part of the wife and sacrificial love on the part of the husband. When those two combinations are at work, you can't help but have harmony. -*Vonette Bright*

There is no more lovely, friendly, and charming relationship, communion, or company than a good marriage. -*Martin Luther*

There is nothing nobler or more admirable than when two people who see eye to eye keep house as man and wife, confounding their enemies and delighting their friends. -*Homer, 900 B.C.*

To have and to hold from this day forward, for better or for worse, for richer, for poorer, in sickness and in health, to love and to cherish, till death do us part.

To have a functional, enjoyable union between two human beings, each has to be able to function independently. -*Paul Franks*

The critical period in matrimony is breakfast time. -*A.P. Herbert*

The secret of happy marriage is simple: Just keep on being polite to one another as you are to your friends. -*R. Quillen*

Though one may be overpowered, two can defend themselves. A cord with three strands is not quickly broken. -*Ecclesiastes 4:12*

To keep your marriage brimming with love in the loving cup, whenever you're wrong, admit it; whenever you're right, shut up. -*Ogden Nash*

To wed is to bring not only our worldly goods but every potential capacity to create more values in living together...In becoming one these two create a new world that had never existed before. -*Paul E. Johnson*

Woe to the house where the hen crows and the rooster keeps still. -*Spanish Proverb*

The goal in marriage is not to think alike, but to think together. -*Robert C. Dodds*

The goal of every married couple, indeed, every Christian home, should be to make Christ the Head, the Counselor and the Guide. -*Paul Sadler*

The key to a good marriage is two good forgivers. -*Dr. Billy Graham*

Sexuality

Studies find that male arousal is strongly visual, and when men engage in sexual activity or even anticipate it, brain structures once thought to have little connection to sex spring into action. The same brain regions, however, remain relatively quiet when women are aroused. -*Anahad O'Conner, New York Times News*

Adultery destroys marriages, destroys families, and destroys lives. -*Bible*

The Bible outlines a specific plan to for human sexuality. Throughout Scripture, God's intention for human sexual relationships is clearly limited to the heterosexual union between a man and a woman in marriage. -*Dr. James Dobson*

Husbands and wives should satisfy each other's sexual needs. -*1 Corinthians 7:3*

In most marriages, at some time, a husband or wife will refuse lovemaking because of distraction, excitement or, most likely, personal hurt. This is a powerful weapon because it touches the innermost sensitivities of the partner. But it is a weapon that should never be used. To do so is a sin against the spirit. -*Dr. Marion Hilliard*

Marriage should be honored by all, and the marriage bed kept pure, for God will judge the adulterer and all the sexually immoral. -*Hebrews 13:4*

People who have an affair with married men or women justify or rationalize their behavior by convincing themselves that the injured party somehow deserves the pain. -*Abigail Van Buren*

The sex instinct is one of the three or four prime movers of all that we are and dream, both individually and collectively. -*Philip Wylie, Author*

When cheated, wife or husband feels the same. -*Euripides, 426 B.C.*

Womanhood: Wives & Mothers

A wife of noble character is her husband's crown, but a disgraceful wife is like decay in his bones. -*Proverbs 12:4*

Be as interested in your spouse's day as you were when you were dating.

A mother cannot unlock all of life's doors for her children but she can help them find the keys. -*Catherine Britton*

A mother's pride is a kind of milk, nourishment that can come from no other source. -*Jeanne Marie Laskas*

A rich child often sits in a poor mother's lap. -*Danish Proverb*

As long as anger lives, she continues to be the fruitful mother of many unhappy children. -*John Glimacus*

A smart mother makes often a better diagnosis than a poor doctor. -*August Bier*

Every beetle is a gazelle in the eyes of its mother. -*Moorish Proverb*

If a woman's adult efforts are concentrated exclusively on her children, she is more likely to stifle than broaden her children's perspective and preparation for adult life. -*Alice S. Rossi*

It is impossible for any woman to love her children twenty-four hours a day. -*Milton R. Sapirstein*

Mothers are the most precious asset of any nation. They are more important than statesmen, than businessmen...They have the most important occupation of any person in this nation. -*Theodore Roosevelt*

She opens her mouth with wisdom, and on her tongue is the law of kindness. She watches over the ways of her household, and does not eat the bread of idleness. Her children rise up and call her blessed; her husband also, and he praises her. -*Proverbs 31:26-28*

Though motherhood is the most important of all professions, requiring more knowledge than any other department in human affairs, there was no attention given to the preparation for this office. -*Elizabeth Cady Stanton*

The ideal mother, like the ideal marriage, is a fiction. - *Milton R. Sapirstein*

What the mother sings to the cradle goes all the way down to the coffin. - *Henry Ward Beecher*

When children are little, they pull at their mother's skirt; when they grow up, they pull at their hearts. -*Italian Proverb*

PARENTING

Advice

It's often different for a daughter to accept suggestions about parenting from her mother or her siblings. -*Dr. Sylvia Rimm, Professor and author*

Age

Allow children to act their age. Speak to your child as respectfully as you would to a friend.

Always treat your child with respect, spend enjoyable time together as a family, and teach your child problem-solving skills. -*Aimee A. Kirsch, School Psychologist*

Ancestors/Descendants

You can't do much about your ancestors, but you can influence your descendants enormously.

Answers/Problems

Too often we give our children answers to remember rather than problems to solve. -*Roger Lewin*

Attitude

Children tend to adopt their parents' attitudes quite early in life. For example, when parents focus on the negative, children tend to do the same. But when parents look for the positive, children will learn that it is what is expected of them. The environment in which children are reared has so much to do with their attitudes about life. -*Editor*

Balance

Try to balance every no with a yes- minimum. -*Editor*

Behavior

The sooner parents expect responsible behavior from their children, the sooner they will come through. -*Editor*

Believe

We never really find out what we believe until we begin to instruct our children. -*Editor*

Blame

Resist the temptation to blame, and thereby set a good example for your children. Teach them to accept responsibility for their actions and not resort to making excuses and blaming others. It's a grave injustice to overlook irresponsible behavior in children and bail them out rather than letting them face the consequences of their actions. -*Editor*

Because children are born with unique personalities, parents often accept too much blame when they turn out "wrong" and take too much credit when they turn out "right." -*Editor*

Character

If good character traits are not instilled in children early, often they are not learned at all. Too often we place more emphasis on what children achieve rather than how they learn and interact with others. -*Editor*

Parents can only give good advice and put children on the right paths, but the final forming of a person's character lies in his or her own hands. -*Anne Franke*

Chores

I think that chores should be given to provide children with a feeling of worth, which is payment enough. If children balk at having chores, don't give in, but insist nicely and let them know that there will be consequence for not doing their chores. -*Cheri Cross, Cleveland*

Children

What the vast majority of American children need is to stop being pampered, stop being indulged, stop being chauffeured, stop being catered to. In the final analysis it is not what you do for your children but what you have taught them to do for themselves that will make them successful human beings. -*Ann Landers*

Church/Children

Adults who attended church regularly as a child are nearly three times as likely to be attending church today as are their peers who avoided the church during childhood (61% to 22%, respectively). -*George Barna Research*

Cleaning

Cleaning your house while your kids are still growing is like shoveling the walk before it stops snowing. -*Phyliss Diller*

Contentment

Typically, kids think that when they get more, then they will be satisfied. The world is filled with disappointed people seeking contentment from material possessions. Contentment is rooted in what people are, not on what they have. -*Editor*

Criticism/Praise

Sandwich every bit of criticism between two layers of praise. -*Mary Kay Ash*

Discipline

Disciplined children are happy children; undisciplined children are not. -*Editor*

He who spares the rod [correction] hates his son, but he who loves him is careful to discipline him. -*Proverbs 13:24*

No discipline seems pleasant at the time, but painful. Later on, however, it produces a harvest of righteousness and peace for those who have been trained by it. -*Hebrews 12:11*

Parents who are afraid to put their foot down usually have children who step on their toes. -*Chinese Proverb*

The rod and rebuke give wisdom, but a child left to himself brings shame to his mother. -*Proverbs 29:15*

Young children are incapable of reasoning. However, they do understand fear. –*Editor*

Mothers and fathers should be united in all aspects of child rearing, otherwise children are quick to take advantage when they fail to speak as one voice. -*Editor*

Do

Where parents do too much for their children, the children will not do much for themselves. -*Elbert Hubbard, 1927*

Education

Contrary to what many people think, the amount of formal education parents have is not the major factor in how children do in school and life. Parents who care about their children and practice Biblical child-rearing principles are the most effective. -*Editor*

Enthusiasm

If you can give your son or daughter only one gift, let it be Enthusiasm. -*Bruce Barton*

Environment

Everything children experience in the environment is recorded in their minds- forever! The more caring the environment the better children will respond and thrive. -*Editor*

Example

As parents, instructors, and coaches, setting the positive example is one of the most important responsibilities we have. -*Joe Dahlheimer*

Live your life in the manner that you would like your children to live theirs.

Expectations

Children don't expect perfect parents. In fact, it's amazing how many negative circumstances they can overcome, especially if they know they're loved. -*Editor*

It's very comforting for children, and adults also, to know that they don't have to be like everybody else. -*Editor*

Friendship

Children need to be taught that friendship just doesn't happen. Seeds have to be planted and cultivated. They have to work at it. -*Editor*

Good/Evil

The first idea that the child must acquire, in order to be actively disciplined, is that of the difference between good and evil. -*Maria Montessori, Educator*

Habits

Helping your children learn good habits is a valuable gift. Because once the bad ones have been established, they're terribly difficult to break. Children's character and personality are greatly determined by their habits. -*Editor*

Heredity/Environment

Since heredity is pre-determined there's little parents can do about it; but, they can do a lot about environment and this can make the biggest difference in how children turn out. -*Editor*

Home

It is in the home that the child learns the basic principle of accountability for actions: first to those around him, and ultimately to God. -*Maxine Hancock*

Honesty

To make your children capable of honesty is the beginning of education. -*John Ruskin*

Housework

I hate housework! You make the beds, you do the dishes—and six months later you have to start all over again. --*Joan Rivers*

Humility

Humility doesn't come naturally to children. They learn it best by example more than by words. Teaching humility is difficult but not impossible. -*Editor*

Indecision

Indecision is like the stepchild: If he doesn't wash his hands, he is called dirty; if he does, he is wasting water. -*Madagascan Proverb*

Independence

Let your children go if you want to keep them. -*M. Forbes*

Laughter

The average child laughs or smiles 400 times a day. The average adult laughs or smiles 15 times a day. Somewhere between childhood and adulthood many of us forget we have a joyful side and aren't sure how to reclaim it. -*Dr. Lee Berk*

Leading

The reason parents no longer lead their children in the right direction is because the parents aren't going that way themselves. -*Kin Hubbard*

Listen

Children have never been very good at listening to their elders, but they have never failed to imitate them. -*James Baldwin*

Love

Parents must get across the idea that I love you always, but sometimes I do not love your behavior. -*Amy Vanderbilt*

God's love is unconditional and people, especially children, need unconditional love. They need to beloved if they are to grow up to be loving. They need love, security, and acceptance from the very beginning. They need praise, encouragement, and instruction more than correction, even when they are not very loving. -*Editor*

How often do you speak kind words of encouragement to your children and assure them of your unconditional love?

Love is spelled T-I-M-E.

Children feel secure only if they have both love and limits. -*Dr. Sylvia Rimm*

Marriage

Children learn about marriage from their parents. This begins very early in life. They use their parents' marriage as a model. This is what they take with them to their marriage and pass on to their children. -*Editor*

Mistakes/Learning

Parents should not make children feel fearful of making mistakes. In fact, mistakes provide opportunities for them to find better ways of doing things. Good parenting welcomes mistakes because children learn so much from them. -*Editor*

Model/Criticism

Children need models more than critics. -*Joseph Joubert*

Motives

Children often think they can fool their brothers, sisters, parents, friends, and teachers. They need to be taught that God knows what they are thinking before they do. -*Editor*

Obedience

Instilling obedience in children is so critical for healthy upbringing that parents need to do whatever it takes- least to most severe measures, including spanking their bottoms; however, one should not assume spanking will always produce favorable measures. -*Editor*

The cost of obedience is small compared to the cost of disobedience.

There was a time when we expected nothing of children but obedience, as opposed to the present, when we expect everything of them but obedience. -*Anatole Broyard*

Parents

A hundred years from now, it will not matter what my bank account was, the sort of house I lived in, or the kind of car I drove; but the world may be different because I was important in the life of a child.

I am my kid's teacher!

In the past, a good parent was someone who spent time with his or her children, teaching them values and manners, and worried about a child's character. Now a good parent is someone who registers you for an activity, pays for it, and then watches from the sidelines. -*Barbara Carlson*

Many parents fear they will lose their children's love by crossing them. But only by helping children curb their impulses, and by guiding them to better use of their energies, can parents gain that love. Parents hear so much criticism of parents that they are afraid of frustrating a child's growing independence of thought, afraid to start a wearing argument, afraid of open rebellion. But parents and children are happiest and most secure when parents are in firm control. -*Sidonie Matsner Gruenberg*

Our children are experiencing a childhood that is no longer just a preparation for adult hood but a full performance in its own right. The definition of "good parenting" began changing in the early Eighties when researchers reported that a lack of stimulation to a child's brain slightly impeded development. -*Dr. Alvin Rosenfeld*

Parentage is a very important profession; but no test of fitness for it is ever imposed in the interest of the children. -*George Bernard Shaw, 1944*

Parenting isn't easy. Parents aren't perfect and neither are children. Sometimes we hurt one another. Fortunately, love can heal hurts. -*Editor*

Parents are the super glue that holds the family together. Pay attention to your kids and be the glue. This is the whole parenting thing in a nutshell. -*Jeanne Marie Laskas, writer and mother of two pre-schoolers*

Parents should work together as efficiently as two book ends.

Praise your children openly, reprove them secretly. -*W. Cecil*

Raising children is a lot like managing a portfolio of stocks: When you look back on what happened, everything you should have done seems perfectly clear, and you can't imagine why it wasn't obvious to you at the time. -*Marilyn vos Savant*

We never know the love of our parents for us till we have become parents. -*Henry Ward Beecher*

You can do anything with children if you only play with them. -*Bismarck*

Reading

It's never too soon to start reading to your children. Good listeners make good readers. They're never too old to be read to either. A good way to stay in touch with your older children is by sharing books that are important to them. -*Judy Blume*

People could read every book written and still be ignorant; but if they only read the Bible they would be wise. They wouldn't want to live their lives without knowing about their salvation as revealed in the Bible. -*Editor*

Relationship

Romance fails us and so do friendships, but the relationship of parent and child, less noisy than all others, remains indelible and indestructible, the strongest relationships on earth. -*Theodor Reik*

Reputation

Children need to be taught the importance of building a good reputation at a very early age because that's when the foundation is laid. -*Editor*

Responsibility

If you want children to keep their feet on the ground, put some responsibility on their shoulders. -*Abigail Van Buren*

Right/Wrong

Wrong comes naturally to children. Right must be taught. Letting children make up their own minds about right and wrong is the source of much confusion. -*Editor*

Roots/Wings

There are only two lasting bequests we can hope to give our children. One of these is roots, the other wings. -*Hodding Carter*

Rules

Parents who fail to set and enforce rules now are actually ordering up problems for later- negative consequences are sure to follow. -*Margaret Bernstein, Plain Dealer Reporter*

Rules without relationships lead to rebellion.

School

A parent's attitude and attention can make all the difference in how a student performs at school. No matter the income level, the most successful students are those whose parents are involved in their educations. -*Colin Greer*

The smaller the gap between what parents teach their children and what the school expects, the easier the adjustment from home to school; and the more children will benefit. -*Editor*

Screamers

Parents who scream a lot at their children usually have kids who don't listen. -*Editor*

Sizing

Children miss nothing in sizing up their parents. If you are only half convinced of your beliefs, they will quickly discern that fact. -*James Dobson*

Sons/Daughters

Your children are not your children. They are the sons and daughters of Life's longing for itself. -*Kahlil Gibran*

Souls

You may give your children love but not your thoughts, for they have their own thoughts. You may house their bodies but not their souls, for their souls dwell in the house of tomorrow, which you cannot visit, not even in your dreams. -*Kahlil Gibran, 1923*

Sternness

Children can stand vast amounts of sternness. It is injustice, inequity, and inconsistency that kill them. -*Robert Capon*

Stretch/Stoop

It's better to make a child stretch to reach your high opinion than stoop to match your disrespect. -*James Dobson*

Talents

Children differ physically, mentally, and emotionally. One of the greatest gifts a parent can give their children is to help them identify their unique talents and nurture and motivate them in those talents. -*Editor*

Talk

Most parents talk to their children too much and act too little. -*Editor*

Television

Television is one of the greatest inventions of all time. Since the 1950s it has affected peoples' lives more than any other technological development. For the first time in history, something other than parents has become the main provider of information, values, and entertainment for children. *-Editor*

Theories

Before I was married I had three theories about raising children. Now I have three children and no theories. *-John Wilmot, Earl of Rochester 1647-1680*

Time

A few years ago, experts were preaching that what's important is "quality time," not "quantity time." More recent research shows that kids need both quality and quantity. In fact, the more involved parents are with their children, the less likely children will have social, emotional or academic problems, use drugs or alcohol, be involved in crime or have premarital sex. *-Dr. Bill Maier*

The typical parent spends less than one hour per week in meaningful interaction with each of his or her children. *-George Barna, Researcher*

In bringing up children, spend on them half as much money and twice as much time. *-Dr. Laurence J. Peter*

Times

Times change. Not too many years ago minding one's children didn't mean obeying them.

Teacher

Parents are the most important teacher a child will ever have. *-Rabbi Daniel Lapin*

Training

A young branch takes on all the bends that one gives it. *-Chinese Proverb*

Children should be led into the right paths, not by severity, but by persuasion. -*Terence, 160 BC*

You train a child until age ten. After that, you only influence them.

Trouble/Joy

Trouble is what you get from children. Joy is what you get from grandchildren. -*Yiddish Proverb*

Truth

One of the hardest things to teach a child is that the truth is more important than the consequences. -*O.A. Battista*

TV

Watching too much television has damaging effects on children's developmental growth. On the average, a preschool child watches 30 hours of television a week. By the time he graduates from high school he has clocked up to 20,000 hours in front of the TV, compared to 13,000 hours spent in school, as the first and most important teachers, parents can help children find more constructive things to do with their time than waste away in front of the TV set. -*Ohio State University Extension*

Values

Cooperation and unity are the most important values we can teach children. -*Nile Rogers*

Knowledge without values is a dangerous thing. Parents: keep teaching values and set guidelines on media viewing until your children are ready. -*Jan Gordon, M. Ed.*

The most important things we can give our kids are our time, our lives, and our values- and values are caught more than they are taught. -*Tim Hansel*

The values we install in our children are more important than the valuables we leave to them. -*Editor*

Waste

Children learn wasteful or conserving habits from their parents' example. For example, energy experts say that we waste as much energy as we really need because lights, appliances, and water are not turned off. -*Editor*

Work

It is very important that children learn to work as soon as possible. IF they don't learn early they may never learn. Good work habits will help them with their school work because school is work. Work teaches responsibility, a sense of accomplishment, self satisfaction, and preparation for life. –*Editor*

Worry

Parents should help their children avoid the worry habit. It's acquired. We aren't born with it. It's destructive. -*Editor*

Yelling

I think one of the biggest mistakes a parent can make is constantly yelling at their kids to get things done. There is not a person out there who will feel like doing something while being screamed at. -*Gina Jarvis*

CHILDREN

Adeptness

Children's ability to grasp the meaning of words and express themselves never ceases to amaze me. -*Editor*

Accountable

Children need to be held accountable for their behavior toward others based on their maturity level. -*Editor*

Babies

Babies are born innocent, not good. -*Dennis Prager*

Everything to a baby is love, food, warm clothing, dry pants, and, in a few months, some measuring cups to play with. A really nice house is nice, too, but not if it's at the expense of love, food, warm clothing, and dry pants. -*Carolyn Hax, Columnist*

Caring

Perhaps a child who is fussed over gets a feeling of destiny; he thinks he is in the world for something important, and it gives him drive and confidence. -*Benjamin Spock*

Exercise

Jumping rope is excellent for cardiovascular fitness, muscular endurance, and coordination. -*American Heart Association*

Children do as you do, not as you say. By being role models physically active parents who practice good nutrition will instill lifelong habits. -*Michael O'Shea, Parade Fitness Editor*

Fatherless

Presently, there is a generation of fatherless, under-supervised, emotionally neglected, and spiritually troubled children! -*Dr. James Kennedy, Ph.D.*

Fitness

The best way to promote vigorous activity is to let kids be kids by allowing them to do activities that require running, jumping, skipping, and hopping. -*Kathleen F. Janz, Researcher*

God's Child

A child that is early taught that he is God's child, that he may live and move and have his being in God, and that he has, therefore, infinite strength at hand for the conquering of any difficulty, will take life more easily, and probably will make more of it. -*Edward Everett Hale*

Gifted

It's a misconception that gifted kids are always model students. -*Jan Davidson, Author*

Growing Up

You know children are growing up when they start asking questions that have answers. -*John J. Plomp*

Illegitimate

There are no illegitimate children- only illegitimate parents. -*Leon R. Yonkwich*

Independent

A child is being properly educated only when he is learning to become independent of his parents.

Injustice

In the little world in which children have their existence, whoever brings them up, there is nothing so finely perceived and so finely felt, as injustices. -*Charles Dickens*

Involvement

Instead of watching television, read to your kids, play board games, take a walk, or just talk to them. -*Dr. Bill Maier*

Kids

I don't want to say anything about my kids...but I go to PTA meetings under an assumed name! -*Robert Orben*

Life/Death

Healthy children will not fear life if their elders have integrity enough not to fear death. -*Erik H. Erikson*

Love

Give a little love to a child, and you get a great deal back. -*John Ruskin*

Manners

A child should always say what's true, and speak when he is spoken to, and behave mannerly at the table: at least as far as he is able. -*Robert Louis Stevenson*

Children are natural mimics: they act like their parents in spite of every attempt to teach them good manners.

Messages

Children are living messages at a time we will not see. -*Dick Hanson*

Need

Children need parents who will hang out with them, with no goal in mind beyond the pleasure of spending time together. -*Dr. Alvin Rosenfeld*

Negative

There is little hope for children who are educated wickedly. If the dye had been in the wool, it is hard to get it out of the cloth. -*Jeremiah Burroughs*

What children wish they never heard from their parents: one parent saying mean things about the other. -*Editor*

Obedience

Children, obey your parents in the Lord, for this is right. "Honor your father and mother" which is the first commandment with promise. -*Ephesians 6:1-2*

Obscenity

Lax enforcement of obscenity laws result in children being infected with vulgar images. -*Coral Ridge Ministries*

Personality

More often than not, we apples don't fall far from our trees. The harder we try to roll away from the dysfunction of our roots, the more likely we are to become mired unconsciously in them. -*Gail Saltz, M.D.*

There is an invisible garment woven around us from our earliest years; it is made of the way we eat, the way we walk, the way we greet people, woven of tastes and colors and perfumes which our senses spin in childhood. -*Jean Giraudoux*

Questions

You know your children are growing up when they stop asking where they came from and refuse to tell you where they're going. -*P. O'Brien*

Reading

Children who learn to love books will grow up to be good readers. The best time for children to learn to love books is when they are young. By making reading a part of your child's life, you can build this love. -*Judy Blume*

Recognition

Children who had been offered rewards and received compliments had markedly higher cognition and IQ test scores than children of equal ability who were not rewarded. -*Dr. Margaret Lloyd*

Relationship

Children begin by loving their parents. After a time they judge them. Rarely, if ever, do they forgive them. -*Oscar Wilde*

Self-Centered

Children are completely egoistic; they feel their needs intensely and strive ruthlessly to satisfy them. -*Sigmund Freud*

Self-Image

Once you see a child's self-image begin to improve, you will see significant gains in achievement areas, but even more important, you will see a child who is beginning to enjoy life more. -*Wayne Dyer*

Sharing

There are only two things a child will share willingly: communicable diseases and his mother's age. -*Dr. Benjamin Spock*

Spiritual Food

You deprive your children when you deny them of spiritual food. -*Charles Stanley, Pastor*

Violations

There is no end to the violations committed by children on children, quietly talking alone. -*Elizabeth Bowen*

Vital Signs

Even a child is known by his actions, by whether his conduct is pure and right. -*Proverbs 20:11*

YOUTH

Adolescence

Adolescence is enough suffering for anyone. -*John Ciardi*

Adolescence and snow are the only problems that disappear if you ignore them long enough.

It's getting tougher to draw attention to yourself when you want to rebel: thus piercing, tattooing, and mutilating. I think the trend will slow when this generation's kids see how bad their parents look as they turn 30 and 40. -*Marilyn Vos Savant*

So much of adolescence is an ill-defined dying, an intolerable waiting, a longing for another place and time, another condition. -*Theodore Roethke*

The thinking that adolescents rebel as they seek more autonomy and push off from their families is a peculiarly well-developed idea in American society. -*Frank Furstenberg, Professor*

What you believe at age 13 is what you're going to die believing. -*George Barna, Researcher*

Adolescence is when children start trying to bring up their parents. -*Richard Armour*

Adolescence is just one big walking pimple. -*Carol Burnett*

Growing Up

Poor judgement is part of growing up, I guess. Kids do dumb things. I did, and my three lovely children will, too. -*John Horton, Plain Dealer*

Preteens are too old for toys and too young for girls and boys.

Instruction

Don't let anyone look down on you because you are young, but set an example for the believers in speech, in life, in love, in faith, and in purity. -*1 Timothy 4:12*

Go straight to the heart of danger and there you will find safety. -*Chinese Proverb*

I maintain, in truth, that with a smile we should instruct our youth, be very gently when we have to blame, and not put them in fear of virtues. -*Moliere, 1661*

The glory of young men is their strength, gray hair the splendor of the old. -*Proverbs 21:29*

Know

It seldom occurs to teenagers that someday they will know as little as their parents.

Parents

A Jewish man with parents alive is a fifteen year old boy, and will remain a fifteen year old boy till they die. *-Philip Roth, Portnoy's Complaint*

Don't laugh at a youth for his affectations; he is only trying on one face after another to find a face of his own. *-Logan Pearsall Smith*

Oh, to be only half as wonderful as my child thought I was when he was small, and only half as stupid as my teenager now thinks I am. *-Rebecca Richards*

Never stop discovering what is amazing about your children. They listen to you, no matter how much their body language says otherwise. Talk with them. So many teens I work with crave the listening ear of their parents. Practice unconditional listening, no interruptions; you'll be amazed at how much they will share with you. *-Bridgette Evans Lempner, Counselor*

Parents need to teach their children the value of money as early as possible. They should be allowed to make as many purchases as possible with the money allotted them and live with mistakes and mismanagement- the price of learning. *-Editor*

Young people are often bad because their parents did not burn their britches behind them.

Priorities

Hopefully our students already realize that their daily attitudes, actions, and spirits are what will really make a difference in today's world. *-John Beutow, Principal*

Repentance

The seeds of repentance are sown in youth by pleasure, but the harvest is reaped in age by pain. *-Charles Caleb Colton, 1825*

Rules

Youngsters who live with a lax set of rules often grow up with a false sense of entitlement and fail to realize they have a responsibility to contribute in positive ways to their household. -*Margaret Bernstein, Plain Dealer Reporter*

Sexuality

Abstinence educators say many youths embrace alternatives to a popular culture that glamorizes teen sex. -*David Briggs, Plain Dealer Reporter*

Free love is seldom free. Teens pay for it in worry- the fear that they'll get caught, or that their partner may tire of them. It's hurried and furtive and not much fun. -*Helen Bottel*

The best contraceptive is the word No repeated frequently. -*Margaret Smith*

Teenagers

Depression is the most common emotional problem in adolescence and the single greatest risk factor for teen suicide. -*Dr. Peter Jensen*

It is not unusual for teens not to listen to advice. -*A Concerned Mom*

It means you're half an adult but still a kid. You want to be an adult, but your parents tell you, "No." So, you try being a kid, and they say you're much too old to be acting like that. -*Heather Smith, 17, Gobles, Michigan*

Perhaps the reason why teenagers know all the answers is that they haven't heard all the questions yet.

Study after study shows that alcohol is the illegal drug of choice for teens, over all other drugs combined. -*Connie Schultz, Plain Dealer Columnist*

Teenage suicide is unfortunately common; more than 3,000 young people, age 10 to 24, kill themselves each year. -*Center for Disease Control and Prevention*

Teenagers are going to test limits; that's just what teenagers do. *-Margaret Bernstein, Plain Dealer Reporter*

The second hardest thing for a teenager to do is become an adult. The hardest thing to do is to die. *-Brent Runyon, suicide survivor and author*

The teenager seems to have replaced the communist as the appropriate target for public controversy and foreboding. *-Edgar L. Friedenbery, 1959*

There's nothing wrong with teenagers that reasoning with them won't aggravate.

When dealing with a troubled teen, parents should be consistent in the way they handle situations. *-Dr. Neil Bernstein*

Violence

Children from single-parent homes, where welfare and low educational attainment are the norm, are more likely to be involved in violent and anti-social behavior. *-Phillip Morris, Associate Editor of The Plain Dealer*

Young men and women must repeatedly be shown desirable alternatives to the air of violence that so often shrouds their daily lives; they have to be made to see that there are good reasons to build good lives. *-Phillip Morris, Associate Editor of The Plain Dealer*

Youth

A boy becomes an adult three years before his parents think he does, and about two years after he thinks he does. *-General Lewis B. Hersley*

A wild colt may become a sober horse. *-Thomas Fuller, M.D., 1732*

A riotous youth, there's little hope for him; that fault his age will, as it grows, correct. *-Ben Jonson, 1603*

All young people want to kick up their heels and defy convention; most of them would prefer to do it at a not too heavy cost. *-Elmer Davis, 1913*

As a result of all his education, from everything he hears and sees around him, youth absorbs such a lot of lies and foolish nonsense, mixed in with essential truths, that the first duty of the adolescent who want to be a healthy man is to disgorge it all. *-Romain Rolland, 1904*

A youth is to be regarded with respect. How do you know that his future will not be equal to our present. *-Confucius, 600 BC*

Having a job and making a living really contribute to their self-esteem. *-Bob Gillingham, Ford Dealer*

He that would pass the latter part of life with honor and decency must when he is young consider that he shall one day be old; and remember when he is old that he has once been young. *-Samuel Johnson, 1750*

Impatience and not inexperience is the greatest handicap of youth. *-Arnold H. Glasgow*

In case you're worried about what's going to become of the younger generation, it's going to grow up and start worrying about the younger generation. *-Roger Allen*

When we are out of sympathy with the young, then our work in this world is over. *– G. Macdonald*

It is not possible for civilization to flow backward while there is youth in the world. Youth may be headstrong, but it will advance its allotted length. *-Helen Keller, 1930*

It is stupid of the young to want to be thought grown up, but it is far more stupid of the old to want to be thought young. *-Hubert van Zeller*

Life should begin with age and its privileges and accumulations, and end with youth and its capacity to splendidly enjoy such advantages. *-Mark Twain, 1901*

Not childhood alone, but the young man till thirty, never feels practically that he is mortal. *-Charles Lamb, 1823*

Man is like palm-wine: when young, sweet but without strength; in old age, strong but harsh. -*Congolese Proverb*

Most men spend the first half of their lives making the second half miserable. -*La Bruyere, 1688*

Our youth now love luxury. They have bad manners, contempt for authority; they show disrespect for their elders and love chatter in places of exercise. They no longer rise when elders enter the room. They contradict their parents, chatter before company, gobble up their food, and tyrannize their teachers. -*Socrates, 5th century BC*

Our youth we can have but today, we may always find time to grow old. -*George Berkeley*

Rise in the presence of the aged; show respect for the elderly and revere your God. -*Leviticus 19:32*

The boy who expects every morning to open into a new world finds that today is like yesterday, but he believes tomorrow will be different. -*Charles Dudley Warner, 1873*

The passions of the young are vices in old age. -*Joseph Joubert, 1842*

The old believe everything, the middle-ages suspect everything, the young know everything. -*Oscar Wilde, 1891*

The right way to begin is to pay attention to the young and make them just as good as possible. -*Socrates, 400 BC*

The young always have the same problem: how to rebel and conform at the same time. They have now solved this by defying their parents and copying one another. -*Quentin Crisk*

There is nothing wrong with the younger generation that the older generation didn't outgrow.

Those who love the young best stay young longest. -*Edgar Z. Friedenberg*

Today's students can put dope in their veins or hope in their brains…If they can conceive it and believe it, they can achieve it. They must know it is not their aptitude but their attitude that will determine their altitude. -*Jesse Jackson*

We were happier when we were poorer, but we were also younger. -*Charles Lamb, 1833*

While we are young the idea of death or failure is intolerable to us; even the possibility of ridicule we cannot bear. -*Isak Dinesen, 1934*

You are what you aspire to be, and not what you are now; you are what you do with your mind, and you are what you do with your youth. -*Maltbie D. Babcock*

Young men have a passion for regarding their elders as senile. -*Henry Adams, 1907*

Young people are thoughtless as a rule. -*Homer, 900 BC*

Young people ought not to be idle. It is very bad for them. -*Margaret Thatcher*

Young people want someone to clearly tell them what God requires and wants. -*Franklin Graham*

Youth is not a time of life; it is a state of mind. -*Benjamin E. Mays*

Youth looks forward, middle-age merely looks startled, and old age looks back. -*Lord Mancroft*

AGING

Advantages

Old age does have some advantages. Not only can you sing while you shower, you can sing while you brush your teeth. -*George Jessel*

Advice

The worst thing about growing old is listening to your children's advice.

Age

At my age, when I order a three-minute egg, they ask for the money up front.
-Milton Berle

Aging

Age is a bad traveling companion. *-English Proverb*

Age is strictly a case of mind over matter. If you don't mind, it doesn't matter. *-Jack Benny*

Do not regret growing older. It is a privilege denied to many.

Don't talk age. It is just a number. It is all about how you feel. Watch nutrition in moderation, exercise in moderation, and everything will fall in place. *-Carol Baker, Aerobics Instructor*

Growing old isn't so bad when you consider the alternative. *-Maurice Chevalier*

I don't feel old. I don't feel anything until noon. Then it's time for my nap. *-Bob Hope*

Inactivity, rather than aging, is responsible for obesity and many diseases. *-Glenn Gaesser, Ph.D.*

In every age the "good old days" were a myth. No one ever thought they were good at the time. For every age has consisted of crisis that seemed intolerable to the people who lived through them. *-Brooks Atkinson*

I warmed both hands before the fire of life; it sinks, and I am ready to depart. *-Walter Savage Landor, 1849*

Let every year make you a better person. *-Benjamin Franklin*

Middle age is when you've met so many people that every new person you meet reminds you of someone else. -*Ogden Nash*

Never grow so old that you cannot change your mind.

Oftener than not the old are uncontrollable; their tempers make them difficult to deal with. -*Euripides, 425 BC*

Old age is not a total misery. Experience helps! -*Euripides, 410 BC*

Older people who are physically active are less likely to become depressed and feel isolated. -*Colin Milner, International Council on Active Aging*

One secret of growing old gracefully is never to lose your enthusiasm for meeting new people and seeing new places.

Osteoporosis is a disease affecting 10 million older Americans plus an estimated 34 million more have low bone mass. Age and sex are significant factors; older females are at greatest risk. -*Chris Hope, Lutheran Home Administration*

People don't grow old. When they stop growing, they become old.

The best thing about getting old is that all those things you couldn't have when you were young you no longer want. -*L.S. McCandles*

There are two kinds of older folks: Those who embrace it and even enjoy making fun of it, and those who deny it and resent all references to old.

To keep the heart unwrinkled, to be hopeful, cheerful, reverent- that is to triumph over old age. -*Thomas Baily Aldrich, 1903*

To me, old age is always fifteen years older than I am. -*Bernard Baruch*

We could certainly slow the aging process down if it had to work its way through Congress.

We ought not to heap reproaches on old age, seeing that we all hope to reach it. -*Bion, 200 BC*

Years ago we discovered the exact point, the dead center of middle age. It occurs when you are too young to take up golf and too old to rush up to the net. -*Franklin P. Adams*

You don't stop laughing because you grow old, you grow old because you stopped laughing.

Experience is a comb which nature gives us when we are bald. -*Chinese Proverb*

Our aches and pains conform to opinion. A man's as miserable as he thinks he is. -*Seneca, 100AD*

He had existed only, not lived, who lacks wisdom in old age. -*Publilius, 100BC*

The years between fifty and seventy are the hardest. You are always being asked to do things, and yet you are not decrepit enough to turn them down. -*T.S. Elliot*

Evidence is mounting that, at any age, physical activity is good for the heart and the mind. -*Molly Wagster, National Institute on Aging*

Regular exercise is a popular way to relieve stress. Twenty to thirty minutes of physical activity benefits both the body and the mind. -*Agency of Aging*

Older adults can obtain significant health benefits with a moderate amount of physical activity, preferably daily. -*The Surgeon General's Report*

A prescription of regular exercise is probably the best insurance that older adults can take to prevent falls. It improves muscle strength, balance, flexibility and endurance, among other things. Walking is an incredibly overlooked form of exercise. -*Mark Grabiner, Researcher*

The golden age was never the present age. -*English Proverb*

You know you're getting old when you stoop to tie your shoes and wonder what else you can do while you're down their. -*George Burns*

Time which diminishes all things increases understanding for the aging. -*Plutarch, 100 AD*

In youth we learn, in old age we understand. -*Marie von Ebner-Eschenbach*

When you're young, your date makes your heart pound, and running up a flight of steps has no effect on you. You know you're getting old when the opposite is true. -*Marilyn vos Savant*

Amused/Shocked

Perhaps one has to be very old before one learns to be amused rather than shocked. -*Pearl S. Buck*

Change

One of the many things nobody ever tells you about middle age is that it's such a nice change from being young. -*Dorothy Canfield Fisher*

Curfew

You know you're growing older when...your children give you a curfew.

Do It

If you can't grow old gracefully, do it any way

Giving

When we grow old, there can only be one regret: not to have given enough of ourselves. -*Eleonora Duse*

Ignored

Old age is when you know all the answers but nobody asks you the questions. -*Laurence J. Peter*

Living

To know how to grow old is the master work of wisdom, and one of the most difficult chapters in the great art of living. -*Frederic Amiel*

Memory

A retentive memory is a good thing, but the ability to forget is the true token of greatness. -*Elbert Hubbard*

People

Things would be a lot nicer if antique people were valued as highly as antique furniture.

Retirement

Don't simply retire from something; have some thing to retire to. -*Harry Emerson Fosdick*

Time

Aging seems to be the only available way to live a long time. -*Daniel François Esprit*

Wisdom

Wisdom doesn't automatically come with old age. Nothing does—except wrinkles. It's true, some wines improve with age. But only if the grapes were good in the first place. -*Abigail Van Buren*

Worry

Old age is like a plane flying through a storm. Once you are aboard there is nothing you can do. -*Golda Meir*

5.
HEALTH MATTERS

Advice

How to avoid high blood pressure: If it starts to rain, let it.

Arthritis

For people with arthritis, regular vigorous exercise halves the risk of being unable to do everyday tasks later on. -*Arthritis and Rheumatism*

Attitude

Scientists have discovered that the small brave act of cooperating with another person, of choosing trust over cynicism, generosity over selfishness, makes the brain light up with quiet joy. -*Natalie Angier*

Depression

Noble deeds and hot baths are the best cures for depression. -*Dodie Smith*

The sooner patients can be removed from the depressing influence of general hospital life, the more rapid the convalescence. -*Dr. Charles H. Mayo*

Diet

All roads to Rome come back to a balanced diet. -*Dr. George Blackburn*

Diets aim at the wrong target- the belly, not the brain. They focus on a symptom rather than its underlying causes. The key to permanent weight loss is changing the attitudes, feelings, and habits that determine what, when, why, how often, and how much you eat. -*Kate Drewry, Social Worker*

Many of us know that we are out of control with out eating habits. We know that we should not indulge certain food except in moderation, yet we reject the overwhelming facts on fresh fruit, vegetables, and water. We eat the way we are taught to eat, whether it be good or bad! -*Sharon Johnson*

Drinking

It is only the first bottle that is expensive. -*French Proverb*

The vine bears three kinds of grapes: the first of pleasure, the next of intoxication, and the third of disgust. -*Anacharsis*

Water taken in moderation cannot hurt anybody. -*Mark Twain*

Eating

It is not the number of minutes you put in at the dining table that makes you fat; it's the seconds.

Let your medicine be your food and your food be your medicine. -*Hippocrates, 2500 BC*

Man is what he eats. -*German Proverb*

My doctor told me to stop having intimate dinners for four. Unless there are three other people. -*Orson Welles*

Studies show that eating the right foods may fortify the immune system against viral diseases such as colds and flues and perhaps other conditions. -*Dr. Isadore Rosenfeld, MD*

The glutton digs his grave with his teeth. -*English Proverb*

We never repent for having eaten too little. -*Thomas Jefferson*

We should eat to live, not live to eat. This is one of the most important things we can do for ourselves. -*Editor*

You're not what you eat after all. It's what eats you. -*Bill Lubinger*

Forgiveness

Forgiveness is healthy for the one who forgives. Actual medical studies document that people who forgive are physically healthier than people who hold grudges. -*Editor*

Everyone has the capacity to forgive; and everyone owes it to himself to do so at every turn in life. Research shows that people who make a habit of forgiving may have lower blood pressure, a stronger immune system, less susceptibility to heart attack, and the upper hand on a number of health issues. They are happier and able to think more clearly. They have unburdened themselves from the weight of anger and freed themselves to go about their lives. -*Edward M. Hallowell, M.D.*

Only true forgiveness will heal wounds caused by others

Ministers, doctors, and psychologists have long prescribed forgiveness as a method of healing oneself and one's relationships. It is extolled as a merciful quality, providing closure and peace. -*Janis Abrahms Spring, Ph D*

The medical profession is convinced that emotions such as anger, hated, resentment, and envy are at the root of most physical ailments. Not forgiving means being imprisoned by the past. Forgiveness frees us from that past. -*Editor*

Giving

Giving is a very good criterion, in a way, of a person's mental health. Generous people are rarely mentally ill people. -*Dr. Karl Menninger*

Gratitude

A research study concluded that gratitude is good for our physical, mental, and moral health. It doesn't seem to matter what you're grateful for, as long as you count your blessings. -*Editor*

Health

For the best physical and mental health: socialize, optimize, and exercise (SOE). *-Dr. Mark Frankel, M.D.*

Healthy eating habits, exercise, and weight management are the keys to long-term health, happiness, and life span. *-Tara Parker-Pope, Wall Street Journal*

If you're healthy, you're a millionaire. *-Polish Proverb*

Only after seeing one go quickly from good to poor health and death can one begin to appreciate one's own health. *-Editor*

New research suggests that prolonged stress reduces our ability to fend off infectious diseases. *-Dr. Isadore Rosenfeld, MD*

People need rest, good food, fresh air, and exercise- the quadrangle of health. *-William Oslet*

People who are always taking care of their health are like misers who are hoarding a treasure which they have never spirit enough to enjoy. *-Lawrence Sterne*

The most powerful and dangerous problem in health care today is denial. Everybody looks around and says, "It's not going to be me." *-Dr. Steven Nissen, Cardiologist*

The trouble about always trying to preserve the health of the body is that it is so difficult to do without destroying the health of the mind. *-G.K. Chesterton*

We are not sensible of the most perfect health as we are of the least sickness. *-Montaigne*

When we are well, we all have good advice for those who are ill. *—Terence, 166 BC*

Heart Health

Fitting in thirty minutes of physical activity on most days of the week will strengthen the heart's pumping power and lower blood pressure. Being active burns calories and helps lower blood sugar levels. This in turn helps the body use food more efficiently for energy. -*Richard Nesto, M.D.*

There is no exercise better of the heart than reaching down and lifting someone else up.

Two things are bad for the heart: running up stairs and running down people. -*Bernard Baruch*

You can improve your odds if you stop smoking, normalize high blood pressure, reduce elevated cholesterol levels, control high blood sugar, lose weight, and exercise regularly. -*Dr. Isadore Rosenfeld*

Hugs

We need four hugs a day for survival. We need eight hugs a day for maintenance. We need twelve hugs a day for growth. -*Virginia Satir*

Hugging is healthy; it helps our body's immune system. It keeps you healthier, cures depression, reduces stress, and induces sleep. It is invigorating, rejuvenating, and has no unpleasant side effects. Hugging is nothing less than a miracle drug. -*Editor*

Love

Love cures people, the ones who receive love and the ones who give it too. -*Karl A. Menninger, M.D.*

Moderation

Balance, moderation in diet and lifestyle, coupled with regular healthy exercise is the best way to deter disease and ensure longevity. -*Hippocrates, Greek Physician, 2500 BC*

Nutrition

Good nutrition makes a difference. Limit intake of caffeine and alcohol (alcohol actually disturbs regular sleep patterns), get adequate rest, exercise, and balance work and play. *-Agency on Aging*

Obesity

America's children are fat because their primary role models are fat. American's children will die premature deaths as adults because their parents are slothful, nutritionally lazy, sedentary, and willing to allow advertizing to dictate their consumption patterns. *-Phillip Morris, Associate Editor of The Plain Dealer*

Because obesity is a worldwide epidemic, the Cleveland Clinic has opened a new weight management center. Studies will address such questions as 'Why do some people become obese and some don't?' and 'Why does obesity cause diabetes?' *-Dr. Philip Schauer, the Clinic's new director of advanced laparoscopic and bariatric surgery*

Gluttony, along with envy, lust, greed, anger, sloth, and pride, is listed by theologians as one of the seven deadly sins. Today, few people seriously consider the idea of eating too much as a profound moral failure in God's eyes. *-Francine Prose, Author*

Imprisoned in every fat man, a thin man is wildly signaling to be let out. *-Cyril Connolly*

I see no objection to stoutness, in moderation. *-W.S. Gilbert*

More die in the United States of too much food than of too little. *-John Kenneth Galbraith, 1958*

New evidence shows that a major cause of the obesity epidemic is the pattern of desk jobs, car pools, suburban sprawl, and other environmental and lifestyle factors that discourage physical activity. *-Rob Stein, Washington Post*

Obesity in mid-life increases the risk of developing Alzheimer's Disease in later life. Lifestyle changes, such as eating a healthy diet and regular exercise which reduce the risk of Alzheimer's, are incredibly difficult to motivate people to change permanently or significantly. It's like trying to keep a new year's resolution. *-Dr. Peter De Golia*

Obesity starts in the brain, not the mouth or stomach. People don't overeat because they're hungry, but as a way of meeting their emotional needs and making it through the day. *-Diane Hales, Editor and Author*

One in three children in the USA is either overweight or at a serious risk of becoming fat. They are becoming fatter at a faster rate; the number of overweight kids between ages six and nineteen has tripled in the last thirty years. *-Sharron Dalton, Associate Professor*

Over the last fifteen years, television, computer games, and the likes have supplanted kids' daily physical activity. The end result is a tripling of childhood obesity. Inactivity and obesity related illnesses now threaten to shorten the life spans of today's kids: four million have above-normal blood pressure, twenty-seven million have high cholesterol, and more than a third get no exercise. Small changes have led to a national energy imbalance, wherein most children take in more daily calories than they burn. Just an extra 100 calories a day can lead to gaining ten pounds of fat yearly. *-Dr. Stephen Daniels, Cincinnati Children's Hospital*

Sticking with a diet and exercise program are central to weight loss, but a positive mind-set is the key. If your mind is keeping you overweight, change it. *-Diane Hales, Editor and Author*

Television: Each of the four major networks now offers fifty-two minutes of commercials in three hours from 8 PM to 11 PM everyday. Children sit on the couch in a stupor, they eat and drink, and alarms are sounded through the nation- our children are becoming obese. *-Norman Mailer, Author*

The double cheeseburger: a weapon of mass destruction. *-Ralph Nader*

To be thinner people have to make permanent changes. *-Dr. James Jill, University of Colorado*

Two-thirds of Americans are overweight or obese, and the number is growing steadily. The percentage of the population that is obese has doubled since 1980; the numbers of those who are morbidly obese (100 pounds or more over the ideal weight) has quadrupled during that period. -*The Centers for Disease Control*

Physical Fitness

Bodily exercises are to be done discreetly; not to be taken evenly and alike by all men. -*Thomas A. Kempis*

Physical training is of some value, but godliness has value for all things, holding promise for both the present life and the life to come. -*1 Timothy 4:8*

We are under-exercised as a nation. We look instead of play. We ride instead of walk. Our existence deprives us of the minimum of physical activity essential for healthy living. -*John F. Kennedy, 1961*

Don't just tell your children to be more active- do it with them. Let them see you being active and eating better. -*Dr. Susan Vincent*

Pain

Much of your pain is self-chosen. It is the bitter potion by which the physician within you heals your sick self. -*Kahlil Gibran, 1923*

Pain is God's megaphone. -*C.S. Lewis*

Pain of mind is worse than pain of body. -*Publilius Syrus*

Sickness

A cigarette is a pinch of tobacco, wrapped in paper, fire at one end, fool at the other.

Do not fail to catch the other's mood; lest you give him pain instead of pleasure. -*Baltasar Grecian*

Excess weight is a major contributor to diabetes (dramatically on the rise in this country), hypertension, heart disease, and cancer. Too many men and women weigh too much. -*Dr. Isadore Rosenfeld*

He sleeps well who knows not that he sleeps ill. -*Publilius Syrus, 100 BC*

If you have symptoms of elevated blood glucose, such as unquenchable thirst and/or frequent urination, or if you have a family history of diabetes, the most important thing you can do now is exercise and lose weight- and have your blood-sugar level tested. An ounce of prevention is better than a pound of cure. -*Dr. Isadore Rosenfeld*

Loneliness definitely has an adverse affect on our well-being. Over the last few decades, medical research has found that people who don't regularly enjoy meaningful relationships with God or others are likely to have lower levels of health. Lonely people are at greater risk for heart attacks, ulcers, strokes, infectious disease, many types of cancer, and other life-threatening illnesses. -*Dr. Walt Larimore*

Show him death, and he'll be content with fever. -*Persian Proverb*

Sickness comes on horseback and departs on foot. -*Dutch Proverb*

Sickness is felt, but health not at all. -*Thomas Fuller, 1640*

Those who have never been ill are incapable of real sympathy for a great many misfortunes. -*Andre Gide, 1930*

We should never derive our self-concept from the limits of our physical form; we are not our bodies. -*Joanne Yeck*

When it comes to your heart, your outlook on life and self-image may be important. For example, chronic stress, anger, and depression make you a candidate for a heart attack. -*Dr. Isadore Rosenfeld, Parade Health Editor*

Sleep

Perhaps one third of all children don't sleep enough, [they probably need nine hours] which can affect mood, behavior, memory, and school performance. Experts recommend parents enforce regular bedtimes and wake times, keep TVs, telephones, and computers out of bedrooms and ban caffeinated drinks. -*Dr. Carol Rosen, Specialist at Rainbow Babies & Children's Hospital*

Sleep is the greatest gift you can give yourself. Scientists say that those who sleep fewer than six hours a night don't live as long as those who sleep seven hours or more. -*Marvin Phillips*

Sleep to the sick is half health. -*German Proverb*

Spirituality

We now know enough, based on solid research, to say that prayer, much like exercise and diet, has a connection with better health. -*Dr. Harold Koenig, Director of Duke University Center for the Study of Religion/Spirituality and Health*

Look at your health, and if you have it, praise God, and value it next to a good conscience. For health is the second blessing that we mortals are capable of- a blessing that money can't buy. -*Izaak Walton*

Exercise daily- walk with God.

It has been increasingly evident, as pointed out by doctors everywhere, that physical health is closely associated with and often dependent upon, spiritual health. -*Dr. Loring T. Swaim*

Stress

While we've long known that stress is a major risk factor for many health problems, marriage stress appears to be a bigger hazard than other types of stress simply because it's so personal. -*Tara Parker-Pope, Wall Street Journal*

Ulcer

You don't get ulcers from what you eat. You get them from what's eating you. -*Vicki Baum*

153

Wealth

The first wealth is health. -*Emerson*

It is only when the rich are sick that they fully feel the impotence of wealth. -*Charles C. Colton*

6.
LEARNING MATTERS

Achievement

If you tell (count) every step you will make a long journey. -*Thomas Fuller, M.D.*

Who begins too much accomplishes little. -*German Proverb*

Action

If you want work well done, select a busy man; the other kind has no time. -*Elbert Hubbard*

To be always ready a man must be able to cut a knot for everything cannot be untied. -*Henri Frederic Amiel*

Advice

There is nothing which we receive with so much reluctance as advice. -*Joseph Addison*

Ambition

I am going to make good use of my time and strive toward getting as many things as I can accomplish. -*Terry Clark*

No bird soars too high, if he soars with his own wings. -*William Blake, 1790*

Anger

A gentle answer turns away wrath, but a harsh word stirs up anger. -*Proverbs 15:1*

Anxiety

We are more often frightened than hurt. Our troubles spring more often from fancy than reality. *-Seneca, 1 BC*

Argument

The best way I know of to win an argument is to start by being in the right. *-Lord Hailsham*

Attitude

A positive attitude is extremely important, no matter what you are doing, no matter what you hope to achieve. *-Ruth Tomkalski*

Beauty

Look for a lovely thing and you will find it. It is not far away. It never will be far. *-Sara Teasdale*

Belief

Man is a credulous animal and must believe something; in the absence of good grounds for belief, he will be satisfied with bad ones. *-Bertrand Russel*

Since faith is never perfect, belief and unbelief are often mixed. "I do believe, help me overcome my unbelief." *-Mark 9:24*

Blessings

The more you count the blessings you have, the less you crave the luxuries you don't have.

Blunder

Better to trip with the feet than with the tongue. *-Zeno of Citium, 300 BC*

Boredom

The prospect of being pleased tomorrow will never console me for the boredom of today. -*Graffito*

Brevity

All pleasantry should be short; and it might even be as well were the serious short also. -*Voltaire*

Men are born with two eyes, but with one tongue, in order that they should see twice as much as they say. -*Charles Caleb Colton*

Bridges

The hardest thing to learn in life is which bridge to cross and which to burn. -*David Russell*

Caution

Fear to let fall a drop and you spill a lot. -*Malay Proverb*

Change

All changes, even the most longed for, have their melancholy; for what we leave behind us is part of ourselves; we must die to one life before we can enter into another. -*Amatole France*

Change is the law of life and those who look only to the past or the present are certain to miss the future. -*John F. Kennedy*

Even in slight things the experience of the new is rarely without some stirring of foreboding. -*Eric Hoffer*

For something new to emerge into the world something old has to die. - *Pastor Kelly Peters*

Nothing will ever be attempted if all possible objections must first be overcome. -*Samuel Johnson*

The more things change the more they remain the same. -*Alphonse Karr*

There is nothing permanent except change. -*Heraclitus, 475BC*

One of the most difficult things to accept, particularly for the old, is change. Change should be seen not as accidental to life but as part of life itself. -*Hubert van Zeller*

We must adjust to changing times and still hold to unchanging principles. -*Jimmy Carter*

Comfort

I will fear no evil, for you are with me; your rod and your staff, they comfort me. *Psalm 23:4*

Courage

The paradox of courage is that a man must be a little careless of his life even in order to keep it. -*G.K. Chesterton*

You cannot step twice into the same river, for other waters are continually flowing. -*Heraclitus, 500BC*

Complacency

Complacency is the enemy of study. We cannot really learn anything until we rid ourselves of complacency. -*Mao Tse Tung*

Complaint

The dogs bark, but the caravan moves on. -*Arabic Proverb*

Conceit

The smaller the mind the greater the conceit. -*Aesop*

Contentment

I have learned to be content whatever the circumstances. -*Philippians 4:11*

Deafness

None so deaf as he that will not hear. -*Thomas Fuller, MD*

Deception

Who will not be deceived must have as many eyes as hairs on his head. -*German Proverb*

Dependence

Every man expects somebody or something to help him and when he finds he must help himself, he says he lacks liberty and justice. -*Edgar Watson Howe*

Development

There is no fruit which is not bitter before it is ripe. -*Publilius Syrus, 100 BC*

Difficulty

He who accounts all things easy will have many difficulties. -*Laotse, 600 BC*

Dissent

We owe almost all our knowledge not to those who have agreed, but to those who have differed. -*Charles Caleb Colton*

Education

A well-educated person ought to know a little about everything, and a lot about something. What's important is not so much what you learn, but that you learn how to learn, and know where to go to find things out. -*Geoffrey Landis, NASA-Glenn physicist and science fiction author*

Educating children can't be left totally in the hands of teachers. We've got to talk about history, science, political science at dinner tables...It has to happen all through childhood. -*David McCullough, Two-time winner of the Pulitzer Prize and twice a winner of the National Book Award*

Give a man a fish and he eats for a day. Teach a man to fish, and he can feed himself for life. -*Chinese Proverb*

Live with those from whom you can learn; let friendly intercourse be a school for knowledge, and social contact, a school for culture. -*Baltasar Grecian*

The illiterate of the 21st century will not be those who cannot read and write, but those who cannot learn, unlearn, and relearn. -*Alvin Toffler*

The mark of a truly educated person is the recognition of how much there really is to learn. Whether learning happens in the classroom, in the boardroom, or in the family room, the future will belong to the people who embrace education. -*Sandra Pianalto, President and CEO of the Federal Reserve Bank of Cleveland*

Enemies

If we could read the secret history of our enemies, we slowly would find in each man's life sorrow and suffering enough to disarm all hostilities. -*Longfellow*

Example

Few things are harder to put up with than the annoyance of a good example. -*Mark Twain*

Excuse

One of man's greatest failings is that he looks almost always for an excuse in the misfortune that befalls him through his one fault before looking for a remedy- which means he often finds the remedy too late. -*Cardinal de Retz*

Expectation

Blessed is he who expects nothing, for he shall never be disappointed. -*Alexander Pope*

Experience

Experience is not what happens to you; it is what you do with what happens to you. -*Reader's Digest*

He who has been bitten by a snake fears a piece of string. -*Persian Proverb*

I have but one lamp by which my feet are guided, and that is the lamp of experience. I know of no way of judging of the future but by the past. -*Patrick Henry*

No man alive can say "this shall not happen to me." -*Menander, 350 BC*

Nothing ever becomes real till it is experienced; even a proverb is no proverb to you till your life has illustrated it. -*John Keats*

Fact

A fact is like a sack which won't stand up when it is empty. In order that it may stand up, one has to put into it the reason and sentiments which have caused it to exist. -*Luigi Pirandello*

Failure

Failure is not an event, but rather a judgement about an event. Failure is not something that happens to us or a label we attach to things. It is a way we think about outcomes. -*John Ortberg*

Focus

When I focus on me, I get myself into a tight package. When I focus on who God is and on His capabilities, which are beyond my comprehension, I can soar. These are lessons I've been learning all my life. *-Willie Dienes*

Friends

Good friends are more difficult to find than buried treasure.

Generous

Good will come to him who is generous. *-Psalm 112:5*

Good

He teaches me to be good that does me good. *-Thomas Fuller, MD*

Nothing is good for him for whom nothing is bad. *-Baltasar Grecian*

Gossip

If what we see is doubtful, how can we believe what is spoken behind the back. *-Chinese Proverb*

Greatness

Lives of great men all remind us; we can make our lives sublime; and departing, leave behind us footprints on the sands of time. *-Longfellow*

Growth

Each day brings opportunity to learn more about myself and the people around me. *- Kris Lewandoski*

There is no growth without change; there is no change without fear or loss; and there is no loss without pain. -*Rick Warren, Pastor*

Remember the mind grows by what it takes in; the heart grows by what it gives out.

Guilt

The gift that keeps on giving. -*Erma Bombeck*

Habit

Old habits die hard. -*Proverb*

Happiness

Happiness is not a state to arrive at, but a manner of traveling. -*Margaret Lee Runbeck*

It has often cost more to make a man unhappy than it would have cost to make him happy. -*Baltasar Grecian*

Helping

As you grow older, you will discover that you have two hands; one for helping yourself and the other for helping others.

History

If there is anything we have learned from history, it's that we learn nothing from history. -*Benjamin E. Mays*

Hope

Hope is necessary in every condition. The miseries of poverty, sickness of captivity, would, without this comfort, be insupportable. -*Samuel Johnson*

Hope sees the invisible, feels the intangible, and achieves the impossible.

Imagination

Imagination grows by exercise and, contrary to common belief, is more powerful in the mature than in the young. -*Somerset Mangham*

Inquiry

There aren't any embarrassing questions- just embarrassing answers. -*Carl Rowan*

Insight

For insight into the <u>real</u> you, ask someone you know, respect, and trust. -*Daniel Taddeo*

Individualism

We need the faith to go a path untrod, the power to be alone and vote with God. -*Edwin Markham*

Innovation

One doesn't discover new lands without consenting to lose sight of the shore for a very long time. -*Andre Gide*

Involvement

I hear and I forget. I see and I remember. I do and I understand. -*Chinese Proverb*

Judging

Men always love what is good or what they find good; it is in judging what is good that they go wrong. -*Rousseau*

No man can justly censure or condemn another, because indeed no man truly knows another. -*Sir Thomas Browne, 1642*

Knowing

Oddly enough, it's the person who knows everything who has the most to learn.

The next best thing to knowing something is knowing where to find it. -*Samuel Johnson*

Knowledge

Knowledge of what is possible is the beginning of happiness. -*George Santayana*

The greater our knowledge increases, the greater our ignorance unfolds. -*John F. Kennedy*

Knowledge speaks, but wisdom listens. -*Jimi Hendrix*

Language

From infancy on, the language we use to think, remember, and describe the world makes each of us unique. -*Diane Ackerman*

Laziness

The lazier a man is, the more he plans to do tomorrow. -*Norwegian Proverb*

Leadership

To further explore your leadership strengths, you might ask people whose opinions you value. -*Daniel Goldeman*

Learning

A little learning is not a dangerous thing to one who does not mistake it for a great deal. -*William Allen White*

Everything I learned about God, I've learned from the poor. -*Mother Teresa*

Every person you meet- and everything you do in life- is an opportunity to learn something. That's important to all of us, but most of all to a writer because a writer can use anything. -*Tom Clancy*

For whatever things were written before were written for our learning, that we through the patience and comfort of the Scriptures might have hope. -*Romans 15:4*

He who adds not to his learning diminishes it. -*The Talmud*

I am defeated, and I know it, if I meet any human being from whom I find myself unable to learn anything. -*George Herbert Palmer*

Learning is a treasure which accompanies its owner everywhere. -*Chinese Proverb*

Learning is discovering that something is possible.

Learn to paddle your own canoe.

My joy in learning is partly that it enables me to teach. -*Seneca, 100AD*

Never too late to learn. -*Proverb*

One's mind is like a knife. If you don't sharpen it, it gets rusty. -*Nien Cheng*

The highest goal in learning is to know God.

There is no limit to learning.

To be fond of learning is to be near to knowledge. -*Tze-sze, 5th centurty BC*

To learn is a natural pleasure, not confined to philosophers, but common to all men. -*Aristotle, 447BC*

What we have to learn to do, we learn by doing. -*Aristotle*

You can teach a student a lesson for a day; but if you can teach him to learn by creating curiosity, he will continue the learning process as long as he lives. -*Clay P. Bedford*

Liberty/Learning

What spectacle can be more edifying or more seasonable, than that of Liberty and Learning, each leaning on the other for their mutual and surest support? -*James Madison*

Love

Learning to love unselfishly is not an easy task! It runs counter to our self-centered nature. -*Pastor Rick Warren*

Meaning

The meaning of things lies not in the things themselves, but in our attitude towards them. -*Saint Exupery*

Mind

Some minds are like concrete, thoroughly mixed up and permanently set.

The mind that has profundity attains immortality. -*Baltasar Grecian*

Mistakes

I think it's good to learn from your mistakes; but I'm getting tired of learning something new everyday. -*Tom Wilson*

Mission Impossible

When the scientific literature says something is impossible, you have to create possibilities that don't exist yet. -*Robert Langer, Research Laboratory at MIT*

Nature

Man masters nature not by force but by understanding. -*Jacob Bronowski*

Need

We don't always recognize that we already have what we need.

Payment

Nothing is to be had for nothing. -*Epictetus, 200 AD*

By paying our debts, we are equal with all mankind; but in refusing to pay a debt of revenge, we are superior. -*Charles Caleb Colton, 1825*

Possession

An object in possession seldom retains the same charm it had in pursuit. -*Pliny The Younger, 100 AD*

Prejudice

We hate some persons because we do not know them; and we will not know them because we hate them. -*Charles Caleb Colton, 1825*

Question

Ask stupid questions. If you don't ask, you remain stupid. -*Dr. Alvan Feinstein*

Quarreling

Most quarrels amplify a misunderstanding. -*Andre Gide*

You can make up a quarrel, but it will always show where it was patched. -*Edgar Watson Howe, 1911*

Rationalization

There's nothing people can't contrive to praise or condemn and find justification for doing so, according to their age and their inclination. -*Moliere, 1666*

Reading

Research shows that children who are read to are far more likely to do well in school and it improve their lives both spiritually and materially by becoming lifetime readers themselves. -*Jim Trelease, Reading Expert and Author*

Sixty years ago, children would read for hours. Their power of concentration developed as naturally as breathing. Good readers became very good readers. The connection between loving to read and doing well in school is no mystery to most students. -*Norman Mailer, Author*

Reality

The sky is not less blue because the blind man does not see it. -*Danish Proverb*

Reform

Reform must come from within, not without. You cannot legislate virtue. -*James Cardinal Gibbons*

Relatives

Blood's thicker than water, and when one's in trouble best to seek out a relative's open arms. -*Euripides, 426 BC*

Relativity

In the ant's house the dew is a flood. -*Persian Proverb*

Remedies

There are some remedies worse than the disease. -*Publilius Syrus, 100BC*

Repression

A poorly extinguished fire is quickly re-ignited. -*Corneille, 1637*

Reproof

Fear not the anger of the wise to raise; those best can bear reproof who merit praise. -*Alexander Pope, 1711*

Reputation

A good name keeps its luster in the dark. -*English Proverb*

Resolution

A resolution to avoid an evil is seldom framed till the evil is so far advanced as to make avoidance impossible. -*Thomas Hardy, 1874*

Respect

If you have some respect for people as they are, you can be more effective in helping them to become better than they are. -*John W. Gardner*

Respectability

The more things a man is ashamed of, the more respectable he is. *-George Bernard Shaw*

Rules

There is no useful rule without an exception. *-Thomas Fuller, MD, 1932*

Scripture

Nobody ever outgrows Scripture; the book widens and deepens with our years. *-Charles Haddon Spurgeon*

Security

Security depends not so much upon how much you have as upon how much you can do without. *-Joseph Wood Krutch*

Self

Self-reflection is the school of wisdom. *-Baltasar Grecian, 1647*

Serendipity

I find that a great part of the information I have acquired by looking up something and finding something else on the way. *-Franklin P. Adams*

Self-Understanding

Everything that irritates us about others can lead us to an understanding of ourselves. *-Carl Jung*

Silence

At times, silence is not golden; it is yellow. *-Senator Zell Miller*

Silence is sorrow's best food. -*James Russell Lowell, 1848*

Simplicity

To be simple is the best thing in the world; to be modest is the next best. I am not sure about being quiet. -*G.K. Chesterton, 1908*

Sincerity

Weak people cannot be sincere. -*La Rochefoucauld, 1665*

Sorrow

Sorrow makes us all children again. -*Emerson, 1843*

Speaking

First learn the meaning of what you say, and then speak. -*Epictetus, 200 BC*

Nobody talks much that doesn't say unwise things- things he did not mean to say; as no person plays much without striking a false note sometimes. -*Oliver Wendell Holmes, Sr., 1858*

Success

Every great achievement was once considered impossible.

Travel

Many will go here and there to increase knowledge. -*Daniel 12:4*

We travel to learn; and I have never been in any country where they did not do something better than we do it, think some thoughts better than we think, catch some inspiration from heights above our own. -*Maria Mitchell*

Trust

It wasn't raining when Noah built the ark. -*Howard Ruff*

Underachievement

Underachievement is a mind-set that's within your control to change. One way to start is to put your goals in writing. -*Susan Battley*

Virtues/Vices

Virtues are learned at a mother's knee; vices are picked up at some other joint.

Wisdom

A wise man will learn something even from the words of a fool. -*Chinese Proverb*

Knowledge is proud that he has learned so much; wisdom is humble that he knows no more. -*William Cowper, 1785*

The longer we live, the more we find we are like other persons. -*Oliver Wendell Holmes, 1891*

If you realize that you aren't as wise today as you thought you were yesterday, you're wiser today.

Pain makes a man think. Thought makes a man wise. Wisdom makes life endurable. -*John Patrick*

The fear (reverence) of the Lord is the beginning of wisdom. -*Proverbs 9:10*

Wisdom is better than rubies, and all the things that may be desired are not to be compared to it. -*Proverbs 8:11*

Wisdom is supreme; therefore, get wisdom. Though it cost all you have, get understanding. -*Proverbs 4:7*

Words

Well to have fine brains, but not a babbling tongue; for too much discourse borders on dispute. -*Baltasar Grecian*

Worry

Worry is the most natural and spontaneous of all human functions. It is time to acknowledge this, perhaps even to learn to do it better. -*Lewis Thomas*

7.
LIFE MATTERS

Abilities

What you are is God's gift to you; what you do with yourself is your gift to God. -*Danish Proverb*

Accountable

Nothing in all creation is hidden from God's sight. Everything is uncovered and laid bare before the eyes of him to whom we must give account. -*Hebrews 4:13*

Action

If you were going to die soon and had only one phone call you could make, who would you call and what would you say? And why are you waiting? -*Stephen Levine*

When I do something kind or when I don't do something hurtful, somebody knows what I've done. Every life touches others. -*Rabbi Harold S. Kushner*

Adversity/Prosperity

Adversity makes men, and prosperity makes monsters. -*Victor Hugo*

Comfort and prosperity have never enriched the world as much as adversity has done. -*Billy Graham*

Advice

Find something to do with your life that makes you happy, and do it with as much passion as you can everyday. -*Lee Marshall, Business Owner*

Affection

Affection is responsible for nine-tenths of whatever solid and durable happiness there is in our lives. -*C.S. Lewis*

Afflicted

All the days of the afflicted are evil, but a cheerful heart has a continual feast. -*Proverbs 15:15*

Anticipation

It is reflection and foresight that assure freedom to life. -*Baltasar Grecian*

A Plea

That we all work together to make our limited time on Earth one of sharing, understanding, tolerance, compassion, and community. -*Robert Schoen*

Appreciation

The deepest principle in human nature is the craving to be appreciated and the desire to be important. -*Dale Carnegie*

Attract/Repel

Goodness and nobility have an inherent power to attract, whereas self-seeking and evil inevitably repel. -*Reverend Francis B. Sayre*

Attitude

Attitudes are more important than facts. -*Karl Menninger, MD*

The difference between success and failure is found in one's attitude toward setbacks, handicaps, discouragements, and other disappointing situations. -*David Joseph Schwartz, Ph. D*

We can be denied every freedom except one- choosing our attitude!

When our attitude is right, our abilities reach a maximum of effectiveness and good results inevitably follow. *-Professor Erwin H. Schell*

Balance

You can go fast through life, or you can go slowly. I think most of us just yearn to master the controls. *-Jeanne Marie Laskas*

Behavior

Anyone can carry his burden for one day. Anyone can be pleasant, courteous, and friendly for one day. And that continued is all there is to life.

Certain behaviors, due to nature or nurture, are fixed early in childhood and, like a leopard's spots, remain unchanged throughout life.

Believe

Be not afraid of life. Believe that life *is* worth living, and your belief will help create the fact. *-William James*

What we repeatedly hear we will believe.

You never know how much you really believe anything until its truth or falsehood becomes a matter of life and death to you. *-C.S. Lewis*

Belong

Do not belong so wholly to others that you no longer belong to yourself. *-Baltasar Grecian*

Beauty

It is better to be first with an ugly woman than the hundredth with a beauty. *-Pearl Buck*

Not only does beauty fade, but it leaves a record upon the face as to what became of it. -*Elbert Hubbard*

Begin

To begin is to be halfway there.

Best

Get up and do your best and God will do the rest.

Bitterness

When you harbor bitterness, happiness will dock elsewhere. -*Andy Rooney*

Bloom

I will bloom where I am planted.

Brevity

When asked his greatest surprise- the brevity of life. -*Billy Graham*

Brotherhood

The universal brotherhood of man is our most precious possession, what there is of it. -*Mark Twain*

Caring

People don't care what we know until they know we care.

Celebration

Life isn't waiting for a celebration. Life is a celebration. -*A man after 9½ months of chemotherapy*

Certain

There is only one thing about which I am certain, and this is that there is very little about which one can be certain.

Character

Character is both developed and rewarded by tests, and all of life is a test. -*Pastor Rick Warren*

Not education, but character is man's greatest need and man's greatest safeguard. -*Herbert Spencer*

Out of our beliefs are born deeds. Out of our deeds we form habits; out of our habits we grow our character; and on our character we build our destiny. -*Henry Hancock*

Temperament is what you are born with. Character is what you make of it. -*Hubert van Zeller*

Your character is essentially the sum of your habits. -*Pastor Rick Warren*

Christianity

If Christianity is false, it is of no importance. If Christianity is true, it is of infinite importance. The one thing it cannot be is of moderate importance. -*C.S. Lewis*

Common Sense

Nothing astonishes men so much as common sense and plain dealing. -*Emerson*

Communication

Five communication killers: fear of rejection, lack of honesty, an explosive response, tears, and silence. -*John Hagee, Pastor*

Compromise

It is better to lose the saddle than the horse. -*Italian Proverb*

Complacency

Most human beings have an almost infinite capacity for taking things for granted. -*Aldono Huxley*

The path is smooth that leadeth on to danger. -*Shakespeare*

Contentment

Contentment begins with thankfulness. -*Editor*

He is a wise man who does not grieve for the things which he has not, but rejoices for those which he has. -*Epictetus*

Control

There are only two things in life that you control and that's what you think and what you do. -*Dr. David Coleman, Dating Doctor*

Consequences

The sin they do by two and two they must pay for one by one. -*Rudyard Kipling*

Corruption

If the camel once gets his nose in the tent, his body will soon follow. -*Arabic Proverb*

Courage

A clay pot sitting in the sun will always be a clay pot. It has to go through the white heat of the furnace to become porcelain. -*Mildred Witte Struven*

Sometimes even to live is an act of courage. -*Seneca*

Crime

He who holds the ladder is as bad as the thief. -*German Proverb*

Cured/Endured

There is an old saying that what can't be cured must be endured, and perhaps we are wise if we learn to accept the inevitable with good grace.

Curiosity

Curiosity is the key to making dreams come true. -*Walt Disney*

Danger

Danger past, God is forgotten. -*Thomas Fuller, MD*

However well organized the foundation of life may be, life must always be full of risks. -*Havelock Ellis*

Death

A man's dying is more the survivors' affair than his own. -*Thomas Mann*

Any man's death diminishes me, because I am involved in mankind; and therefore never send to know for whom the bell tolls; it tolls for thee. *-John Donne*

Death does not blow a trumpet. -*Danish Proverb*

Death is just a distant rumor to the young. -*Andy Rooney*

Death sneaks up on you like a windshield sneaks up on a bug.

If we live, we live to the Lord; and if we die, we die to the Lord. So, whether we live or die, we belong to the Lord. -*Romans 14:8*

If you aren't fit to face death today, it's very unlikely you will be by tomorrow; besides, tomorrow is an uncertain quantity; you have no guarantee that there will be any tomorrow-for you. -*Thomas A. Kempis*

In the midst of life we are in death. -*The Book of Common Prayer*

What we can learn from death is how to live. -*Dick Feagler, Columnist*

Those who believe heaven is a real place makes a big difference on how they view death. -*Editor*

To think of death and to prepare for death is not a surrender. It is a victory over fear. -*Paul Wilhelm Von Keppler*

When you accept that you can die at any time, you focus on the essentials. Once you learn how to die, you learn how to live. -*Morrie Schwartz, on his death bed.*

He hath lived ill that knows not how to die well. -*Thomas Fuller, MD*

It hath often been said, that it is not death but dying, which is terrible. -*Henry Fielding*

It is death that is the guide of our life, and our life has no goal but death. -*Maurice Maeterlinck, 1869*

It is a myth to think death is just for the old. Death is there from the very beginning. -*Herman Feifel*

Let us endeavor so to live that when we come to die even the undertaker will be sorry. -*Mark Twain*

Neither the sun nor death can be looked at steadily. -*La Rochefoucauld*

Nobody knows, in fact, what death is, nor whether to man it is not perchance the greatest of all blessings; yet people fear it as if they surely knew it to be the worst of all evils. -*Socrates, 400 BC*

Precious in the sight of the Lord is the death of his saints.

Reflect frequently on death and impermanence. If you are conscious of the certainty of death, it will not be difficult for you to avoid evil, and it will not be difficult for you to practice virtue. -*Ge-She-Pu-to-pa*

Rich man and poor move side by side toward the limit of death. -*Pindar, 500 BC*

Suicide is not abominable because God forbids it: God forbids it because it is abominable. -*Immanuel Kant*

Then shall the dust return to the earth as it was, and the spirit shall return unto God who gave it. -*Ecclesiastes 12:7*

The end of all is death, and man's life passeth away suddenly as a shadow. -*Thomas A. Kempis, 1426*

The perpetual work of your life is but to lay the foundation of death. -*Montaigne*

The old man has death before his eyes; the young man behind his back. -*Proverb*

The goal of life is to die young as old as possible.

To the Christian, death is not the end, but an event in life; a new start with an extended knowledge and a purer love. -*Bishop of Lincoln*

When the cancer that later took his life was first diagnosed, Senator Richard L. Neuberger remarked upon his "new appreciation of things I once took for granted- eating lunch with a friend, scratching my cat Muffet's ears and listening to his purrs, the company of my wife, reading a book or magazine in the quiet of my bed lamp at night, raiding the refrigerator for a glass of orange juice or a slice of toast. For the first time, I think I actually am savoring life. -*Senator Richard L. Neuberger*

Debt

It is hard to pay for bread that has been eaten. -*Danish Proverb*

The rich rule over the poor, and the borrower is servant to the lender. -*Proverbs 22:7*

Deception

We are never so easily deceived as when we imagine we are deceiving others. -*La Rochefoucauld*

Decline

The passing years steal from us one thing after another. -*Horace, 8 BC*

Deeds

Though men pride themselves on their great actions, often they are not the result of any great design but of chance. -*La Rochefoucauld*

Defeat

Being defeated is often a temporary condition. Giving up is what makes it permanent. -*Robert H. Schuller*

Dependence

The younger we are, the more people we need so that we may live; the older we become, the more people we again need to live. Life is lived from dependence to dependence. -*Henri J.M. Nouwen*

There is not a soul who does not have to beg alms of another, either a smile, a handshake, or a fond eye. -*Edward Dahlberg*

Despair

Modern man's despair is not despair of God at all, but despair of all that is not God. Beyond that certain despair lies Christian hope, the certainty that God alone is enough for man. -*William McNamara*

Destination

If you don't know where you're going, every road will get you nowhere. -*Henry Kissinger*

Development

The shell must break before the bird can fly. -*Alfred, Lord Tennyson*

Different

It's very comforting for people to know that they don't have to be like everybody else. -*Editor*

When two people are the same, one is unnecessary.

Difficulty

A smooth sea never made a skillful mariner. -*English Proverb*

I walk firmer and more secure up hill than down. -*Montaigne*

What's too hard for a man must be worth looking into. -*Kenyan Proverb*

Discord

The ultimate measure of a man is not where he stands in moments of comfort and convenience, but where he stands at times of challenge and controversy. -*Martin Luther King, Jr.*

Discouragement

Don't let life discourage you; everyone who got where he is had to begin where he was. -*Richard L. Evans*

Disillusionment

Hope is the only good thing that disillusion respects. -*Vauvenargues*

Driven

Many people are driven by guilt, resentment and anger, fear materialism and the need for approval; all lead to the same dead end: without a purpose, life is trivial, petty, and pointless. -*Pastor Rich Warren*

Duty

God obligeth no man to more than he hath given him ability to perform. -*Koran*

Rich men are to bear the infirmities of the poor. Wise men are to bear the mistakes of the ignorant. -*Henry Ward Beecher*

When habit has strengthened our sense of duties, they leave us no time for other things; but, when young we neglect them, and this gives us time for anything. -*Thomas Jefferson*

Effort

Despite one's own best efforts- things can and do go wrong. -*Dr. Paul Hinko*

Enemies

Our enemies approach nearer to truth in their judgement of us than we do ourselves. -*La Rochefoucauld*

Enthusiasm

There is a real magic in enthusiasm. It spells the difference between mediocrity and accomplishment. -*Norman Vincent Peale*

Envy

A heart at peace gives life to the body, but envy rots the bones. -*Proverbs 14:30*

Excellence

Men of genius do not excel in any profession because they labor in it, but they labor in it because they excel. -*William Hazlitt*

Excuses

Excuses are the nails used to build a house of failure. -*Don Wilder*

Existence

As long as any man exists, there is some need of him; let him fight for his own. -*Emerson*

Exit

Every exit is an entrance to someplace else.

Expectations

Expect people to be better than they are; it helps them to become better. But don't be disappointed when they are not; it helps them to keep trying. -*Merry Browne*

Nothing is so good as it seems before hand. -*George Eliot*

The best of our lives we pass in counting on what is to come. -*William Hazlitt*

Experience

Experience is not what happens to you. It is what you do with what happens to you. -*Aldous Huxley*

Facts

Though we face the facts of sex, we are more reluctant than ever to face the fact of death or the crueler facts of life, either biological or social. -*Joseph Wood Krutch*

Failure

A man can fail many times, but he isn't a failure until he begins to blame somebody else. -*John Burroughs*

Many of life's failures are people who did not realize how close they were to success when they gave up. -*Thomas Edison*

You have only failed when you have failed to try.

Faith

But always, if we have faith, a door will open for us, not perhaps one that we ourselves would ever have thought of, but one that will ultimately prove good for us. -*A.J. Cronin*

If you do what you know how to do, the things you don't know how to do will work themselves out; this is faith.

It is faith that makes every tomorrow a reason for hope, not despair, a reason to be thankful, not bitter. -*Gloria Haynes*

Familiarity

The song is best esteemed with which our ears are most acquainted. -*William Byrd*

Faults

No man is born without faults; he is the best who has the fewest. -*Horace*

Favor

If you do a favor, forget it; if you receive one, remember it.

Fear

Nothing in life is to be feared; it is only to be understood. -*Madame Curie*

We fear that which we don't understand.

Feast/Fast

Feast, and your halls are crowded; fast, and the world goes by. -*Ella Wheeler Wilcox*

First Impression

You never get a second chance to make a first impression.

Fools

Fools rush in where angels fear to tread. -*Alexander Pope*

No one is a fool always, everyone sometimes.

The greatest lesson in life is to know that even fools are right sometimes. -*Winston Churchill*

Forgetting

Matters best forgotten are those best remembered. At times the only remedy for evil lies in forgetting it, and to be able to forget is the remedy; wherefore, train your memory to these comfortable manners, for she can bring you heaven or hell. -*Baltasar Grecian*

Forgiveness

He who cannot forgive others breaks the bridge over which he must himself pass.

One of the most lasting pleasures you can experience is the feeling that comes over you when you genuinely forgive an enemy- whether he knows about it or not. -*A. Battista*

Fortune/Misfortune

From fortune to misfortune is but a step; from misfortune to fortune is a long way. -*Yiddish Proverb*

Friends

Fate chooses your relations; you choose your friends. -*Jacques Delille*

One friend in a lifetime is much; two are many; three are hardly possible. -*Henry Adams*

The happiest miser on earth is one who saves friends.

Two are better than one, because they have a good return for their work: If one falls down, his friend can help him up. -*Ecclesiastes 4:9*

Without friends no one would choose to live, though he had all other goods. -*Aristotle, 400 B.C.*

Friendship

Flowers of friendship bloom year around.

Friendship is born at that moment when one person says to another: "What? You too? I thought I was the only one." -*C.S. Lewis*

Fulfillment

True personal fulfillment never comes through self-gratification.

Future

The best thing about the future is that it comes only one day at a time. - *Abraham Lincoln*

The future is full of doubt, indeed, but fuller still of hope.

Giving

Anyone can give- if not money, then your time. -*John Scardino, L. A Land Developer*

Then give to the world the best you have, and the best will come back to you. -*Madeline Bridges*

Goal

You become successful the moment you start moving toward a worthwhile goal.

To keep on the cutting edge, a list of goals is critical: things you want to do, places you want to go, people you want to see, skills you want to learn, and issues you think are important. -*Win Arn, Author*

Golden Rule

We have committed the Golden Rule to memory; let us now commit it to life.
-Edwin Markham

Goodness

There's no bad from which some good doesn't come.

A good man isn't good for everything. *-John W. Gardner*

Graduation

It is ironic that we spend our school days yearning to graduate and our graduation day yearning to remember our school days. *-Isabel Waxman*

Grateful

As we've traveled along life's path, how grateful I am for your company and how grateful I am for your bringing along what I lack, but most of all, I'm grateful for what you've left behind when we had to part. For those provision sustain me on my journey and lighten my burden. *-Tom Wilson*

Greatness

Great men with great truths have seldom had much support from their associates. *-Philip Wylie*

No great thing is created suddenly. *-Epictetus*

Some are born great, some achieve greatness, and some have greatness thrust upon them. *-Shakespeare*

Grudge

A grudge is not being able to get out of your mind some injustice you think somebody committed against you. The only way to let go of a grudge is through forgiveness. It is absolutely essential if people are going to move forward in their lives. *-Professor Maurice Elias*

Habit

A man's habit clings, and he will wear tomorrow what today he wears. *-Edna St. Vincent Millay*

Happiness

Everyone wants to live on top of the mountain, but all the happiness and growth occurs while you're climbing it. *-Andy Rooney*

It is not how much we have, but how much we enjoy, that makes happiness. *-Charles H. Spurgeon*

Happiness is the practice of the virtues. *-Clement of Alexandria*

Happiness is when what you think, what you say, and what you do are in harmony. *-Gandhi*

No man is happy who does not think himself so. *-Publilius Syrus, 100B.C.*

Not only do we have a right to be happy; we have an obligation to be happy. Our happiness has an effect on the lives of everyone around us; it provides them with a positive environment in which to thrive and to be happy themselves. *-Dennis Prager, Talk Show Host*

Remember happiness doesn't depend upon who you are or what you have; it depends solely upon what you think. *-Dale Carnegie*

Remember that you are responsible for your happiness.

The door to happiness opens outward.

The bird of paradise alights only upon the hand that does not grasp. *-John Berry*

The pursuit of happiness is a most ridiculous phrase: if you pursue happiness, you'll never find it. -*C.P. Snow*

There is no better time than right now to be happy.

What a wonderful life I've had! I only wish I'd realized it sooner. -*Colette*

What really matters is what happens in us, not to us. -*Reverend James W. Kennedy*

Happenings

You can't always choose what happens to you in life, but you can choose how you react to it. Choose your attitude. -*Jeanine S. Hein*

Hatred/Love

Hatred paralyzes life; love releases it. Hatred confuses life; love harmonizes it. Hatred darkens life; love illuminates it. -*Martin Luther King, Jr.*

Heredity

The seed of the cedar will become cedar. The seed of the bramble can only become bramble. -*Saint Exupery*

History

History never looks like history when you are living through it. It always looks confusing and messy, and it always feels uncomfortable. -*John W. Gardner*

The only lesson history has taught us is that man has not yet learned anything from history.

Home

Home is the place where, when you go there, they have to take you in. -*Robert Frost*

The dog is a lion in his own house. -*Persian Proverb*

Honored

No person was ever honored for what he received. Honor has been the reward for what he gave. -*Calvin Coolidge*

Hope

Everything that is done in the world is done by hope. -*Martin Luther*

If winter comes, can spring be far behind? -*Shelley*

Hope inspires the good to reveal itself. -*Emily Dickinson*

Hope is a necessity for normal life and the major weapon against the suicide impulses. Hope is not identical with optimism. Optimism is distant from reality: like pessimism, it emphasizes the importance of "I." Hope is modest, humble, selfless; it implies progress; it is an adventure, a going forward- a confident search for a rewarding life. -*Dr. Karl Menninger*

The hopeful man sees success where others see failure, sunshine where others see shadows and storm. -*O.S. Marden*

Hospitality

A guest sees more in an hour than the host in a year. -*Polish Proverb*

Unbidden guests are often welcomest when they are gone. -*Shakespeare*

Hour

One of the illusions of life is that the present hour is not the critical decisive hour. Write it on your heart that every day is the best day of the year. -*Ralph Waldo Emerson*

Houses

Small rooms or dwellings discipline the mind; large ones weaken it. -*Leonardo Da Vinci*

Humor

They say hard work never hurt anybody, but I figure why take the chance. -*Ronald Reagan*

Life is like a roll of toilet paper. The closer it gets to the end, the faster it goes. -*Andy Rooney*

The old believe everything; the middle-aged suspect everything; the young know everything. -*Oscar Wilde*

Human Nature

It is usually the case with most men that their nature is so constitute that they pity those who fare badly and envy those who fare well. -*Spinoza*

Most men have low regard for what they understand and venerate only what is beyond them; they honor most what they cannot grasp. -*Baltasar Grecian*

Hunger

An empty stomach will not listen to anything. -*Spanish Proverb*

Hypochondria

An imaginary ailment is worse than a disease. -*Yiddish Proverb*

Hypocrisy

All are not saints that go to church. -*Proverb*

Ideals

Every dogma has its day, but ideals are eternal. -*Israel Zangwill*

The ideals that have lighted my way, and time after time have given me new courage to face life cheerfully, have been kindness, beauty, and truth. -*Albert Einstein*

Idleness

The hardest work is to go idle. -*Yiddish Proverb*

Ignorance

He that knows least commonly presumes most. -*Thomas Fuller, MD*

Not to know is bad; not to wish to know is worse. -*Nigerian Proverb*

Imitation

We are, in truth, more than half what we are by imitation. -*Lord Chesterfield*

When people are free to do as they please, they usually imitate each other. -*Eric Hoffer*

Immortality

Surely God would not have created such a being as man to exist only for a day! No, no, man was made for immortality. -*Abraham Lincoln*

If something comes to life in others because of you, then you have made an approach to immortality. -*Norman Cousins*

Imperfection

A good garden may have some weeds. -*Thomas Fuller, MD*

The best brewer sometimes makes bad beer. -*German Proverb*

Important

Only after watching a person go from good health to fragile death, over an extended period of time, can one begin to know and appreciate what is <u>really</u> important in life. -*Editor*

What's important is not the years in your life but the life in your years.

Indispensable

The eye cannot say to the hand, "I don't need you!" And the head cannot say to the feet, "I don't need you!" On the contrary, those parts of the body that seem to be weaker are indispensable. -*1 Corinthians 12:21-22*

Ingratitude

Men are slower to recognize blessings than evils. -*Livy*

Influence

The best effect of fine persons is felt after we have left their presence. -*Emerson*

Injury

Everyone suffers wrongs for which there is no remedy. -*Edgar Watson Howe*

Who offends writes on sand, who is offended on marble. -*Italian Proverb*

Insight

Would some power the gift to give us to see ourselves as others see us! It would from many a blunder free us. -*Robert Burns*

Inspiration

Ninety percent of inspiration is perspiration. -*Proverb*

Intelligence

Most of us make two basic errors with respect to intelligence: We underestimate our own brain power, and we overestimate the other fellow's brain power. -*David Joseph Schwartz, Ph.D.*

Introspection

The unexamined life is not worth living. -*Socrates, 400 BC*

Jobs

There are no menial jobs, only menial attitudes. -*William J. Bennett*

Judgment

You are judged by the company you keep. -*Aesop*

The good judgment of some people will never wear out. They don't use it often enough.

Knowledge

Since we cannot be universal and know all that is to be known of everything, we ought to know a little about everything. -*Pascal*

Kindness

Being in a hurry is always the death of kindness.

Kindness can become its own motive. We are made kind by being kind. -*Eric Hoffer*

Kindness is the oil that takes the friction out of life.

Practicing kindness and letting go of prejudice have a deep impact on everyone around us and on society as a whole. -*Arthur Caliandro*

Leniency

If we had to tolerate in others all that we permit in ourselves, life would become completely unbearable. -*George Courteline*

Lesson

Everyone has something to contribute and will if given the opportunity. -*Randell McShepard*

Lesson Learned

Life is precious, never take it for granted. -*Herb de la Porte, Business owner*

Liberty

Liberty is always dangerous, but it is the safest thing we have. -*Henry Emerson Fosdick, Pastor*

Life

Life is the greatest bargain; we get it for nothing. -*Yiddish Proverb*

A living dog is better than a dead lion. -*Ecclesiastes 9:4*

As we voyage along through life, tis the set of soul that decides its goal and not the calm or the strife. -*Ella Wheeler Wilcox*

Life is half spent before one knows what life is. -*French Proverb*

The purpose of life is to discover your gift. The meaning of life is giving your gift away. -*David Viscott*

The measure of a life is not its duration but its donation. -*Corrie Ten Boom*

Life is what happens to you while you're busy making plans. -*John Lennon*

The lust for comfort, that stealthy thing that enters the house a guest, and then becomes a host, and then a master. -*Kahlil Gibran*

Relationships, not achievements or acquisition of things, are what matter most in life. -*Rick Warren, Pastor*

As we travel through life…what we begin the journey with…what we take with us…and what we pick up along the way is never more important than what we leave behind. -*Tom Wilson*

We are shifting from 'material want' to 'meaning want.' Lack of things can make us unhappy; getting them does not necessarily make us happy. And so we feel our lives deficient in significance. If life is getting better, why do we feel worse? -*Gregg Easterbrook, Author, 2004*

Life is a war of attrition. You have to stay active on all fronts. It's one thing after another…I've tried to control a chaotic universe. And it's a losing battle. -*Harvey Pekar, author*

We don't see things as they are, we see them as we are. -*Anais Nin*

On the holy ground of our heritage let us, in brotherhood, sustain our commitment to seek a nobler life for all mankind. -*Alfred Bryan Bonds, Jr.*

Live (the moment) like there's no tomorrow; love like you've never been hurt; dance like no one is watching.

Life may begin at 40, but everything else starts to wear out, fall out, or spread out!

It ought to be the business of every day to prepare for our final day. -*Matthew Henry*

How far you go in life depends on your being tender with the young and compassionate with the aged, sympathetic with the striving, and tolerant of the weak and the strong, because someday you will have been all of these. - *George Washington Carver*

We must all take our place in the circle of life- for each one of us has a place which is ours and ours alone. -*The Lion King*

Life is hard by the yard; but by the inch, life is a cinch

Look at life through the windshield, not the rearview mirror.

The secret of life: do something for somebody else.

Life is a coin. You can spend it any way you wish, but you can only spend it once.

Life is a series of choices. No matter where you are in life you always have choices. -*Cynthia Earl*

One voice can make a song. One life can change the world, so let your light shine!

Getting up each morning and simply trying to do the next right thing equips one with the strength and comfort to get through life a day at a time. -*Dick Feagler, Columnist*

Somewhere there's someone who dreams of your smile, and finds in your presence that life is worthwhile. So when you are lonely, remember it's true. Somebody somewhere is thinking of you. -*K. Blackburn*

Nobody can ruin your life if you don't let them. -*Joyce Meyer, Speaker*

When life hands you a bad deal, learn and grow from it. If we embrace the good that can come from whatever life hands us, we have come a long way in embracing uncertainty. -*Susan Jeffers*

Life can only be understood backwards, but it must be lived forwards. -*Soren Kierkegaard*

It's a shallow life that doesn't give a person a few scars. -*Garrison Keillor*

Life is a mirror: if you frown at it, it frowns back; it you smile, it returns the greeting. -*Thacheray*

Life is a mystery to be lived, not a problem to be solved. -*Van Kaam*

Life will sooner or later show its claws. -*Anton Chekhov*

Life was not given to be used up in the pursuit of what we must leave behind us when we die. -*Joseph May*

Treasure life in yourself, and you give it to others; give it to others, and it will come back to you. For life, like love, cannot thrive inside its own threshold but is renewed as it offers itself. Life grows as it is spent. -*Ardis Whitman*

Only a life lived for others is a life worth while. -*Albert Einstein*

The grand essentials in this life are something to do, something to love, and something to hope for. -*Addison*

The life of every man is a diary in which he means to write one story, and writes another; and his humblest hour is when he compares the volume as it is with what he vowed to make it. -*J.M. Barrie*

There is no wealth but life. -*John Ruskin*

Life is an adventure in forgiveness. -*Norman Cousins*

Whatever is at the center of your life is your God. -*Pastor Rick Warren*

The best portion of a good man's life is his little, nameless, unremembered acts of kindness and love. -*William Wordsworth*

Life is just a minute, only sixty seconds in it, forced upon you, can't refuse it. Didn't seek it, didn't choose it, but it's up to you to use it. You must suffer if you lose it, give an account if you abuse it, just a tiny little minute, but eternity is in it. -*Dr. Benjamin Elijah Mays*

Life is no straight and easy corridor along which we travel free and unhampered, but a maze of passages, through which we must seek our way, lost and confused, now and again checked in a blind alley. -*A.J. Cronin*

One of the tragedies of life is that once a deed is done, the consequences are beyond our control. -*Benjamin E. Mays*

Life is 10% what happens to you, 90% how you respond to it. -*Charles Swindoll, Pastor*

The game of life is not so much in holding a good hand as playing a poor hand well. -*H.T. Leslie*

Life is full of unexpected second chances. -*Martha Stewart*

Life: in spite of the cost of living, it's still popular. -*Kathleen Norris*

I [Jesus] have come that you may have life- and have it more abundantly. -*John 10:10*

Life is the art of drawing without an eraser. -*John Christian*

Life/Death

A good life fears not life or death. -*Thomas Fuller, MD*

Sometimes the best preparation for life is a preparation for death. -*Carolyn Nystrom*

Living

The only real invalid is the person who thinks she or he is one. I take nothing away from anyone's real suffering by saying this. I simply mean, if you can't completely put mind over matter, you can at least tend your mind. -*Margaret Blackstone, Author*

Longevity

It is vanity to desire a long life and to take no heed of a good life. *-Thomas A. Kempis*

Loneliness

The man who spends his life building walls instead of bridges has no right to complain if he is lonely.

Man's loneliness is but his fear of life. *-Eugene O'Niell*

No one would choose a friendless existence on condition of having all the other things in the world. *-Aristotle, 400 BC*

Love

Love is life and if you miss love, you miss life. *-Leo Buscaglia*

The best use of life is love. The best expression of love is time. The best time to love is now.

Lose

Whatever you can lose reckon of no account. *-Publilius Syrus, 100 BC*

Lying

Dogs bark, cats meow, and children lie. Your neighbor's children lie. Your sisters's children lie. And yes, your children lie. *-Chick Moorman*

Mankind

There are three classes of men: lovers of wisdom, lovers of honor, and lovers of gain. *-Plato, 400 BC*

We should expect the best and the worst from mankind as from the weather. -*Vauvenargues, 1746*

Manners

A bad manner spoils everything, even reason and justice; a good one supplies everything, gilds a no, sweetens truth, and adds a touch of beauty to old age itself. -*Baltasar Grecian*

Materialism

You've never seen a hearse with luggage racks.

Matters

Matters of the heart matter most in life.

Means/Ends

When we deliberate, it is about means and not ends. -*Aristotle, 400 BC*

Melancholy

That the birds of worry and sadness fly above your head, this you cannot change. But that they build nests in your hair, this you can prevent. -*Chinese Proverb*

Memory

Memory is the dairy that we all carry about with us. -*Oscar Wilde*

Men/Women

Women, as they grow older, rely more and more on cosmetics. Men, as they grow older, rely more and more on a sense of humor. -*George Jean Nathan, 1925*

Minds

Minds differ still more than faces. -*Voltaire*

Strongest minds are often those of whom the noisy world hears least. -*William Wordsworth*

The mind covers more ground than the heart but goes less far. -*Chinese Proverb*

The mind has great influence over the body, and maladies often have their origins there. -*Moliere, 1665*

Minority/Majority

The test of courage comes when we are in the minority; the test of tolerance comes when we are in the majority. -*Ralph W. Sockman*

Misfortune

Let us be of good cheer, remembering that the misfortunes hardest to bear are those which never come. -*James Russell Lowell*

Mistake

The greatest mistake you can make in life is to be continually fearing you will make one. -*Elbert Hubbard*

Moderation

Moderation, after all, is only the belief that you will be a better man tomorrow than you were yesterday. -*Murray Kempton*

Money

The darkest hour of any man's life is when he sits down to plan how to get money without earning it. -*Horace Greeley*

There are people who have money and people who are rich. -*Coco Chanel*

To learn the value of money, it is not necessary to know the nice things it can get for you; you have to have experienced the trouble of getting it. -*Phillippe Herieat*

When money speaks, the truth keeps silent. -*Russian Proverb*

When reason rules, money is a blessing. -*Publilius Syrus, 100 B.C.*

Whoever loves money never has enough money; whoever loves wealth is never satisfied with his income. -*Ecclesiastes 5:10*

Morality

Our lives…are but a little while, so let them run as sweetly as you can and give no thought to grief from day to day. -*Euripides, 422 BC*

Right is right, even if everyone is against it; wrong is wrong, even if everyone is for it. -*William Penn*

Where morality is present, laws are unnecessary. Without morality, laws are unenforceable.

Without civic morality communities perish; without personal morality their survival has no value. -*Bertrand Russel*

Mortality

All is transitory- fame and the famous as well. -*Marcus Aurelius, 200 AD*

Motivation

There have been two great motivators in my life: Jesus Christ and adversity. -*J.C. Penny*

Motives

I saw that if one's motives are wrong, nothing can be right.

Mourning

When we lose one we love, our bitterest tears are called forth by the memory of hours when we loved not enough. -*Maurice Maeterlinck*

Mystery

Mystery lies under the surface of the ordinary. We just have to look for it. -*Frederich Buecher*

Without mysteries, life would be very dull indeed. -*Charles de Lint*

Nature

Nature takes no account of even the most reasonable human excuses. -*Joseph Wood Krutch*

Never does nature say one thing and wisdom another. -*Juvenal, 100 AD*

Needs

They say a person needs just three things to be truly happy in this world: someone to love, something to do, and something to hope for. -*Tom Bodett*

Neighbors

Every man's neighbor is his looking glass. -*English Proverb*

It is one of the most beautiful compensations in life that one cannot sincerely try to help another without helping himself. -*Ralph Waldo Emerson*

You're never quite sure how you feel about a neighbor until a "For Sale" sign suddenly appears in front of his house. -*O.A. Battista*

News

Evil report carries farther than any applause. -*Baltasar Grecian, 1647*

Nobility

Virtue is the only true nobility. -*Thomas Fuller, MD, 1732*

Non-Conformist

To lead the orchestra one must turn one's back to the crowd.

Novelty

It is always the latest song that an audience applauds the most. -*Homer, 900 BC*

Obstacles

Obstacles are those frightful things you see when you take your eyes off the goal. -*Hannah More*

Obscurity/Competence

Obscurity and a competence: that is the life that is best worth living. -*Mark Twain*

Open-Mind

Where there is an open mind, there will always be a frontier. -*Charles F. Kettering*

Opinions

New opinions are always suspected, and usually opposed, without any other reason but because they are not already common. -*John Locke*

Opportunity

Opportunities multiply as they are seized. -*Sun Tzu*

The opportunity that God sends does not wake up him who is asleep. -*Senegalese Proverb*

There is no security on this earth; there is only opportunity. *-Douglas MacArthur, 1955*

Optimism

In this tumult of change, one of the hardest things to remember is that some things do endure: Reason remains a constant force; civilization is cumulative, not rebuild overnight; work and merit deserve rewards; progress relies on honesty and virtue. *-Robert L. Bartley, Editor of Wall Street Journal*

Order

Order marches with weighty and measured strides; disorder is always in a hurry. *-Napoleon, 1804*

Originality

All good things which exist are the fruits of originality. *-John Stuart Mill, 1859*

When people are free to do as they please, they usually imitate each other.

Originality is deliberate and forced, and partakes of the nature of a protest. -*Eric Hoffer*

Outlook

A pessimist sees the difficulty in every opportunity; an optimist sees the opportunity in every difficulty. *-Winston Churchill*

One thing I do, forgetting those things which are behind and reaching forward to those things which are ahead. *-Philippians 3:13*

Overcoming

Be still, sad heart, and cease repining; behind the cloud is the sun still shining; thy fate is the common fate of all, into each life some rain must fall, some days must be dark and dreary. -*H.W. Longfellow*

Whatever reason you had for not being somebody, there's somebody who had that same problem and overcame it.

Past

One may return to the place of his birth; he cannot go back to his youth. -*John Burroughs*

Passion

Nothing great in the world has been accomplished without passion. -*Hegel, 1832*

Parting

The return makes one love the farewell. -*Alfred De Musset*

Patience

Have patience with all things, but chiefly have patience with yourself. Do not lose courage in considering your imperfections, but instantly set about remedying them- everyday begin the task anew. -*St. Francis de Sales*

Patience is hard because it takes time- time to listen, time for circumstances to change, time to wait for God to move. -*Marshall Beale*

The future has a way of repaying those who are patient with it. -*Reverend Arthur Pringle*

Peace

You may call for peace as loudly as you wish, but where there is no brotherhood there can, in the end, be no peace. -*Max Lerner, 1949*

People

People will forget what you said, people will forget what you did, but people will never forget how you made them feel.

Personality

When we recognize that people respond to others because of their personality, we can allow ourselves to not take their reactions personal. -*Jan Hoffbauer*

Person

To the world, you may be one person, but to one person, you may be the world.

Philosophy

I must create a system or be enslaved by another man's. -*William Blake, 1804*

Plans

Do not plan for ventures before finishing what's at hand. -*Euripides, 455 BC*

Plans get you into things but you got to work your way out. -*Will Rogers, 1949*

Play

There are toys for all ages. -*English Proverb*

Pleasure

Everyone is dragged on by their favorite pleasure. -*Virgil*

Where pleasure prevails, all the greatest virtues will lose their power. -*Cicero*

Politeness

Politeness is worth much and costs little. -*Spanish Proverb*

Poor

There is none so poor as he who knows not the joy of what he has. -*Ben Franklin*

Positive

Keep your face to the sunshine and you cannot see the shadow. -*Helen Keller*

Positive people radiate goodwill and make everyone around them seem important, creating an atmosphere of respect, creativity, and possibility. -*Joe Dahlheimer*

Poverty

An empty purse frightens away friends. -*Thomas Fuller, MD, 1732*

He that is poor, all his kindred scorn him; he that is rich, all are kind to him. -*Thomas Fuller, MD, 1732*

Poverty is no virtue; wealth is no sin. -*C.H. Spurgeon*

There is always more misery among the lower classes than there is humanity in the higher. -*Victor Hugo, 1862*

Power

Never underestimate the power of a smile, a kind word, a listening ear, an honest compliment, of any small act of caring that may just 'make someone's day,' everyday. -*Jim Stevens*

Praise

Praise is always pleasing; let it come from whom or upon what account it will. -*Montaigne, 1580*

Prepare

I will study and get ready, and someday my chance will come. -*Abraham Lincoln*

Prejudice

Everyone is a prisoner of his own experiences. No one can eliminate prejudices- just recognize them. -*Edward R. Murrow, 1955*

Present

Each day provides its own gifts. -*Martial, 86 AD*

Pride

Pride is a kind of pleasure produced by a man thinking too well of himself. -*Baruch Spinoza*

Priorities

I want to learn to be happy with what I have and avoid the curse of 'somewhere over the rainbow' thinking. True and lasting treasure is built in those moments when we focus on the things that are eternal, when we take the time to really be with family, friends, and God. -*Susan Reedy*

If you want to know a person's priorities, just look at how they use their time. -*Pastor Rick Warren*

The great use of life is to spend it for something that will outlast it. -*William James*

Problems

Problems are only opportunities in work clothes. -*Henry J. Kaiser*

Problems do not make us or break us; they merely reveal us. -*Pastor Gary Woodard*

Profiteering

He who wishes to be rich in a day will be hanged in a year. -*Leonardo Da Vinci*

Progress

The way to progress is never swift or easy. -*Madame Curie*

Restlessness and discontent are the first necessities of progress. -*Thomas A. Edison*

Promiscuity

I consider promiscuity immoral. Not because sex is evil, but because sex is too good and too important. -*Ayn Rand*

Property

Men honor property above all else; it has the greatest power in human life. -*Euripides, 400 BC*

Prosperity

Prosperity is having enough provisions to take me to my destiny in life.

In prosperity friends do not leave you unless desired, whereas in adversity they stay away of their own accord. -*Demetrius, 400 BC*

Proud

Be proud of who you are. You are someone who can make a difference in this world. -*Dr. Robert Schuller*

Punctuality

Better three hours too soon than a minute too late. -*Shakespeare, 1597*

Purpose

He who would make a serious use of his life must always act as though he had a long time to live and must schedule his time as though he were about to die. -*Emile Littre, 1877*

We all have a purpose and a place in life, and finding that purpose is the key to life and to success. -*Ricky Skaggs*

The secret to success is constancy to purpose. -*Benjamin Disraeli, 1870*

The soul that has no established aim loses itself. -*Montaigne, 1580*

Without God, life has no purpose, and without purpose, life has no meaning. Without meaning, life has no significance or hope. -*Pastor Rick Warren*

Quality

Quality of life depends on what happens in the space between stimulus and response. -*Stephen R. Covey*

Quarrels

Quarrels would not last long if the fault was only on one side. -*La Rochefoucauld, 1665*

Rational Thought

Emotions 'color thoughts,' so one must be capable of feeling completely calm about the subject. This is one reason outsiders can give valuable advice to a person struggling to make a decision. -*Marilyn Vos Savant*

Realism

It is only by knowing how little life has in store for us that we are able to look on the bright side and avoid disappointment. -*Ellen Glasgow, 1932*

Reality

In my life, I have suffered many terrible experiences. Some of which actually happened. -*Mark Twain*

Reciprocity

Evidence of trust begets trust, and love is reciprocated by love. -*Plutarch, 100 AD*

Rejection

The biggest disease today is not leprosy or tuberculosis, but rather the feeling of being unwanted, uncared for, and deserted by everybody. The greatest evil is the lack of love and charity. -*Mother Teresa*

To be happy with human beings, we should not ask them for what they cannot give. -*Triston Bernard*

Responsibilities/Consequences

Dodge responsibilities, and get hit by consequences. -*Ancient Proverb*

Reputation

A good reputation is a person's greatest asset. -*Publilius Syrus*

A man is known by the company he keeps. Goodness rubs off- as does wickedness. -*Manual*

Life is for one generation; a good name is forever. -*Japanese Proverb*

Resignation

We must like what we have when we don't have what we like. -*Roger De Bussy Rabutin*

Respect

Respect yourself if you want others to respect you. -*Baltasar Grecian*

Restraint

It's a good idea to keep your words soft and sweet- you never know when you may have to eat them.

Retirement

Retirement is a journey, not a destination. -*Dr. David A. Loop, Cleveland Clinic*

Riches

Riches are not from an abundance of worldly good, but from a contented mind. - *Mohammed*

There is no one so rich that he does not still want something. -*German Proverb*

Said/Done

After all is said and done, more is said than done.

Satisfaction

He is well paid that is well satisfied. -*Shakespeare*

Self-Concept

No one can make you know your self-worth; all of us have to come to our own discovery of our importance and value. -*Bridgette Evans Lempner*

Self-Conscious

Those people who are uncomfortable in themselves are disagreeable to others. -*William Hazlitt, 1839*

Self-Centeredness

Self-centeredness seems to come quite naturally to us. We are so used to egocentric thinking that it's hard to imagine being otherwise. -*Max Lucado*

You cannot play with the animal in you without becoming wholly animal, play with falsehood without forfeiting your right to truth, play with cruelty without losing your sensitivity of mind.

Self-Contained

I learned that, to keep your life from becoming self-contained and useless, you have to feel other people's pain and act to help them. That is what faith and love are about. -*Martin Sheen*

Self-Esteem

A man cannot be comfortable without his own approval. -*Mark Twain*

Self-Important

Half of the harm that is done in this world is due to people who want to feel important. -*T.S. Eliot*

We would rather speak badly of ourselves than not talk about ourselves at all. -*La Rochefoucauld*

Self-Sufficient

The greatest thing in the world is to know how to be self-sufficient. -*Michel deMontaigne*

Serve

Everybody can be great...because anybody can serve. You don't have to have a college degree to serve. You don't have to make your subject and verb agree to serve. You only need a heart full of grace. A soul generated by love. -*Martin Luther King, Jr.*

Every kind of service necessary to the public good becomes honorable by being necessary. -*Nathan Hale*

The only really happy people are those who have learned how to serve. -*Albert Schweitzer*

You will never know what you're good at until you try. -*Pastor Rick Warren*

Secret

Nothing is so burdensome as a secret. -*French Proverb*

Seed

Keep on sowing your seed, for you never know which will grow- perhaps it all will. -*Ecclesiastes 11:6*

Shame

He that is shameless is graceless. -*Thomas Fuller, MD, 1732*

I think that man is lost indeed who has lost the sense of shame. -*Plautus*

Simple

Life is really simple, but we insist on making it complicated. –*Confucius, 500 BC*

God meant for life to be simple and basic so that man could enjoy God's beautiful earth, as well as one another. We live in such a fast paced world that is full of stress. This kind of lifestyle is proven to induce sickness. -*Amanda DiBenedetto*

Sin

Undeservedly you will atone for the sins of your fathers. -*Horace*

We are punished by our sins, not for them. -*Elbert Hubbard, 1927*

Single-Mindedness

A straight path never leads anywhere except to the objective. -*Andre Gide*

Sleep

The sleep of a laborer is sweet, whether he eats little or much, but the abundance of a rich man permits him no sleep. (Greater wealth brings greater anxiety) -*Ecclesiastes 5:12*

Snobbery

Snobbery: A fine imitation of self-esteem for those who can't afford the real thing. -*Frederic Morton*

Society

The world is made of people who never quite make the first team and who just miss the prizes at the flower show. *-Jacob Bronowski*

Solitude

He never is alone that is accompanied with noble thoughts. *-Beaumont, 1647*

One can acquire everything in solitude except character. *-Stendhal, 1832*

Source

Before you drink at a brook, it is best to know its source.

Speaking

What is uttered is finished and done with. *-Thomas Mann, 1903*

Deep rivers move in silence, shallow brooks are noisy. *-English Proverb*

Sports

If the people don't want to come out to the park, nobody's going to stop 'em. *-Yogi Berra*

Stress

If you experience stress, you're doing it wrong. *-Jay Conrad Levinson*

Success

Every great achievement was once considered impossible.

I don't know the secret of success, but I do know the secret of failure- try to please everybody!

You have reached the pinnacle of success as soon as you become uninterested in money, compliments, and publicity. -*Thomas Wolfe*

Success is more attitude than aptitude.

The secret of success is to do the common things uncommonly well. -*John D. Rockefeller*

The cask can only yield the wine it contains.

The secret of getting ahead is getting started. The secret of getting started is breaking your complex, changing overwhelming tasks into small manageable tasks, and then starting on the first one. -*Mark Twain*

There are no secrets to success. It is the result of preparation, hard work, and learning from failure. -*General Colin Powell*

Coming together is a beginning, keeping together is progress, and working together is success. -*Henry Ford*

Why should we be in such desperate haste so succeed and in such desperate enterprises? If a man does not keep pace with his companions, perhaps it is because he hears a different drummer. -*Henry David Thoreau*

The only place where success comes before work is in the dictionary.

Suffering

Although the world is full of suffering, it is full also of the overcoming of it. -*Helen Keller*

Nine-tenths of our suffering is caused by others not thinking so much of us as we think they ought. -*Mary Lyon*

Suicide

The one who, in a fit of melancholy, kills himself today, would have wished to live had he waited a week. -*Voltaire, 1764*

Surprise

Surprise is the greatest gift which life can grant us. *-Boris Pasternak, 1936*

Sympathy

There is nothing sweeter than to be sympathized with. *-George Santayana, 1905*

Talk

Talk is cheap because the supply always exceeds the demand. *-Sam Ewing*

People who know little are usually the greatest talkers, while people who know much say little. *-Jean Jacques Rousseau*

Temptation

All men are tempted. There is no man that lives that can't be broken down, provided it is in the right temptation, put in the right spot. *-Henry Ward Beecher, 1887*

I have a simple principle for the conduct of life- never to resist an adequate temptation. *-Max Lerner, 1959*

So long as we live in this world we cannot escape suffering and temptation. *-Thomas A. Kempis*

Things

The most valuable things in life are not things.

Things turn out best for the people who make the best of the way things turn out. *-John Wooden, Coach*

Thinking

Thinking is the hardest work there is, which is the probable reason why so few engage in it. -*Henry Ford*

Our life is what our thoughts make it. -*Marcus Aurelius, 200 AD*

As a man thinks in his heart, so is he.

Time

Sometime you'll know what it is to wish you had another day, even another hour, to put your life straight; and will you get it? There's no saying. -*Thomas A. Kempis*

There is only one time that is important- NOW! It is the most important time because it is the only time we have power over. -*Leo Tolstoy*

Time makes more converts than reason. -*Thomas Paine, 1776*

Time is too slow for those who wait, too swift for those who fear, too long for those who grieve, too short for those who rejoice, but for those who love- time is eternity. -*Henry Van Dyke*

Time heals grief and quarrels, for we change and are no longer the same persons. -*Pascal, 1670*

What a day may bring a day make take away.

Thoughts

Change your thoughts, and you change your world. -*Norman Vincent Peale*

Tolerance

Imagine what your life might be like if you were a person of another race, gender, or sexual orientation. How might 'today' have been different? -*Rob Collinet*

Tradition

It's when you do the same old thing- only it's still fun. -*Michael, 7 year old*

Tranquility

When we are unable to find tranquility within ourselves, it is useless to seek it elsewhere. -*La Rochefoucauld, 1665*

Trials

People are like tea bags: You have to put them in hot water to know how strong they are.

Trying times tend to bring out the best in people. -*Editor*

You can't smooth out the surf, but you can learn to ride the waves.

Thrift

People are divided between those who are as thrifty as if they would live forever, and those who are as extravagant as if they were going to die the next day. -*Aristotle, 400 BC*

A man who both spends and saves money is the happiest man, because he has both enjoyments. -*Dr. Samuel Johnson*

Trifles

Trifles make up the happiness or the misery of human life. -*Alexander Smith, 1863*

Trivia

Trivial matters take up more time for discussion because some of us know more about them than we do about important matters. -*Thomas S. Weiss*

Trouble

Nothing is troublesome that we do willingly. -*Thomas Jefferson*

May your troubles be few and your blessings many. -*Irish Proverb*

Truth

Every truth has two sides; it is well to look at both before we commit ourselves to either. -*Aesop, 600 BC*

To thine own self be true, and it must follow, as the night the day. Thou canst not then be false to any man. -*Shakespeare*

To be persuasive we must be believable. To be believable we must be credible. To be credible we must be truthful. -*Edward R. Murrow*

Truth and oil always come to the surface. -*Spanish Proverb*

If you tell the truth you don't have to remember anything. -*Mark Twain*

Truth sits upon the lips of dying men. -*Matthew Arnold, 1835*

He that does not speak truth to me does not believe me when I speak truth. -*Thomas Fuller, MD, 1732*

The man who fears no truths has nothing to fear from lies. -*Thomas Jefferson*

Pretty much all the honest truth-telling there is in the world is done by children. -*Oliver Wendell Holmes*

Trust

A man who doesn't trust himself can never really trust anyone else. -*Cardinal De Retz, 1718*

Tyranny

He who despises his own life is soon master of another. -*English Proverb*

You have not converted a man because you have silenced him. -*John Morley, 1874*

Unhappiness

If you are bitter at heart, sugar in the mouth will not help you. - *Yiddish Proverb*

Uneducated

He who knows little often repeats it. -*Proverb*

Unique

Everyone, especially those we know well, deserves his or her own chapter in our book of life. -*Daniel Taddeo*

Usefulness

A cloak is not made for a single shower of rain. -*Italian Proverb*

Use/Lose

Whatever you have, you must either use or lose. -*Henry Ford*

Value

Those things are dearest to us that have cost us most. -*Montaigne, 1580*

We never know the worth of water till the well is dry. -*Thomas Fuller, MD, 1732*

Vice

We tolerate without rebuke the vices with which we have grown familiar. -*Publilius Syrus, 100* BC

Vices are their own punishment. -*Aesop, 600 BC*

For lawless joys a bitter ending waits. -*Pindar, 500 BC*

Virtue

Virtue herself is her own fairest reward. -*Silius Italicus*

I never was so rapid in my virtue, but my vice kept up with me. -*Thoreau, 1841*

Vocation

Blessed is he who has found his work; let him ask no other blessedness. -*Thomas Carlyle, 1843*

The vocation of every man and woman is to serve other people. -*Leo Tolstoy*

Wants

My belief is that to have no wants is divine. -*Socrates*

War/Peace

We must be at war with evil, but at peace with men. -*J.E.E. Dalberg*

Weakness

You cannot run away from a weakness; you must some time fight it out or perish; and if that be so, why not now, and where you stand? -*Robert Louis Stevenson*

Welfare

It usually happens, within certain limits, that to get a little help is to get a notion of being defrauded of more. -*Dickens*

Wealth

To acquire wealth is difficult, but to spend it wise is most difficult of all. Wealth is no insurance against discontent.

He is rich who hath enough to be charitable. -*Sir Thomas Browne, 1642*

Riches rather enlarge than satisfy appetites. -*Thomas Fuller, MD, 1732*

The larger a man's roof, the more snow it collects. -*Persian Proverb*

That glittering hope is immemorial and beckons many men to their undoing. -*Euripides, 414 BC*

There is nothing wrong with people possessing riches; the wrong comes when riches possess people. -*Billy Graham*

The wealthy people are those who are content with what they have.

Wealth brings many friends. -*Proverbs 19:4*

Whoever loves wealth is never satisfied with his income. -*Ecclesiastes 5:10*

Wickedness

There is no peace, saith the Lord, unto the wicked. -*Isaiah 48:22*

Winning

Anybody can win, unless there happens to be a second entry. -*George Ade*

Wisdom

It is the province of knowledge to speak and it is the privilege of wisdom to listen. -*Oliver Wendell Holmes, 1872*

It requires wisdom to understand wisdom; the music is nothing if the audience is deaf. - *Walter Lippmann, 1929*

The heart of a fool is in his mouth, but the mouth of a wise man is in his heart. -*Benjamin Franklin, 1732*

What is evident to the wise is not evident to all. -*Thomas Aquinas*

Not by years but by disposition is wisdom acquired. -*Plautus, 194 BC*

Words/Wisdom

Where there is a feast of words there is often a famine of wisdom. -*Catherine of Siena*

Worldliness

If you keep in step with God, you'll be out of step with the world.

The world has forgotten, in its preoccupation with Left and Right, that there is an Above and Below. -*Franz Werfel*

Work

All work is empty save when there is love. -*Kahlil Gibran, 1923*

Far and away the best prize that life offers is the chance to work hard at work worth doing. - *Theodore Roosevelt, 1903*

No race can prosper till it learns there is as much dignity in tilling a field as in writing a poem. -*Booker T. Washington, 1895*

When work is a pleasure, life is a joy! When work is a duty, life is slavery. -*Maxim Gorky, 1903*

Work spares us from three great evils: boredom, vice, and need. -*Voltaire, 1759*

The secret joy in work is contained in one word: excellence. To know how to do something well is to enjoy it. -*Pearl Buck*

You're working hard to make a good life for yourself. Put at least as much effort [and more] into your spiritual life. -*Editor*

Work is the least important thing and family is the most important. -*Jerry Seinfeld*

Worry

Therefore do not worry about tomorrow, for tomorrow will worry about itself. Each day has enough trouble of its own. -*Matthew 6:34*

If you want to test your memory, try to remember what you were worrying about a year ago today. -*Leonard Thomas*

Worry is interest paid on trouble before it falls due.

Ninety-nine percent of things people worry about never happen. The other one percent is unavoidable.

Wrongdoing

A good man can be stupid and still be good. But a bad man must have brains, absolutely. -*Maxim Gorky*

Xenophobia

Do not fret because of evil men or be envious of those who do wrong; for like the grass they will soon wither like green plants; they will soon die away. -*Proverbs 37:1-2*

Zeal

Never be lacking in zeal, but keep your spiritual fervor, serving the Lord. - *Romans 12:11*

8.
LIVING MATTERS

Ability

Everyone must row with the oars he has. *-English Proverb*

Action

Desire is a treasure map; knowledge is the treasure chest; wisdom is the jewel. Yet, without action they all stay buried.

If you don't pick up the ball and run with it, someone else will.

No matter what you may say, it's your actions that speak for you.

Whatever you do, strive to do it so well that no man living and no man dead and no man yet to be born could do it any better. *-Benjamin E. Mays*

When you do the common things in life in an uncommon way, you will command the attention of the world. *-George Washington Carver*

Advice

Advice is seldom welcomed, and those who need it the most always like it the least. *-Chesterfield*

He who builds to every man's advice will have a crooked house. *-Danish Proverb*

Adjustment

Dance to the tune that is played. *-Spanish Proverb*

Adversity

People don't ever seem to realize that doing what's right is no guarantee against misfortune. *-William McFee*

Agree

We seldom attribute common sense except to those who agree with us. *-La Rouchefoucauld*

Ambition

There is always room at the top. *-Daniel Webster*

You'll miss 100% of the shots you don't take. *-Wayne Gretzsky, Hockey player*

Anger

Be not angry that you cannot make others as you wish them to be, since you cannot make yourself as you wish to be. *-Thomas A. Kempis*

He who angers you, controls you!

Many of us crucify ourselves between two thieves- regret for the past and fear for the future.

Apathy

Bad officials are elected by good citizens who do not vote. *-George Jean Nathan*

Appearance

Even though most things are far different from what they appear, a good exterior is the best recommendation of the excellence of the interior. *- Baltasar Grecian*

How anybody dresses is indicative of his self-concept. If students are dirty and ragged, it indicated they are not interested in tidying up their intellects either. -*S.I. Kayakawa, President of San Francisco State College*

Of all the things you wear, your expression is the most important.

Someone who looks slovenly probably doesn't care about himself or other people. -*Sam Fulwood, Columnist*

Apology

Apology is one of the most profound interactions between human beings. -*Dr. Aaron Lazare*

Once you realize you don't have to make yourself wrong to deliver an apology, you'll feel a new power. -*Rosamund Stone Zander*

The best way to have the last word is to apologize.

Approval

Lean too much upon the approval of people and it becomes a bed of thorns. -*Tenyi Hsien*

Please all, and you will please none. -*Aesop, 600 BC*

Asset

Know your chief asset, your great talent; cultivate it, and help along the others. -*Baltasar Grecian*

Assistance

It is one of the beautiful compensations of this life that no one can sincerely try to help another without helping himself. -*Charles Dudley Warner*

Association

By associating with good and evil persons, a man acquires the virtues and vices which they posses, even as the wind blowing over different places takes along good and bad odors. -*Panchatantra, 5 BC*

If you live with a cripple, you will learn to limp. -*Plutarch, 100 AD*

Attitude

Keep a green tree in your heart, and perhaps the singing bird will come. -*Chinese Proverb*

Nothing can stop the man with the right mental attitude from achieving his goal; nothing on earth can help the man with the wrong mental attitude. -*Thomas Jefferson*

If life gives you lemons, make lemonade. -*Dale Carnegie*

Learn to win graciously and lose with honor. Gloating after a win or making excuses after a loss doesn't work in tennis or in life. -*Jack L. Groppel, Ph.D.*

The remarkable thing we have is a choice every day regarding the attitude we will embrace for that day. We cannot change the inevitable. The only thing we can do is play on the one string we have, and that is our attitude. -*Charles Swindoll, Pastor*

Whether you think you can or think you can't, you're right. -*Henry Ford*

If you can live with the worst, the rest will take care of itself. -*Donald Trump*

Awareness

Take time to be aware; it is an opportunity to help others.

Balance

Try to balance every negative with a positive- minimum! -*Editor*

238

We have to acquire a peace and balance of mind such that we can give every word of criticism its due weight, and humble ourselves before every word of praise. -*Dag Hammarskjold*

Beauty

Beauty, or lack thereof, is in the eye of the beholder.

Becoming

We become what we practice most.

Begin

To have begun makes the work half done. Half still remains, again begin this, and you will complete the task. *Ausonius*

It is better to begin in the evening than not at all. -*English Proverb*

The journey of a thousand miles starts with a single step. -*Chinese Proverb*

A good beginning makes a good ending. -*English Proverb*

Believe

Seek not to understand that you may believe, but believe that you may understand. -*Saint Augustine*

When you believe something is impossible, your mind goes to work for you to prove why. But, when you believe, really believe, something can be done, your mind goes to work for you and helps you to find the ways to do it. -*David Joseph Schwartz, Ph.D.*

Best

Don't settle for average. Bring your best to the moment. -*Angela Bassett*

Heed not the worst in a person, seek out and love that is the best in him.

If a man does his best, what else is there? -*General George S. Patton*

You get the best out of others when you give the best of yourself. -*Henry Firestone*

Why do we often think that the best is what someone else should do? -*Daniel Young*

Blacks

We will not be satisfied until justice rolls down like waters and righteousness like a mighty stream. -*Martin Luther King, Jr.*

Blunders

Great blunders are often made, like large ropes, of a multitude of fibers. -*Victor Hugo*

Boasting

He who killeth the lion when absent feareth a mouse when present. -*English Proverb*

Boldness

It is easy to frighten a bull from the window. -*Italian Proverb*

Unless you enter the tiger's den you cannot take the cubs. -*Japanese Proverb*

When the mouse laughs at the cat, there is a hole nearby. -*Nigerian Proverb*

Bore

The secret to being a bore is to tell everything. -*Voltaire*

Borrower

Neither a borrower nor a lender be; for loan oft loses both itself and friend. -*Shakespeare (Hamlet)*

Burden

None knows the weight of another's burden. -*George Herbert*

Buy

Never buy what you do not need because it is cheap; it will be costly to you. -*Thomas Jefferson*

Care

If I care about someone, I will want to listen to that person. I will want to find out what that person is thinking, feeling, believing, and experiencing.

If you don't care for yourself, you're less able to care for others. -*Alice Domar*

Cause

A just cause is not ruined by a few mistakes. -*Dostoevsky*

It is better to fail in a cause that will ultimately succeed than to succeed in a cause that will ultimately fail. -*James Elliot, Missionary*

In a just cause the weak will beat the strong. -*Sophocles, 401 BC*

Calling

Don't waste time after you know what you want to be, where you want to go, whatever you want to accomplish. Make dust- or eat it. -*J.B. Hunt, Trucking Corporation*

Candle

Blowing out another person's candle won't make yours shine any brighter.

Chance

The only time you run out of chances is when you stop taking them. -*Patti La Belle*

Challenge

Above all, challenge yourself. You may well surprise yourself at what strengths you have, what you can accomplish. -*Cecile M. Springer*

Sometimes you have to take the test before you've finished studying.

Change

Be the change you want to see in the world!

You can take the boy out of the country, but you can't take the country out of the boy. -*American Proverb*

Love of neighbor is the *most* powerful means of changing things for good. -*Foster S. Friess*

Not everything that is faced can be changed. But nothing can be changed until it is faced. -*James Baldwin*

Character

You can't give character to another person, but you can encourage him to develop his own by possessing one yourself. -*Artemus Calloway*

Charity

Charity is twice blessed- it blesses the one who gives and the one who receives.

Through your conscientious efforts, you enable a less fortunate person to rise up in life, earn a livelihood, and gain self-respect. This is the highest grade of charity, the level at which one helps others to help themselves. -*Moses Maimonides*

Cheerfulness

Cheerfulness bears the same friendly regard to the mind as to the body. It banishes all anxious care and discontent, soothes and composes the passions, and keeps the soul in a perpetual calm. -*Joseph Addison, 1672-1719*

Cheating

People who are secretive usually have a lot to hide.

Choices

As a man thinketh so is he, and as man chooseth so is he. -*Emerson*

Choices have consequences, and you are today what you decided yesterday to become. -*John Hagee, Pastor*

Do you want to be the statue or the bird? -*Frances Weaver*

Constantly choose rather to want less, than to have more. -*Thomas A. Kempis*

Too much of anything has negative consequences. -*Editor*

We often experience more regret over that part we have left, than pleasure over the part we have preferred. -*Joseph Roux*

Church

Don't wait for six strong men to take you to church.

If I should go out of church whenever I hear a false sentiment, I could never stay there five minutes. -*Emerson*

When you find the perfect church, join it. But remember, after you do it will no longer be perfect. -*Andrew Greeley*

Going to church doesn't make a person Christian any more than going to a garage makes a person a car. -*Billy Sunday, Evangelist*

Circumstances

Concern yourself with circumstances as they are, not how you wish them to be. Then, proceed with courage, confidence, and cheerfulness. -*Editor*

Comfort

To ease another's heartache is to forget one's own. -*Abraham Lincoln*

Commitment

Commitment has to do with faithfulness, responsibility, and loyalty. Self-centeredness is the eternal enemy of commitment. -*Pastor Larry D. Jones*

The need for devotion to something outside ourselves is even more profound than the need for companionship. If we are not to go to pieces or wither away, we all must have some purpose in life; for no man can live for himself alone. -*Rosa Parmenter*

We become whatever we are committed to. -*Pastor Rick Warren*

Company

Man loves company even if only that of a small burning candle. -*Georg C. Licltenberg*

Comparing

I murmured because I had no shoes until I met a man who had no feet. -*Persian Proverb*

Comparison, more than reality, makes men happy or wretched. -*Thomas Fuller, MD*

None but himself can be his parallel. -*Lewis Theobald*

Instead of comparing our lot with that of those who are more fortunate than we are, we should compare it with the lot of the great majority of our fellow men. It then appears that we are among the privileged. -*Helen Keller*

The man with a toothache thinks everyone happy whose teeth are sound. The poverty stricken man makes the same mistake about the rich man. -*George Bernard Shaw*

Competition

If you don't run, you won't trip but you may never get there. -*Cynthia Copeland Lewis*

Do as adversaries do in law: strive mightily but eat and drink as friends. -*Shakespeare*

Complain

The crying cat catches nothing.

Howsoever every man may complain occasionally of the hardships of his condition, he is seldom willing to change it for any other on the same level. -*Samuel Johnson*

There are two kinds of complainers: men and women.

He that falls by himself never cries. -*Turkish Proverb*

Compliance

He that complies against his will is of his own opinion still. -*Samuel Butler*

Compliment

When you cannot get a compliment in any other way, pay yourself one. -*Mark Twain*

Composure

Calmness is always Godlike. -*Emerson*

Computer

I can be upgraded. Can you?

Concealment

Everyone is a moon and has a dark side which he never shows to anybody. -*Mark Twain*

He who conceals his disease cannot expect to be cured. -*Ethiopian Proverb*

We are so accustomed to disguise ourselves to other, that in the end we become disguised to ourselves. -*La Rochefoucauld*

Conceit

Those who know the least of others think the highest of themselves. -*Charles Caleb Colton*

Conduct

Brighten the corner where you are. -*Old Proverb*

Holy living consists in doing God's work with a smile. -*Mother Teresa*

Do not withhold good from those to whom it is due when it is in the power of your hand to do so. -*Proverbs 3:26*

Live in each season as it passes; breathe the air, drink the drink, taste the fruit, and resign yourself to the influence of each! -*Henry David Thoreau*

The heart has no secret which our conduct does not reveal. -*French Proverb*

People spend too much time finding other people to blame, too much energy finding excuses for not being what they are capable of being, and not enough energy putting themselves on the line, growing out of the past, getting on with their lives. -*J. Michael Straczynski*

If you would be interesting, be interested; if you would be pleased, be pleasing; if you would be loved, be lovable; if you would be helped, be helpful. -*William Arthur Ward*

Confession

Confession of our faults is the next thing to innocence. -*Publilius Syrus, 100 BC*

Confide

To whom you tell your secrets, to him you resign your liberty. -*Spanish Proverb*

We rarely confide in those who are better than we are. -*Albert Camus*

Confidence

If you wait until you're really sure, you'll never take off the training wheels. -*Cynthia Copeland Lewis*

No one is born with confidence. Those people you know who radiate confidence, who have conquered worry, who are at ease everywhere and all the time, acquired their confidence, every bit of it. -*David Joseph Schwartz, Ph.D.*

Confidant

Divide with another your burdens and your sorrows, for misfortune is doubly unbearable to him who stands alone. -*Baltasar Grecian*

Conflict

In resolving conflict, how you say it is as important as what you say. -*Pastor Rick Warren*

If you run after two hares, you will catch neither. -*Thomas Fuller, MD*

When conflict is handled correctly, we grow closer to each other by facing and resolving our differences. -*Pastor Rick Warren*

Conformity

We are half ruined by conformity, but we should be wholly ruined without it. -*Charles Dudley Warner*

We are created different; they lose their social freedom and their individual autonomy in seeking to become like each other. -*David Reisman*

Conscience

A quiet conscience sleeps in thunder. -*English Proverb*

There is no pillow so soft as a clear conscience. -*French Proverb*

Consider

We can live our lives either as a thermostat or thermometer. We can either blend in with the crowd, or we can change the crowd. We are influencing others, or they are influencing us.

Contentment

Be content with your lot; one cannot be first in everything. -*Aesop*

Do not spoil what you have by desiring what you have not; but, remember that what you now have was once among the things only hoped for. -*Epicurus, 300 BC*

He is a wise man who does not grieve for the things which he has not, but rejoices for those which he has. -*Epictetus, 300 BC*

Nothing will content him who is not content with a little. -*Greek Proverb*

Poor and content is rich and rich enough. -*Shakespeare*

To find contentment, enjoy your own life without comparing it with that of another. -*Condorcet*

If you cannot catch a bird of paradise, better take a wet hen. -*Nikita Khrushchev*

Conversation

To listen closely and reply well is the highest perfection we are able to attain in the art of conversation. -*La Rochefoucauld*

Coping

When you least feel like it do something for someone else. You forget about your own situation. It gives you a purpose, as opposed to being sorrowful and lonely. It makes me feel better when things are too hard for me. -*Dana Reeve, Widow of actor Christopher Reeve*

Cooperation

Alone we can do little. Together we can do so much. -*Helen Keller*

Courage

Courage is doing right when everyone around you is doing wrong.

It is easy to be brave from a safe distance. *-Aesop, 600 BC*

Courtesy

Everyone has to think to be polite; the first impulse is to be impolite. *-Edgar Watson Howe*

Coward

Cowards die many times before their deaths; the valiant never taste of death but once.

Credit

God can do great things through the person who doesn't care who gets the credit. *-Dr. Robert Schuller*

Credibility

Give your word and keep it, because a personal credibility is everything. *- Tom Lasorda, Chrysler Corporation*

Credulity

People can be induced to swallow anything, provided it is sufficiently seasoned with praise. *-Moliere*

Crime

Commit a crime and the earth is made of glass. There is no such thing as concealment. *-Emerson*

Great crimes never come singly; they are linked to sins that went before. -*Racine*

Crisis

Your success in handling a crisis depends to a larger extent on how you picture and value yourself. -*William Arthur Ward*

Criticism

Be sure to expose yourself to criticism: A fine polish requires an abrasive. -*Marilyn vos Savant*

If one person calls you a donkey, forget it. If five people call you a donkey, buy a saddle. -*Arab Proverb*

It is much easier to be critical than to be correct. *Benjamin Disraeli*

Judge not, that you be not judged. -*Matthew 7:1*

They have a right to censure that have a heart to help. -*William Penn*

When we see ourselves as we really are, we are less likely to be critical of others. -*Editor*

Why do you worry about a speck in your friend's eye when you have a log in your own? -*Matthew 7:3*

Curiosity

Enquire not what boils in another's pot. -*Thomas Fuller, MD*

Curse

A thousand curses never tore a shirt. -*Arabic Proverb*

Cynicism

A cynic is not merely one who reads bitter lessons from the past; he is one who is prematurely disappointed in the future. -*Sydney J. Harris*

A thankful heart can not be cynical. -*A.W. Tozer, Theologian*

Darkness

When the train in your life goes through a dark tunnel, don't jump! There is a light at the end. -*Torrie Ten Boom*

Debt

I'm living so far beyond my income that we may almost be said to be living apart. -*E.E. Cummings*

Owe no one anything (except to love one another).

One of the first things financial advisors recommend to families with spending problems is to destroy their credit cards. Sometimes the best solution is to just eliminate temptation. -*Larry Burkett, Author*

There are but two ways of paying debt: increase of industry in raising income or increase of thrift in laying out. -*Thomas Carlyle*

Part of our problem with debt is that we have confused needs with wants. Yesterday's luxuries are today's necessities. -*Billy Graham*

People who are never to sacrifice or deny impulses to spend will always be in financial bondage. -*Larry Burkett, Author*

Deception

A clean glove often hides a dirty hand. -*English Proverb*

Decision

Decision making is easy if there are no contradictions in your value system. -*Robert Schuller*

Deeds

He that returns a good for evil obtains the victory. -*Thomas Fuller, MD*

Men are all alike in their promises. It is only in their deeds that they differ. -*Moliere*

The greatest pleasure I know is to do a good action by stealth and to have it found out by accident. -*Charles Lamb*

What I must do is all that concerns me, not what the people think. -*Emerson*

Defeat

Misfortunes in themselves do not defeat a man; it is his attitude towards them that defeat him. -*Hubert van Zeller*

Dependence

He who is being carried does not realize how far the town is. -*Nigerian Proverb*

Depression

No matter how low you feel, if you count your blessings, you'll always show a profit.

An anxious heart weighs a man down, but a kind word cheers him up. -*Proverbs 12:25*

Deprivation

To be without some of the things you want is an indispensable part of happiness. -*Bertrand Russel*

Desire

It is easier to suppress the first desire than to satisfy all that follow it. -*Benjamin Franklin*

Despair

When water covers the head, a hundred fathoms are as one. -*Persian Proverb*

Where there is no hope there can be no endeavor. -*Samuel Johnson*

Destiny

It is a mistake to look too far ahead. Only one link of the chain of destiny can be handled at a time. -*Sir Winston Churchill*

Devil

The devil is a gentleman who never goes where he is not welcome. -*John A. Lincoln*

Difficulty

Every path has its puddle. -*English Proverb*

Direction

You got to be careful if you don't know where you're going, because you might not get there. -*Yogi Berra*

Disappointment

Don't let today's disappointments cast a shadow on tomorrow's dreams.

Not to get what you have set your heart on is almost as bad as getting nothing at all. *-Aristotle, 400 BC*

Discontentment

He that is discontented in one place will seldom be happy in another. *-Aesop*

What a miserable thing life is: You're living in clover, only the clover isn't good enough. *-Bertolt Brecht*

Discipline

Discipline yourself and others won't have to.

Dogmatism

We are least open to precise knowledge concerning the things we are most vehement about. *-Eric Hoffer*

Doing

I am only one, but still I am one. I cannot do everything, but still I can do something. *-Helen Keller*

If a thing is worth doing, it's worth doing well. *-Lord Chesterfield*

Dreams

Dreams are faithful interpreters of our inclinations but there is art required to sort and understand them. *-Montaigne*

Never to tire, never to grow cold; to be patient, sympathetic, tender; to look for the budding flower and the opening heart; to hope always, like God, to love always- this is duty. -*H.F. Amiel*

Dying

The things I valued most became worthless, and the things that I considered of little value are now the most important things in the world to me. *Death bed*

Eating

One should eat to live, not live to eat. -*Moliere*

Effort

Effort is only effort when it begins to hurt. -*Jose Ortega*

When we do the best that we can, we never know what miracle is wrought in our life or in the life of another. -*Helen Keller*

Emotions

Reason guides but a small part of man, and that the least interesting. The rest obeys feeling, true or false, and passion, good or bad. -*Joseph Roux*

Endurance

He that can't endure the bad will not live to see the good. -*Yiddish Proverb*

Who would wish for hardship and difficulty? You command us to endure these troubles, not to love them. No one loves what he endures when though he may be glad to endure it. -*Augustine of Hippo*

Enterprise

If you don't crack the shell, you can't eat the nut. -*Russian Proverb*

Roasted pigeons will not fly into one's mouth. -*Pennsylvania Dutch Proverb*

Enthusiasm

Every great and commanding movement in the annals of the world is the triumph of enthusiasm. Nothing great was ever achieved without it. -*Ralph Waldo Emerson*

If you aren't fired with enthusiasm, you will be fired with enthusiasm. -*Vince Lombardi, Coach*

Man never rises to great truths without enthusiasm. -*Vauvenaruges*

Envy

As iron is eaten away by rust, so the envious are consumed by their own passion. -*Antisthenes*

Our envy always lasts much longer than the happiness of those we envy. -*La Rochefoucauld*

For where you have envy and selfish ambition, there you find disorder and evil practice. -*James 3:16*

Equality

We clamor for equality chiefly in matters in which we ourselves cannot hope to attain excellence. -*Eric Hoffer*

Exaggeration

Exaggeration is akin to lying; and through it you jeopardize your reputation for good taste which is much, and for good judgment, which is more. -*Baltasar Grecian*

To exaggerate is to weaken.

There is no one who does not exaggerate. -*Emerson*

Example

The example of good men is visible philosophy. -*English Proverb*

Excellence

Excellence is a result of caring more than others think is wise, risking more than others think is safe, dreaming more than others think is practical, and expecting more than others think is possible.

Excess

To go beyond is as wrong as to fall short. -*Confucius, 600 BC*

Excuses

He that is good for making excuses is seldom good for anything else. -*Benjamin Franklin*

Excuses are a way of dodging responsibility. -*James Mol, Psychologist*

You will find that the more successful the individual, the less inclined he is to make excuses. -*David Joseph Schwartz, Ph.D.*

Experience

Only the wearer knows where the shoe pinches. -*English Proverb*

Explanation

Never explain. Your friends do not need it and your enemies will not believe you anyway. -*Elbert Hubbard*

Extraordinary

Ordinary people do extraordinary things. -*Robert Schuller*

Falsehood

A liar will not be believed, even when he speaks the truth. -*Aesop*

Failure

Fall seven times, stand up eight. -*Japanese Proverb*

It's better to try and fail than to sit back and never take a chance. -*Nathan Shay, 13*

Nobody is a total failure if he dares to try to do something worthwhile. -*Robert Schuller*

There is no failure except in no longer trying. -*Elbert Hubbard*

He that lies on the ground cannot fall.

I would prefer to fail with honor than win by cheating. -*Sophocles, 409 BC*

Faith

Faith is not a formula which is agreed to if the weight of evidence favors it. -*Walter Lippmann*

Faith is not being afraid of death, but embracing the true life that awaits us after we die. -*Michelle Borsz*

Faithful

Unless you are faithful in small matters, you won't be faithful in large ones. -*Luke 16:10*

Fame

A celebrity is a person who works hard all his life to become known, then wears dark glasses to avoid being recognized. -*Fred Allen*

There is no business in this world so troublesome as the pursuit of fame: life is over before you have hardly begun your work. -*La Bruyere*

People that seem so glorious are all show; underneath they're like anybody else. -*Euripides, 426 BC*

Don't confuse fame with success. One is Madonna; the other is Helen Keller. -*Erma Bombeck*

Familiarity

A rose too often smelled loses its fragrance. -*Spanish Proverb*

Fasting

Everything tastes better after fasting. -*Baltasar Grecian*

Faults

The greatest of faults, I should say, is to be conscious of none. -*Thomas Carlyle*

Those see nothing but faults that seek for nothing else. -*Thomas Fuller, MD*

Nothing is easier than fault-finding; no talent, no self-denial, nor brains are required to set up in the grumbling business. -*Robert West*

Fear

He will never have true friends who is afraid of making enemies. -*William Hazlitt, 1823*

The only thing we have to fear is fear itself…which paralyzes needed effort to convert retreat into advance. -*Franklin Roosevelt*

What is more mortifying than to feel that you have missed the plum for want of courage to shake the tree. -*Logan Pearsall, 1931*

Fellowship

Every time you understand and affirm someone's feelings you build fellowship. -*Pastor Rick Warren*

Fish Bowl

Even when alone, work as though the eyes of the world were upon you, because everything comes to be known. -*Baltasar Grecian*

Flattery

We despise no source that can pay us a pleasing attention. -*Mark Twain*

He who rebukes a man will find more favor afterward than he who flatters with the tongue. -*Proverbs 28:23*

Flexibility

A wise man changes his mind; a fool never will. -*Spanish Proverb*

Focus

If we're wise, we focus on our achievements rather than our failures. We appreciate our loved ones even more, go easier on ourselves, and live more fully in the moment. -*Dr. Brothers*

Fool

No one is a fool always, everyone sometimes.

To never see a fool you lock yourself in your room and smash the looking glass. -*Carl Sandburg*

Forgetting

Forgetting of a wrong is a mild revenge. *-English Saying*

Forgive

To forgive is to set the prisoner free and discover the prisoner was you.

Forgiveness is perfect when the sin is not remembered. *-Arabic Proverb*

To forgive does not mean you have to forget what the person did to you. With forgiveness, the memory remains, but not their power to hurt us. *-Hamilton Beazley, Author*

"I can forgive, but I cannot forget," is only another way of saying, "I will not forgive." A forgiveness ought to be like a cancelled note, torn in two and burned up, so that it can never be shown against the man. *-Henry Ward Beecher*

Frankness

Plain dealing is a jewel, but they that wear it are out of fashion. *-Thomas Fuller, MD*

Forethought

A danger foreseen is half avoided. *-Thomas Fuller, MD*

Affairs are easier of entrance than exit; and it is but common prudence to see our way out before we venture in. *–Aesop*

Freedom

If you cannot be free, be as free as you can. *-Emerson*

The greatest freedom man has is the freedom to discipline himself. *-Bernard M. Baruch*

Unless a man exercises his talents to make something of himself, freedom is an irksome burden. *-Eric Hoffer*

We can choose how we respond to circumstances. *-Pastor Rick Warren*

Friendship

Think twice before burdening a friend with a secret.

A true friend is someone who believes in you after he has seen you at your worst.

Friendship is like money, easier made than kept. *-Samuel Butler*

Wishing to be friends is quick work, but friendship is a slow-ripening fruit. *-Aristotle, 400 BC*

Your friend is the man who knows all about you and still likes you. *-Elbert Hubbard*

Friends show their love in times of trouble, not in happiness. *-Euripides, 408 BC*

True friendship is like sound health: The value of it is seldom known until it be lost. *-Charles Caleb Colton*

The friendships which last are those wherein each friend respects the other's dignity to the point of not really wanting anything from him. *-Cyril Connolly*

Frugality

Use it up. Wear it out. Make it do. Put it off. Do without. *-New England Proverb*

Future

He that fears not the future may enjoy the present. *-Thomas Fuller, MD*

We steal if we touch tomorrow. It is God's. *-Henry Ward Beecher*

Gain/Pain

There are no gains without pain. -*Benjamin Franklin*

Generosity

Generosity gives assistance, rather than advice. -*Vauvenargues*

Gentleness

It is the weak who are cruel. Gentleness can only be expected from the strong. -*Leo Roskin*

Gentleness is the strongest force in the world. -*Alexander Maclaren*

Gentleness washes away all that is harsh and austere. -*Billy Graham*

Giving

A generous man will prosper; he who refreshes others will himself be refreshed. -*Proverbs 11:25*

If you give what you do not need, it isn't giving. -*Mother Teresa*

You give but little when you give your possessions. It is when you give yourself that you truly give. -*Kahlil Gibran*

It is more blessed to give than to receive. -*Acts 20:35* This happens to be the most disbelieved verse in the Bible. -*Dr. Tom Ahlersmeyer*

You can give without loving, you cannot love without giving. -*Amy Carmichael, Missionary*

Blessed are those who can give without remembering and take without forgetting. -*Elizabeth Bibesco*

Glory

Glory ought to be the consequences not the motive of our actions. -*Pliny The Younger*

Goal

In trying to reach your goal, expect to make mistakes. Plan ahead to provide a safety margin for those mistakes you make. -*Bobby Jones, Businessman and Athlete*

Golden Rule

Do not choose for anyone what you do not choose for yourself. -*Persian Proverb*

Golf

Have you ever noticed what golf spells backwards? -*Al Bolinksa*

Goodness

Live not as though there were a thousand years ahead of you. Fate is at your elbow; make yourself good while life and power are still yours. -*Marcus Aurelius, 200 AD*

Good-Natured

Of cheerfulness or good temper: the more it is spent, the more it remains. -*Emerson*

Gossip

Out of some little thing, too free a tongue can make an outrageous wrangle. -*Euripides, 426 BC*

You cannot always prevent people from speaking evil about you, but you can live so that their stories will be false. -*Egyptian Proverb*

Grateful

If you haven't all the things you want, be grateful for the things you don't have that you didn't want.

It is to be able to live in the present, rather than longing for the past or wondering anxiously about the future. To live in the present and notice what is good about it is to be grateful. -*Pastor Kelly Peters*

Greatness

To vilify a great man is the readiest way in which a little man can himself attain greatness. -*Edgar Allan Poe*

Greed

Big mouthfuls often choke. -*Italian Proverb*

If your desires be endless, your cares and fears will be so too. -*Thomas Fuller, MD*

Grief

Grief expressed is a beginning of the process of healing.

Everyone can master a grief but he that has it. -*Shakespeare, 1598*

Gratitude

The practice of the attitude of gratitude will make gratitude your basic attitude. -*Norman Vincent Peale*

Grudge

Holding a grudge is like taking poison and hoping it will kill someone else.

Habit

Habit is a cable; we weave a thread of it everyday and at last we find we cannot break it.

Good habits are hard to acquire but easy to live with. Bad habits are easy to acquire but hard to live with.

Old habits die hard. *-Proverb*

Happiness

A man is happy so long as he chooses to be happy and nothing can stop him. *-Alexander Solzhenitsyn*

Happiness is like honey: You can pass it around, but some of it will stick to you.

Happiness depends upon ourselves. *-Aristotle, 400 BC*

If happiness truly consisted in physical ease and freedom from care, then the happiest individual would not be either a man or a woman; it would be, I think, an American cow. *-William Lyon Phelps*

Happiness is itself a kind of gratitude. *-Joseph Wood Krutch*

It is not easy to find happiness in ourselves, and it is not possible to find it elsewhere. *-Agnes Repplier*

True happiness comes from the work we do to make the world a better place. *-Pastor Kelly Peters*

We possess only the happiness we are able to understand. *-Maurice Maeterlinck*

Look around and you'll agree that the really happy people are those who have broken the chains of procrastination, those who find satisfaction in doing the job at hand. They're full of eagerness, zest, and productivity. You can be, too. *-Norman Vincent Peale*

Hate

Hating people is like burning your own house down to get rid of a rat. *-Harry Emerson Fosdick*

To wrong those we hate is to add fuel to our hatred. Conversely, to treat an enemy with magnanimity is to blunt our hatred for him. *-Eric Hoffer*

Hell

The road to hell is paved with good intentions.

Hero

A hero is a man who does what he can. *-Romain Rolland*

We can't all be heroes because somebody has to sit on the curb and clap as they go by. *-Will Rogers*

Home

Let a man behave in his own house as a guest. *-Emerson*

Honesty

I hope I shall always possess firmness and virtue enough to maintain what I consider the most enviable of all titles, the character of an "honest man." *- George Washington*

Hospitality

Do not neglect to show hospitality to strangers, for thereby some have entertained angels unaware. *-Hebrews 13:2*

It is equally offensive to speed a guest who would like to stay and to detain one who is anxious to leave. *-Homer, 900 BC*

House

Our houses are such unwieldy property that we are often imprisoned rather than housed in them. -*Thoreau*

Humanitarian

He that gives his heart will not deny his money. -*Thomas Fuller, MD*

Humor

Good humor is one of the best articles of dress one can wear in society. -*Thackeray*

Identity

Resolve to be thyself: and know: that, he who finds himself loses his misery. -*Arnold Matthew*

Important

Pretend that every person you meet has a sign around his or her neck that says, 'Make me feel important.' -*Mary Kay Ash*

Improve

If each one sweeps in front of his own door, the whole street is clean. -*Jewish Proverb*

There is only one corner of the universe you can be certain of improving and that is your own self. -*Aldous Huxley*

Inconvenience

What may look like an inconvenience might be no less than the beginning of a life-changing opportunity. -*Erwin Raphael McManus*

Indecision

When not sure which course of action to take regarding others, put yourself in their place. -*Editor*

Indifference

The worst sin toward our fellow creatures is not to hate them, but to be indifferent to them: that's the essence of inhumanity. -*George Bernard Shaw*

Individuality

We forfeit three-fourths of ourselves in order to be like other people. -*Arthur Schopenhauer*

Inferiority

No one can make you feel inferior without your consent. -*Eleanor Roosevelt*

Influence

Associating with bad people will ruin decent people. -*1 Corinthians 15:33*

Inquiry

Better ask twice than lose your way once. -*Danish Proverb*

I keep six honest serving men; they taught me all I know; their names are what and why and when and how and where and who. -*Rudyard Kipling*

Insight

Know the kink in your armor. -*Baltasar Grecian*

Integrity

The man of integrity walks securely, but he who takes crooked paths will be found out. -*Proverbs 10:9*

Interacting

I believe that by interacting with others in the world, we all become stronger. -*Cellist Yo-yo Ma*

Introspection

What lies behind us and what lies before us are small matters compared to what lies within us. -*Ralph Waldo Emerson*

Involvement/Commitment

The difference between 'involvement' and 'commitment' is like an eggs-and-ham breakfast: the chicken was 'involved', pig was 'committed.'

Jealous

You shall not covet...-*Deuteronomy 5:21*

Jest

I talk to myself because I like dealing with a better class of people. -*Jackie Mason, Comedian*

Joy

The road's not so important as the how-I-live my days; because the joy is in the journey not the road I've traveled on. -*Jack McGuane, Poet*

Happiness comes and goes in life, but joy persists; joy endures through every dark night.

The root of joy is gratefulness. For it is not joy that makes us grateful; it is gratitude that makes us joyful.

Two of the greatest joys experienced are the joy of being different from others and the joy of being the same as others. *-Henri J.M. Nouwen*

By sharing the joy of another, we increase it. By sharing the woe of another, we diminish it.

Judging

Do not judge, and you will not be judged. Do not condemn, and you will not be condemned. Forgive, and you will be forgive. *-Luke 6:37*

People who live in glass houses shouldn't throw stones. *-Geoffrey Chaucer*

Such as every man is inwardly so he judgeth outwardly. *-Thomas A. Kempis*

Justice

When those who are not injured are as indigent as those who are!

Kindness

Constant kindness can accomplish much. As the sun makes ice melt, kindness causes misunderstanding, mistrust, and hostility to evaporate. *-Albert Schweitzer*

Kindness it is that brings forth kindness always. *-Sophocles, 477 BC*

Kind words can be short and easy to speak, but their echoes are truly endless. *-Mother Teresa*

One can either look at life and think there's nothing I can do that would really make a difference, or one can do small acts of kindness that would make a big difference in the lives of those touched. *-Editor*

One kind word can warm three winter months.

The unfortunate need people who will be kind to them; the prosperous need people to be kind to. -*Aristotle*

The world is full of people who could use a joke, a compliment, an expression of compassion. -*Karen Sandstrom*

Those who bring sunshine into the lives of others cannot keep it from themselves. -*Sir James M. Barrie*

Laughter

Laughter is the shortest distance between two people. -*Comedian Victor Borge*

Laziness

A river becomes crooked by following the line of least resistance. So does man.

Leadership

Decisive people with judgment, who aren't afraid to tell other people who don't have such good judgment that their judgment isn't very good, make good leaders. -*Bobby Knight*

When you have got an elephant by the hind legs and he is trying to run away, it is best to let him run. -*Abraham Lincoln*

Light

Light one candle, and no matter how dark it is, the darkness cannot overcome the light.

There are two ways of spreading light: to be the candle, or the mirror that reflects it. -*Edith Wharton*

Like

Getting people to like you is merely the other side of liking them. *-Norman Vincent Peale*

Listen

Everyone should be quick to listen, slow to speak, and slow to become angry. *-James 1:19*

Life

If you wish to live, you must first attend your funeral. *-Katherin Mansfield*

Make sure the thing you're living for is worth dying for. *-Charles Mayes*

Highway of life…expect delays. *-Tom Wilson*

Live

For yesterday is over, tomorrow's far away, and I remain committed to the good I do today!

If you hope to live well and wisely, try to be, here and now, the man you would want to be on your deathbed. *-Thomas A. Kempis*

Live as if everything you do will eventually be known and treat others as if you can see the effects before you act. *-Hugh Prather*

It's a fact that if we fail to make the most of the moment, right here and now, then it becomes next to impossible to do so in the future. *-Editor*

Live in this world like some stranger from abroad; keep your heart free, and trained up toward God in heaven. You have no lasting citizenship here. *-Thomas A. Kempis*

Many people live their lives in a cycle of fear, shame, guilt, and regret, never experiencing the power of forgiveness, grace, and love. *-Pastor Kelly Peters*

My grandfather always said that living is like licking honey off a thorn. -*Louis Adamic*

We can't choose how we're going to die; but, we can choose how we're going to live.

Wherever you are, be all there! -*Jim Elliot, Missionary*

We were not born just to be surviving, but we are to be constantly in a state of functioning actively, not passively. We are not to let time go swiftly by without using any talents, skills, or abilities that we were born with or acquired along the way. -*Laura Moore, Columnist*

Loneliness

Often we know the lonely and fail to reach out in love. We may be shy or find it hard to show love. We may feel that we are being insincere if we try. Then let us accept ourselves as we are- God's imperfect instruments- and pray that he will use us despite our shortcomings. -*Mother Teresa*

Losing

You can't ask to start over just because you're losing the game.

Love

It's not what you do, but how much love you put into it that matters. -*Mother Teresa*

If you'd beloved, be worthy to be loved. -*Ovid, 8 AD*

How you treated other people, not your wealth or accomplishments, is the most enduring impact you can leave on earth. -*Pastor Rick Warren*

If you want to love better, you should start with a friend you hate. -*Nikka, age 6*

Tell me again, do you love me or do you not? You told me once, but I forgot. -*Wife to Husband*

Love dies only when growth stops. -*Pearl S. Buck*

So often when we say "I love you" we say it with a huge "I" and a small "you." -*Antony, Russian Orthodox Archbishop*

Those who deserve love the least need it the most.

You really shouldn't say I love you unless you mean it. But if you mean it, you should say it a lot. People forget. -*Jessica, age 8*

The great acts of love are done by those who are habitually performing small acts of kindness. -*American Proverb*

So loving my enemies does not apparently mean thinking them nice either. That is an enormous relief. For a good many people imagine forgiving your enemies means making out that they are really not such bad fellows after all, when it is quite plain that they are. -*C.S. Lewis*

Love moves us to come to the aid of those who are in real need.

We are not the same person this year as last; nor are those we love. It is a happy change if we, changing, continue to love a changed person. -*Somerset Maugham*

Low

When you feel you're at your lowest, remember this: There is nowhere to go but up. -*Dr. Robert Schuller*

Lying

It is often the case that a man who can't tell a lie thinks that he is the best judge of one. -*Mark Twain*

I'm convinced it's less costly to tell the truth and get on with life, even if it means doing some time. -*R. Fosterwinans*

Luxury

How many things I can do without. -*Socrates*

Making A Difference

Act as if what you do makes a difference. It does. -*William James*

Mass Media

I hate television. I hate it as much as peanuts, but I cannot stop eating peanuts. -*Orson Welles*

Materialism

The more people acquire, the more they want and the less satisfied they become with what they have. When they get it, it's never enough. -*Herbert W. Armstrong*

Maturity

If you are looking for painless ways to grow toward each other and toward maturity, call off the search. -*J. Grant*

The ability to stick with a job until it's finished. The ability to do a job without being supervised. The ability to carry money without spending it. And, the ability to bear an injustice without wanting to get even. -*Abigail Van Buren*

A man at his best you are not so born: Strive daily to develop yourself in your person, in your calling. -*Baltasar Grecian*

To live with fear and not be afraid is the final test of maturity. -*Edward Weeks*

You are only young once, but you can be immature forever.

Meditate

Whatever things are true, whatever things are noble, whatever things are just, whatever things are pure, whatever things are lovely, whatever things are of good report, if there is any virtue and if there is anything praiseworthy-meditate on these things. *-Philippians 4:8*

Meekness

Meekness is not weakness; meekness is power submitting to love. *-Dr. Jim Long*

Memory

A memory is something that you can pull from the file in your head. A memory is something that you can relive over and over again. A memory is something that no one can ever take away. *-Barbara Tate*

The things we remember best are those better forgotten. *-Baltasar Grecian*

Better by far you should forget and smile, than that you should remember and be sad. *-Christina Rossetti, 1862*

We do not remember days, we remember moments. *-Cesare Pavese*

We should never remember the benefits we have conferred, nor forget the favors received. *-Proverb*

What was hard to bear is sweet to remember. *-Portugese Proverb*

Mercy

In case of doubt, it is best to lean on the side of mercy. *-Legal Maxim*

Method

Better one safe way than a hundred which you cannot reckon. *-Aesop*

If there are obstacles, the shortest line between two points may be the crooked line. -*Bertolt Brecht*

Minds

Minds are like parachutes…they only function when open!

Mistake

A man who has committed a mistake and doesn't correct it is committing another mistake. –*Confucius, 500 BC*

Convert mistakes into learning opportunities. -*Editor*

Learn from mistakes of others; you can't make them all yourself.

Measure twice, cut once. -*An Old Carpenter's Saw*

Manage mistakes by learning to play within your abilities and realizing that managing and minimizing mistakes in life is critical. -*Jack L. Groppel, Ph.D.*

Sulking about your mistakes only leads to future ones. -*Bill Rancic*

When in doubt, cut the piece of wood long and the piece of iron short. -*Carmine Taddeo*

You may never make a discovery if you're afraid to make a mistake.

Moderation

Enough is as good as a feast. -*John Heywood, 1546*

You never know what is enough unless you know what is more than enough. -*William Blake, 1790*

Nothing in excess. -*Solon, 700 BC*

Modesty

A modest man is usually admired, if people ever hear of him. -*Edgar Watson*

It's good to be clever, but not to show it. -*French Proverb*

Who would succeed in the world should be wise in the use of his pronouns. Utter the you twenty times, where you once utter the I. -*John Hay, 1871*

Money

Money can't buy you happiness, but it does bring you a more pleasant form of misery. -*Spike Milligan*

Never work just for money or for power. They won't save your soul or build a decent family or help you sleep at night. -*Marian Wright Edelman*

The moment you stop worrying about money, life gets better. -*Ken Robinson*

Spend what you have left after saving instead of saving what you have left after spending. -*Patti Labelle*

Motivation

People are more motivated to call or write about a negative experience than a positive experience. -*Packy Longfellow, Account Supervisor*

Motive

But when you do a charitable deed, do not let your left hand know what your right hand is doing. -*Matthew 6:2*

Mourning

Let mourning stop when one's grief is fully expressed. -*Confucius*

Mundane

Every day cannot be a feast of lanterns.

Many eyes go through the meadows but few see the flowers in it. *-Emerson*

Music

Music is a beautiful opiate, if you don't take it too seriously. *-Henry Miller*

Naive

He who does not open his eyes must open his purse. *-German Proverb*

Name

A good name is more desirable than great riches; to be esteemed is better than silver or gold. *-Proverbs 22:1*

Necessity

Necessity turns lion into fox. *-Persian Proverb*

Where necessity speaks it demands. *-Russian Proverb*

Needs

Understanding human needs is half the job of meeting them. *-Adlai Stevenson*

One of the weaknesses of our age is our apparent inability to distinguish our needs from our greeds. *-Don Robinson*

Neighbor

Mix with the neighbors, and you learn what's doing in your own house. *-Yiddish Proverb*

The correlative to loving our neighbors as ourselves is hating ourselves as we hate our neighbors. -*Oliver Wendell Holmes, Sr.*

Nonsense

A little nonsense now and then is cherished by the wises men. -*Raold Dahl*

Obstinacy

No man is good for anything who has not some particle of obstinacy to use upon occasion. -*Henry Ward Beecher*

Open-Mindedness

To get others to come into our ways of thinking, we must go over to theirs; it is necessary to follow in order to lead. -*William Hazlitt, 1850*

Opinion

A difference of opinion alienates only little minds. -*Scottish Proverb*

We credit scarcely any person with good sense except those who are of our opinion. -*La Rochefoucauld, 1665*

Opportunity

Opportunity doesn't even need to knock if you just leave your door open. -*Tom Wilson*

A wise man will make more opportunities than he finds. -*Francis Bacon*

It is better to be prepared for an opportunity and not have one than to have an opportunity and not be prepared. -*Whitney Young, Jr.*

If opportunity doesn't knock, build a door. -*Joe Mazur*

Opportunities are usually disguised as hard work, so most people don't recognize them. -*Ann Landers*

Great opportunities may come once in a lifetime, but small opportunities, such as acts of telling the truth, being kind, and encouraging others, surround us every day. -*Pastor Rick Warren*

When one door closes another door opens; but we so often look so long and so regretfully upon the closed door that we do not see the ones which open for us. -*Alexander Graham Bell*

Opportunity seldom knocks twice. -*Proverb*

Great opportunities often disguise themselves in small tasks. -*Pastor Rick Warren*

Opportunity may knock once, but temptation bangs on your front door forever.

Opposition

Men naturally despise those who court them, but respect those who do not give way to them. -*Thucydides, 400 BC*

Optimism

An optimist is an accordionist with a beeper. -*Johnny Carson*

Order

It is best to do things systematically, since we are only human, and disorder is our worst enemy. -*Hesiod, 800 BC*

Organize

Organizing is what you do before you do something, so that when you do it, it's not all mixed up. -*Christopher Robin in Winnie the Pooh*

Outlook

Learn from yesterday, live for today, and make reasonable plans for tomorrow. -*Paul Franks*

Pardon

We pardon in the degree that we love. -*La Rochefoucauld*

Passion

When the passions become masters, they are vices. -*Pascal, 1670*

Past

It's futile to talk too much about the past; it's something like trying to make birth control retroactive. -*Charles Edward Wilson, 1955*

We have to do with the past only as we can make it useful to the present and the future. -*Frederick Douglass*

The farther backward you can look, the farther forward you are likely to see. -*Winston Churchill*

Patience

A man's wisdom gives him patience; it is to his glory to overlook an offense. -*Proverbs 19:11*

Be patient in little things. Learn to bear the everyday trials and annoyances of life quietly and calmly, and then, when unforeseen trouble or calamity comes, your strength will not forsake you. -*William Swan Plumer*

Patience serves as protection against wrongs as clothes do against the cold. For if you put on more clothes, as the cold increases it will have no power to hurt you. So in like manner you must grow in patience when you meet with great wrongs, and they will then be powerless to vex your mind. -*Leonardo Da Vinci*

Peace

A harvest of peace is produced from a seed of contentment. -*Indian Proverb*

Peace begins with a smile- smile five times a day at someone you don't really want to smile at, at all- do it for peace. -*Mother Teresa*

People

Walk briskly away from destructive people and find generous people to hang out with. You are whom you associate with. -*Bill O'Reilly*

Perception

We like to read others, but we do not like to be read. -*La Rochefoucauld, 1665*

Perfection

The perfect does not lie in quantity, but in quality. All that is best is always scant and rare, for mass in anything cheapens it. -*Baltasar Grecian*

We shall never have friends if we expect to find them without fault. -*Thomas Fuller, MD*

Performance

People do their best in the situation they find themselves. -*Daniel Taddeo*

Perseverance

Great works are performed not by strength, but by perseverance. -*Samuel Johnson*

The person who makes a success of living is the one who sees his goal steadily and aims for it unswervingly. This is dedication. -*Cecil B. DeMille*

Perspective

The field cannot well be seen from within the field. *-Emerson*

Persuasion

Would you persuade, speak of interest, not of reason. *-Benjamin Franklin*

Pick-Me-Up

Stop and find at least one thing in your life that you can be grateful for. *-Tina Hovan, Staff Reporter*

Piety

A tear dries quick, especially when it is shed for the troubles of others. *-Cicero, 55 BC*

Pity

It's all right to sit on your pity pot every now and again. Just be sure to flush when you are done.

Plans

Nobody ever drew up his plans for life so well but what the facts, and the years, and experience always introduce some modification. *-Terence, 160 BC*

Our plans miscarry because they have no aim. When a man does not know what harbor he is making for, no wind is the right wind. *-Seneca, 4 BC*

Play

In our play we reveal what kind of people we are. *-Ovid, 8 AD*

Plain Living

Reduce the complexity of life my eliminating the needless wants of life, and the labors of life reduce themselves. -*Edwin Way Leals*

Pleasure

All the things I really like to do are either immoral, illegal, or fattening. -*Alexander Woollcott*

Many seek good nights and lose good days. -*Dutch Proverb*

No pleasure is evil in itself, but the means by which certain pleasures are gained bring pain many times greater than the pleasures. -*Epicurus, 300 BC*

The fly that prefers sweetness to a long life may drown in honey. -*George Santayana*

There is more of fear than delight in secret pleasure. -*Publilius Syrus, 100 BC*

There is no such thing as pure pleasure; some anxiety always goes with it. -*Ovid, 43 BC*

After pleasant scratching comes unpleasant smarting. -*Danish Proverb*

There is no gathering the rose without being pricked by the thorns. -*Fables of Bidpai, 750 AD*

Poor

It is not the man who has little, but he who desires more, that is poor. – *Seneca, 4 BC*

Positive

Think positive. Find the bless in the mess.

Always look at what you have left; never look at what you have lost. -*Dr. Robert Schuller*

Positive anything is better than negative nothing. -*Elbert Hubbard*

Surround yourself with positive people who don't make you feel inferior or defensive, and train yourself to tune out the negative words of others. -*Susan Battley*

Possession

The more you have, the more you are occupied, the less you give. But the less you have, the more free you are. -*Mother Teresa*

Poverty

Poverty is no disgrace, but no honor either.

War on nations change maps. War on poverty maps change. -*Muhammad Ali*

Practice

Practice is one of the things that keeps one attentive. -*Peter Steinhart, Author*

Praise

Refusal of praise is a desire to be praised twice. -*La Rochefoucauld*

Once in a century a man may be ruined or made insufferable by praise. But surely once in a minute something generous dies for want of it. -*John Masefield*

Generally we praise only to be praised. -*La Rochefoucauld*

Prayer

If we pray for help to do the next right thing, everything will turn out the way it should. -*Dick Feagler, Columnist*

Preach

He preaches well that lives well. *-Don Quixote, 1605*

Prejudice

Dogs bark at a person whom they do not know. *-Heraclitus, 500 BC*

Prepare

It's easier to prepare and prevent than to repair and repent.

Present

Wherever you are, be all there. Live to the hilt every situation you believe to be the will of God. *-Elisabeth Elliot*

Pride

When pride comes, then comes disgrace, but with humility comes wisdom. *-Proverbs 11:2*

Priorities

Live like you were dying. [Everyone actually is.]

When we eat out, most of us expect to tip the waiter or waitress fifteen percent. When we suggest ten percent as a minimum church offering, some folks are aghast. *-Felix A. Lorenz*

Your calendar and your checkbook reveal your priorities.

Privacy

A hedge between keeps friendship green. *-German Proverb*

Problems

Never let a problem become an excuse. -*Robert Schuller*

Don't duck the most difficult problems. That just insures that the hardest part will be left when you're most tired. Get the big one done- it's all downhill from then on. -*Norman Vincent Peale*

If there were no problems, there would be no opportunities.

If a problem has no solution, it may not be a problem but a fact not to be solved, but to be coped with over time. -*Shimon Peres*

The only people without problems are those in cemeteries. -*Fred Taddeo*

Procrastination

A ripe crop must not wait for tomorrow. -*Latin Proverb*

Procrastination is my sin. It brings me naught but sorrow. I know that I should stop it. In fact, I will- tomorrow! -*Gloria Pitzer*

A procrastinator suffers from hardening of the oughteries.

Profiteering

Prefer a loss to a dishonest gain: the one brings pain at the moment, the other for all time. -*Chilon, 600 BC*

Progress

The person determined to achieve maximum success learns the principle that progress is made one step at a time. -*Eric Sevareid*

You're not very smart if you're not a little kinder and wiser than yesterday. -*Abraham Lincoln*

Prosperity

It is not a sin to have riches, but it is a sin to fix our hearts upon them. -*John Baptist De La Salle*

Purpose

Living on purpose is the only way to really live. Everything else is just existing. -*Pastor Rick Warren*

The man without a purpose is like a ship without a rudder- a waif, a nothing, a no man. -*Thomas Carlyle*

Quarrels

Don't have anything to do with foolish and stupid arguments, because you know they produce quarrels. -*2 Timothy 2:23*

Racial Prejudice

There is a tendency to judge a race, a nation, or any distant group by its least worthy members. -*Eric Hoffer, 1951*

Reciprocity

Men seldom give pleasure when they are not pleased themselves. -*Samuel Johnson, 1750*

The sort of thing you say is the thing that will be said to you. -*Homer, 900 BC*

Reconciliation

When we focus on reconciliation the problem loses significance and often becomes irrelevant. -*Pastor Rick Warren*

Relationships

The problems start when one of you wishes the other were different; wishes you yourself could be different. -*Carolyn Hax*

Reprove/Praise

Reprove a friend in secret, but praise him before others. -*Leonardo da Vinci*

Reputation

Associate yourself with men of quality if you esteem your own reputation, for 'tis better to be alone than in bad company. -*George Washington*

It is easier to add to a great reputation than to get it. -*Publilius Syrus, 100 BC*

If you would not be known to do anything, never do it. -*Emerson*

You're known by the company you keep.

Resentment

Nothing on earth consumes a man more quickly than the passion of resentment. -*Nietzoche*

Resignation

Happy he who learns to bear what he cannot change. -*Schiller, 1793*

What cannot be altered must be borne, not blamed. -*Thomas Fuller, MD, 1732*

Responsibility

God will hold us responsible as to how well we fulfill our responsibilities to this age and take advantage of our opportunities. -*Billy Graham*

Responsibility is the price of greatness. -*Winston Churchill*

Unto whomever much is given, of him shall much be required. -*Luke 12:48*

Results

The results you achieve will be in direct proportion to the effort you apply. - *Dennis Waitley*

Revenge

Men are more prone to revenge injuries than to requite kindness. -*Thomas Fuller, MD, 1732*

Rich

A man is rich in proportion to the number of things he can afford to let alone. -*Henry David Thoreau*

He is rich who owes nothing. -*Hungarian Proverb*

Get rich quick: count your blessings.

Right

You cannot make yourself feel something you do not feel, but you can make yourself do right in spite of your feelings. -*Pearl S. Buck*

Rights

I am the inferior to any man whose rights I trample under foot. -*Robert G. Ingersoll, 1884*

Right/Wrong

We don't have to get so caught up with figuring out who is right and who is wrong that we forget what matters. -*Rosamund Stone Zander*

It's O.K. to think you're right, but it's not O.K. to think others are wrong.

Risk

Those of us who refuse to risk and grow get swallowed up by life. -*Patty Hansen*

To love is to risk not being loved in return. To hope is to risk pain. To try is to risk failure, but risk must be taken because the greatest hazard in life is to risk nothing.

Rules

For most people trying to find the road to success, breaking the rules is a shortcut to failure. -*Marilyn vos Savant*

Secret

Another person's secret is like another person's money: You are not so careful with it as you are of your own. -*Edgar Watson*

Sex

Civilized people cannot fully satisfy their sexual instinct without love. -*Bertrand Russel*

Self

He that falls in love with himself will have no rivals. -*Benjamin Franklin*

Make the most of yourself, for that is all there is to you. -*Ralph Waldo Emerson*

We are all serving a life-sentence in the dungeon of self. -*Cyril Connoll*

Self-Control

Man who man would be, must rule the empire of himself. -*Shelley, 1821*

The word teaches us to say "No" to ungodliness and worldly passions and to live self-controlled, upright, and godly lives in this present age. -*Titus 2:12*

Self-Deception

The greatest deception men suffer is from their own opinions. -*Leonardo da Vinci, 1500*

Until the donkey tried to clear the fence, he thought himself a deer. -*Arthur Guitarman, 1924*

Selfishness

Men are not against you; they are merely for themselves. -*Gene Fowler*

Self-Esteem

Respect yourself if you would have others respect you. -*Baltasar Grecian, 1647*

Be a friend to thyself, and others will be so too. -*Thomas Fuller, MD, 1732*

Self-Importance

The big drum only sounds well from afar. -*Persian Proverb*

When they came to shoe the horses, the beetle stretched out his leg. -*English Proverb*

Self-Indulgent

I can be worldly without necessarily being self-indulgent. But I cannot be consistently self-indulgent without being worldly. -*Hubert van Zeller*

Self-Injury

The bow too tensely strung is easily broken. -*Publilius Syrus, 100 BC*

Self-Knowledge

He who knows others is learned; he who knows himself is wise. -*Laotse, 600 BC*

Self-Love

In another's, yes, but in his own eye, he sees no dirt. -*Burmese Proverb*

People fall in love with themselves almost immediately after birth. This is invariably the beginning of a life-long romance. There is no record of infidelity, separation, or divorce between humans and their egos. -*Harry Singer*

Self-Made

A cold, self-righteous prig who goes regularly to church may be nearer to hell than a prostitute. But, of course, it is better to be neither. -*C.S. Lewis*

Like all self-made men, he worships his creator.

Self-Sufficiency

Be thine own palace or the world's thy jail. -*John Donne*

Every tub must stand upon its own bottom. -*Thomas Fuller, MD, 1732*

We never reflect how pleasant it is to ask for nothing. -*Seneca, 100 AD*

Sermon

The average man's idea of a good sermon is one that goes over his head and hits a neighbor.

Service

Most people wish to serve God, but only in an advisory capacity.

Age, health, and stage in life have nothing to do with serving or not serving. In each season of life there are attributes and qualities of life and experience that God values in service. -*Bruce Kemper*

When we stop focusing on our own needs, we become aware of the needs around us. -*Pastor Rick Warren*

Shame

The only shame is to have none. -*Pascal, 1640*

When we use shame as an impetus for growth our sense of self becomes stronger. -*Dr. Joyce Brothers*

Shame seems to be even more powerful than guilt, though the two emotions are linked. While guilt is the feeling that you have done something wrong, shame is the feeling that there's something wrong *about* you. -*Dr. Joyce Brothers*

Significance

If you want to increase you significance, focus your energies on significant activities: those which will remain for eternity. -*Neil Anderson*

Simplify

The ability to simplify means to eliminate the unnecessary so that the necessary may speak. -*Hans Hofmann*

Sincerity

Sincerity is the highest compliment you can pay. -*Emerson, 1836*

Single-Mindedness

When you are at sea, keep clear of the land. -*Publilius Syrus, 100 BC*

Silence

Better say nothing than say nothing to the purpose. *-English Proverb*

No one realizes what you don't know until you open your mouth. *-Fred Nance, Squire, Sanders & Dempsey, Cleveland*

Silence will save me from being wrong (and foolish), but it will also deprive me of the possibility of being right. *-Igor Stravinsky, 1966*

Sin

Little sins add up to big trouble.

Sin always has its negative consequences. *-Editor*

Sleep

The pillow is a silent Sibyl [prophet], and it is better to sleep on things before than lie awake about them afterwards. *-Baltasar Grecian, 1647*

Smile

The warmest kind of welcome is a smile.

Smile at people. It takes 72 muscles to frown and only 14 to smile.

Snobbery

All the people like us are "we" and everyone else is "they". *-Rudyard Kipling, 1926*

Sour Grapes

Sour grapes can ne'er make sweet wine. *-Thomas Fuller, MD, 1732*

Speech

Let thy speech be better than silence, or be silent. *-Dionysus the Elder, 400 BC*

One never repents of having spoken too little, but often of having spoken too much. *-Philippe De Commynes, 1524*

Too much talk will include errors. *-Burmese Proverb*

There is always time to add a word, never to withdraw one. *-Baltasar Grecian, 1647*

The recipe for a good speech contains shortening.

Stress

There are four different ways to tackle a stressful situation: change your attitude, avoid the situation, alter the situation, or adapt to the situation. *-Jodi Sivon, Health and Wellness Campus Manager*

Struggle

"Inside of me there are two dogs. One of the dogs is mean and evil. The other dog is good. The mean dog fights the good dog all the time." When asked which dog wins, he reflected for a moment and replied, "The one I feed the most." *-A Native American Elder*

You learn from struggling.

Success

If a man has a talent and cannot use it, he has failed. If he has a talent and uses only half of it, he has partially failed. If he has a talent and learns somehow to use the whole of it, he has gloriously succeeded and won a satisfaction and a triumph few men ever know. *-Thomas Wolfe*

He who would climb the ladder must begin at the bottom. *-English Proverb*

I can give you a six word formula for success: Think things through- then follow through. *-Edward Rickenbacker*

It takes twenty years to make an overnight success. *-Eddie Cantor*

Never take "no" for an answer. If you don't succeed the first or second time, keep on trying until you find the right way. *-Carmelita A. Thomas, Western Campus President, Cuyahoga Community College*

No person can succeed without helping people. *-Dr. Robert Schuller*

Secret to success: staying the course against the critics. *-Jim Stevens*

Success is speaking words of praise…in cheering other people's ways…in doing just the best you can…with every task and every plan.

To be successful you must be willing to do all the things that unsuccessful people won't do. *-Troy Walker, Director of Cox Communications, Cleveland*

There is no success without hardship. *-Sophocles, 418 BC*

To reach the port of success we must sail, sometimes with the wind and sometimes against it- but we must sail, not drift or lie at anchor. *-Oliver Wendell Holmes*

There are no shortcuts to any place worth going.

Success without honor is an unseasoned dish; it will satisfy your hunger, but it won't taste good. *-Joe Paterno, Coach*

Suffering

If you are distressed by anything external, the pain is not due to the thing itself but to your own estimate of it; and this you have the power to change at any moment. *-Marcus Aurelius, 800 AD*

It is the fire of suffering that brings forth the gold of godliness. (We learn things in suffering that we cannot learn any other way). *-Madame Guyon*

Suffering can soften our own hearts. We become more compassionate toward others. We become less judgmental, less self-centered, and more willing to walk that mile in someone else's shoes. -*Greg Albrecht, Theologian*

We feel and weigh soon enough what we suffer from others; but how much others suffer from us, of this we take no heed. -*Thomas A. Kempis, 1426 AD*

Support Group

Having a support group is a valuable asset to carry us when we are buried under a load of troubles. -*Billy Graham*

Sympathy

Before an affliction is digested, consolation ever comes too soon; and after it is digested, it comes too late. -*Laurence Sterne, 1759*

When you live next to the cemetery, you cannot weep for everyone. -*Russian Proverb*

Tact

A tactless man is like an axe on an embroidery frame. -*Malay Proverb*

Tact is the art of changing the subject without changing your mind.

Taste

One man's poison is another man's spinach. -*George Ade, 1980*

There isn't one life flavor that suits every taste. -*Carolyn Hax, Columnist*

Temptation

When temptation calls you on the phone, don't argue with it. Just hang up. -*Pastor Rick Warren*

When you flee temptation, don't leave a forwarding address.

Thankfulness

I complained about having no shoes, until I met a man who had no feet.

Thanksgiving

Not what we say about our blessings but how we use them is the true message of our thanksgiving. -*W.T. Purkiser*

Things

There are many things in life that will catch your eye, but only a few that will catch your heart. Pursue those!

The best things are nearest: breath in your nostrils, light in your eyes, flowers at your feet, duties at your hand, the oath of God just before you. -*Robert Louis Stevenson*

While we know that things cannot provide lasting happiness, the act of buying gives consumers deep emotional satisfaction. -*Pam Danzinger*

Think/Action

We know what a person thinks not when he tells us what he thinks, but by his actions. -*Isaac Bashevis Singer*

Thoughts

I have no riches but my thoughts, yet these are wealth enough for me. -*Sara Teasdale*

Thoughts, like fleas, jump from man to man, but they don't bite everybody. -*Stanislaw Lec, 1962*

Right thoughts will lead to right actions. -*Editor*

Thrift

Frugality is the sure guardian of our virtues. -*Brahman Proverb*

Time

Yesterday is history. Tomorrow is a mystery. Today is a gift. That's why we call it the present. -*Babatunde Olatunji*

Dost though love life, then do not squander time, for that's the stuff life is made of. -*Benjamin Franklin, 1757*

The greatest gift you can give someone is your time. -*Pastor Rick Warren*

Half our life is spent trying to find something to do with the time we have rushed through life trying to save time. -*Will Rogers, 1949*

Those who make the worst use of their time are the first to complain of its brevity. -*La Bruyere, 1688*

Yesterday is a cancelled check; tomorrow is a promissory note; today is the only cash you have- so spend it wisely. -*Kay Lyons*

Time is more valuable than money. You can get more money, but you can't get more time.

Tomorrow

Finish each day and be done with it. You have done what you could; some blunders and absurdities have crept in; forget them as soon as you can. Tomorrow is a new day; you should begin it serenely and with too high a spirit to be encumbered with your old nonsense. -*Ralph Waldo Emerson*

Tough Times

Sometimes life hands you situations when all you can do is put one foot in front of the other and live moment to moment.

When the going gets tough, the tough get going. *-Maxim*

Tradition

A tradition without intelligence is not worth having. *-T.S. Eliot, 1934*

I have yet to meet a tradition that wasn't enhanced by interacting with others; and we all become stronger. *-Cellist Yo-Yo Ma*

Travel

He that travels much knows much. *-Thomas Fuller, MD, 1732*

He who would travel happily must travel light. *-Saint Exupery*

Trials

A calm sea does not make a skilled sailor. *-African Proverb*

It's good to remember that the tea kettle, although up to its neck in hot water, continues to sing.

The gem cannot be polished without friction, nor man perfected without trials. *-Chinese Proverb*

Trifles

Those who apply themselves too much to little things usually become incapable of great ones. *-La Rochefoucauld*

Trouble

A trouble shared is a trouble halved. *-Proverb*

Trust

Love all, trust few. *-Shakespeare, 1602*

Thrust ivrbody- but cut th' ca-ards. -*Finley Peter Dunne, 1900*

We do not have it in our power to make someone trust us. We can behave in a trustworthy manner- or not- and therefore deserve someone's trust -or not. -*Carolyn Hax*

Truth

It would be wrong to put friendship before truth. -*Aristotle, 400 BC*

Nowadays flattery wins friends, truth hatred. -*Terence, 166 BC*

To love the truth is to refuse to let oneself be saddened by it. -*Andre Gide, 1940*

When in doubt, tell the truth. -*Mark Twain*

Trying

For us there is only the trying. The rest is not our business. -*T.S. Eliot*

Uncertain

Do the next best thing. -*Elizabeth Elliot*

Understanding

Be not disturbed at being misunderstood; be disturbed rather at not being understanding. -*Chinese Proverb*

To understand is to forgive, even oneself. -*Alexander Chase*

Understatement

Never give the Devil a ride; he will always want to drive.

Unhappiness

One cloud is enough to eclipse all the sun. *-Thomas Fuller, MD, 1732*

When we sing, everybody hears us; when we sigh, nobody hears us. *-Russian Proverb*

Unity

How good and pleasant it is when brothers live together in unity. *-Psalm 133:1*

Unknown

Grieve not, because though understandest not life's mystery; behind the veil is concealed many a delight. *-Hafiz, 1400 AD*

Usefulness

It is a great misfortune to be of use to nobody; scarcely less to be of use to everybody. *-Baltasar Grecian, 1647*

Useless

No one is useless in this world who lightens the burden of anyone else.

Value

Men understand the worth of blessings only when they have lost them. *-Plautus, 300 BC*

Too many people overvalue what they are not and undervalue what they are.

Vanity

There are no grades of vanity; there are only grades of ability in concealing it. *-Mark Twain*

Virtue

Happiness cannot be the reward of virtue; it must be the intelligible consequence of it. -*Walter Lippmann, 1929*

The good opinion of our fellow men is the strongest, though not the purest motive to virtue. -*Charles Caleb Colton, 1825*

The superior man thinks always of virtue; the common man thinks of comfort. –*Confucius, 500 BC*

A thankful heart is not only the greatest virtue, but the parent of all other virtues. -*Cicero*

Vision

Vision without action is a daydream. Action without vision is a nightmare. -*Japanese Proverb*

Visitors

Unbidden guest are welcomest when they are gone. *Scottish Proverb*

Vocation

Every calling is great when greatly pursued. -*Oliver Wendell Holmes, 1885*

If at first you don't succeed you're running about average. -*M.H. Alderson*

The test of a vocation is the love of the drudgery it involves. -*Logan Pearsall, 1931*

Vulnerability

One always knocks oneself on the sore place. -*French Proverb*

Waiting

He who waits to do a great deal of good at once will never do anything. -*Samuel Johnson*

They also serve who only stand and wait. -*Milton, 1655*

Want

When you can't have what you want, it's time to start wanting what you have. -*Kathleen A. Sutton*

People who have little and want less are happier than those who have much and want more. -*Thomas A. Kempis*

Wealth

There are men who gain from their wealth only to fear of losing it. -*Antoine Rivaroli, 1808*

Wealth unused might as well not exist. -*Aesop, 600 BC*

Wealth is like seawater: the more we drink, the thirstier we become. The same is true for fame. -*Arthur Schopenhauser*

The difference between the wealthy and the poor is this: The wealthy invest their money and spend what's left; the poor spend their money and invest what's left.

Weeping

Waste not fresh tears over old griefs. -*Euripides, 415 BC*

Willing

Nothing is troublesome that we do willingly. -*Thomas Jefferson, 1825*

Winner

Winners never quit and quitters never win.

Wish

It is never wise to seek or wish for another's misfortune. If malice or envy were tangible and had a shape, it would be the shape of a boomerang. - *Charley Reese*

Wisdom

It is easier to be wise on behalf of others than to be so for ourselves. *-La Rochefoucauld, 1665*

Nine-tenths of wisdom is being wise in time. *-Theodore Roosevelt, 1917*

Words

The Scriptures repeatedly remind us that, with our words, we can either encourage or discourage, forgive or condemn, lift up or tear down. *-James C. Dobson, Ph.D.*

Work

He who considers his work beneath him will be above doing it well. - *Alexander Chase*

His brow is wet with honest sweat, he earns whate'er he can, and looks the whole world in the face, for he owes not any man. *-Longfellow, 1839*

Laziness may appear attractive, but work gives satisfaction. *-Anne Frank*

Most people spend most of their days doing what they do not want to do in order to earn the right, at times, to do what they may desire. *-John Mason Brown, 1960*

Thank God every morning when you get up that you have something to do that day which must be done, whether you like it or not. *-James Russell Lowell*

There can be intemperance in work just as in drink. *-C.S. Lewis*

Where our work is, there let our joy be. *-Tertullian*

World

All the world's a stage, and all the men and women merely players. They have their exits and their entrances, and one man in his time plays many parts. *-Shakespeare, 1599*

Worldliness

Don't be squeezed into the mold of this world. *-Romans 12:2*

Worry

If the grass is greener in the other fellow's yard, let him worry about cutting it. *-Fred Allen*

There are only two things in the world to worry over: the things you can control and the things you can't control. Fix the first, forget the second.

Whatever the circumstances, if it's out of your hands, dismiss it from your mind, totally. *-Editor*

Worry less about cholesterol and more about gratitude, forgiveness, and optimism. We need to see the glass as half full, not half empty. *-Dr. George E. Vailliant*

Worriers can become so occupied with the past and future that the present gets ignored. Living is not unlike driving a car. Occasionally, drivers should look back and far ahead, but mostly they should look at the road immediately in front of them. *-Editor*

Wrongdoing

For a wrongdoer to be undetected is difficult; for him to have confidence that his concealment will continue is impossible. -*Epicurus, 300 BC*

The sinner sins against himself; the wrongdoer wrongs himself, becoming the worse by his own action. -*Marcus Aurelius, 200 AD*

There is no shame in the accidents of chance, but only in the consequences of our own misdeeds. -*Phaedrus, 100 AD*

Those who are once found to be bad are presumed to be so forever. -*Latin Proverb*

There is scarcely any man sufficiently clever to appreciate all the evil he does. -*La Rochefoucauld, 1665*

Zeal

Too much zeal is a bad soldier who fires before the word of command.

Zeal will do more than knowledge. -*William Hazlitt, 1826*

9.
RELATED MATTERS

Ability

Natural abilities are like natural plants: They need pruning by study. *-Francis Bacon*

Achievement

Mighty rivers can easily be leaped at their source. *-Publilius, 100 BC*

Acquaintance

A person whom we know well enough to borrow from, but not well enough to lend to. *-Ambrose Bierce*

Adversity

Wise are they who have learned these truths: Trouble is temporary. Time is tonic. Tribulation is a test tube. *-William Arthur Ward*

Advertising

Doing business without advertising is like winking at a girl in the dark. You know what you are doing, but nobody else does. *-Steward H. Britt*

Age/Youth

He who is of a calm and happy nature will hardly feel the pressure of age; but to him who is of an opposite disposition youth and age are equally a burden. *-Plato*

Ambition

There is a loftier ambition than merely to stand in the world. It is to stoop down and lift those around us a little higher. -*Henry Van Dyke*

Appearance

The face is the mirror of the heart. -*Japanese Proverb*

Most of us mask our true identity to ourselves and the world, thus depriving us of a fulfilling life that includes the kind of relationships with God and others we are meant to have. This behavior is attributed to today's emphasis on appearance. -*Bill Thrall, Author*

Approval

Remove those "I want you to like me" stickers from your forehead and, instead, place them where they truly will do the most good- on your mirror.

Association

He that lies down with dogs shall rise up with fleas. -*Latin Proverb*

It is better to weep with wise men than to laugh with fools. -*Spanish Proverb*

Atheist

Antony Flew, one of the world's leading philosophical atheists, has concluded at age 81 that there must be a God. -*D. James Kennedy, Ph.D.*

Beauty

The art of inventing beauty transcends class, intellect, age, profession, geography- virtually every cultural and economic barrier. -*Estee Lauder*

Behavior

The greatest pleasure of a dog is that you can make a fool of yourself with him and not only will he not scold you, but he will make a fool of himself too. -*Samuel Butler*

We have all failed to practice ourselves the kind of behavior we expect from other people. -*C.S. Lewis*

Believing/Dying

Every man must do two things alone: He must do his own believing and his own dying. -*Martin Luther*

Birth

Blessed is the man who knows why he was born. -*Danny Thomas*

The day of our birth is one day's advance toward our death. -*Thomas Fuller, MD*

Body

Though it be disfigured by many defects, to whom is his body not dear. -*Panchatantra, 500 BC*

Blunder

Half of our mistakes in life arise from feeling where we ought to think and thinking where we ought to feel. -*John Churton Collins*

The man who makes no mistakes does not usually make anything. -*William Connor Mager*

Books

You can't tell- but you can sell- a book by its cover. -*The Wall Street Journal*

Boredom

Man is the only animal that can be bored. -*Erich Fromm*

Brotherhood

We are so bound together that no man can labor for himself alone. Each blow he strikes in his own behalf helps to mold the universe. -*Jerome K. Jerome*

Bribery

A conscience which has been bought once will be bought twice. -*Norbert Wiener*

He that bringeth a present findeth the open door. -*Thomas Fuller, MD*

Caliber

Your greatness is measured by your kindness, your education and intellect by your modesty; your ignorance is betrayed by your suspicions and prejudices; your real caliber is measured by the consideration and tolerance you have for others. -*Wm. J.II. Boetcker*

Can'ts

What many of us need is a good vigorous kick in the seat of the can'ts! -*Ame Babcock*

Cautious

Measure a thousand times and cut once. -*Turkish Proverb*

Change

Change always begins with changed thinking. It's human nature to resist change. -*Pastor Rick Warren*

The absurd man is he who never changes. -*Auguste Barthelemy*

Wood may remain ten years in the water, but it will never become a crocodile. -*Congolese Proverb*

Character

Character is tested by the true sentiments more than conduct. A man is seldom better than his word. -*Lord Acton*

Character cannot be developed in ease and quiet. Only through experience of trial and suffering can the soul be strengthened, vision cleared, ambition inspired, and success achieved. -*Helen Keller*

When wealth is lost, nothing is lost; When health is lost, something is lost; When character is lost, all is lost! -*German Proverb*

Charm

The quality in others of making us more satisfied with ourselves. -*Henri F. Amiel*

Choice

Research indicated that the explosion of choice plays an important role. It seems that as we become freer to pursue and do whatever we want, we get less and less happy. Settle for a choice that is "good enough" rather than searching for the elusive "best." Limit how much you think about the choices or options you reject. -*Barry Schwartz*

We who lived in the concentration camps can remember the men who walked through the huts comforting others, giving away their last piece of bread. They have been few in number, but they offer sufficient proof that everything can be taken from a man but one thing: The last of his freedoms-to choose one's attitude in any given set of circumstances, to choose one's own way. -*Dr. Viktor E. Frankl*

Class

Class is real. You can't fake it. Class never tries to build itself up by tearing others down. Class is already up and need not attempt to look better by making others look worse. Everyone is comfortable with the person who has class because he is comfortable with himself. *-Ann Landers*

Committee

A committee is a group that keeps the minutes and loses the hours. *-Milton Berle*

Common Sense

Common sense tells us nothing is free. *-Cheryl Ehlers*

There is nothing more uncommon than common sense. *Frank Lloyd Wright*

Community

No man is an island, entire of itself; every man is a piece of the continent. *-John Donne*

Competition

He may well win the race that runs by himself. *-Benjamin Franklin*

Compliment

To say a compliment well is a high art and few posses it. *-Mark Twain*

Composure

He is a first rate collector who can, upon all occasions, collect his wits. *-George Dennison Prentice*

Compromise

Such an adjustment of conflicting interests as gives each adversary the satisfaction of thinking he has got what he ought not have, and is deprived of nothing except what was justly his due. *-Ambrose Bierce*

Conclusion

At some point, failure to reach a conclusion is a conclusion.

Conduct

Act the way you want to be and soon you will be the way you act. *-Dr. Johnnie Coleman*

Concealment

Talking about oneself can also be a means to conceal oneself. *-Nietzsche*

Conscience

Conscience is the compass of the soul. *-John Hagee, Pastor*

Consequences

All systems of morality are based on the idea that an action has consequences that legitimize or cancel it. *-Albert Camus*

The sower may mistake and sow his peas crookedly; the peas make no mistake, but come up and show his line. *-Emerson*

The influence of sin touches the innocent as well as the guilty. *-Billy Graham*

Console

In order to console, there is no need to say much. It is enough to listen, to understand, to love. *-Paul Tournier*

Conversation

A gossip is one who talks to you about others; a bore is one who talks to you about himself; a brilliant conversationalist is one who talks to you about yourself. *-Lisa Kirk, Journal-American*

Say only those things about people that you would say if they were present. -*Editor*

Courage

Courage mounteth with occasion. *-Shakespeare*

Coward

Perfect courage and utter cowardice are two extremes which rarely occur. -*La Rochefoucauld*

Creativity

The secret of creativity is knowing how to hide your sources. *-Albert Einstein*

Credulity

Our credulity is greatest concerning the things we know least about. Since we know least about ourselves, we are ready to believe all that is said about us. Hence the mysterious power of flattery and calumny. *-Eric Hoffer*

Critic

A critic is someone who is quick on the flaw.

It's not the critic who counts; not the man who points out how the strong man stumbles, or where the doer of deeds could have done better. The credit belongs to the man who is actually in the arena...who, at best, knows in the end the triumph of great achievement, and who, at worst, if he fails, at least fails while daring greatly. So that his place will never be with those cold timid souls who know neither victory nor defeat. -*Theodore Roosevelt*

Criticism

Honest criticism is hard to take, particularly from a relative, a friend, an acquaintance, or a stranger.

If it's very painful for you to criticize your friends, you're safe in doing it. But if you take the slightest pleasure in it, that's the time to hold your tongue. -*Alice Duer Miller*

If someone criticizes you, see if there is any truth to what they are saying; if so, make changes. If there is no truth to the criticism, ignore it and live so that no one will believe the negative remark.

Cruelty

A cruel story runs on wheels, and every hand oils the wheels as they run. -*Ouida*

Deadly Sins

According to a BBC poll, Brits believe that sloth, gluttony, envy, anger, pride, and lust should no longer be black marks on a person's soul. Only greed remains from the original Seven Deadly Sins, described by Thomas Aquinas (1225-74). The Brits rank cruelty, adultery, selfishness, bigotry, dishonesty, and hypocrisy as the other worst "sins." -*Lyric Wallwork Winik*

Death

Death is the destiny of every man; the living should take this to heart. -*Ecclesiastes 7:2*

Debt

People spend up to a third more when paying with credit instead of cash. -*Joan W. Lawrence, Ohio Department of Aging Director*

Decline

Statesman and beauties are very rarely sensible of the gradations of their decay. -*Lord Chesterfield*

Deed

An evil deed, like freshly drawn milk, does not turn sour at once. -*Dhammapada*

Deliberation

That done with deliberation is done quickly enough, and better: what is made in haste is unmade soon. -*Baltasar Grecian*

Doctor

There is no better surgeon than one with many scars. -*Spanish Proverb*

Dress

A man becomes the creature of his uniform. -*Napoleon*

Know first who you are; and then adorn yourself accordingly. -*Epictetus*

A man cannot dress, but his ideas get clothes at the same time. -*Laurence Sterne*

Nobody dresses for himself; everyone dresses to impress someone other than himself. -*Clothing Store Manager*

Earth

The Earth is given as a common stock for man to labor and live on. -*Thomas Jefferson*

The Earth is like the breast of a woman: useful as well as pleasing. -*Nietzsche*

Emotions

There are seven major negative emotions to be avoided: fear, jealously, hatred, revenge, greed, superstition, and anger. -*Napoleon Hill*

There are seen major positive emotions: desire, faith, love, sex, enthusiasm, romance, and hope. -*Napoleon Hill*

Endurance

There is an old saying that what can't be cured must be endured, and perhaps we are wise if we learn to accept the inevitable with good grace.

Envy

For where you have envy and selfish ambition, there you find disorder and every evil practice. -*James 3:16*

Equality

Equality is a futile pursuit: equality of opportunity is a noble one. -*Iain Macleod*

Men their rights and nothing more; women their rights and nothing less. -*Susan B. Anthony*

Error

It is one thing to show a man that he is in an error, and another to put him in possession of the truth. -*John Locke*

Evil

All that is necessary for evil to triumph is for good people to do nothing. -*Edmund Burke*

Excitement

There is a pleasure in being in a ship beaten by a storm, when we are sure that it will not flounder. -*Pascal*

Expectations

Most of us are carrying far too many expectations. Let go of those created by society's demands. -*Dr. Brothers*

Experience

Nothing ever becomes real till it is experienced- even a proverb is no proverb to you till your life has illustrated it. -*John Keats*

Experience is a good teacher, but she send in terrific bills. -*Menna Antrim*

Falsehood

A liar should have a good memory. -*Quintilian, 95 AD*
One falsehood spoils a thousand truths. -*Ashanti Proverb*

A single lie destroys a whole reputation for integrity. -*Baltasar Grecian*

I do myself a greater injury in lying than I do him of whom I tell a lie. -*Montaigne*

People lie because they can't help making a better story than it was the way it happened. -*Carl Sandburg*

Repetition does not transform a lie into the truth. -*Franklin D. Roosevelt*

To tell a falsehood is like the cut of a saber: for though the wound may heal, the scar of it will remain. -*SA'DI*

Failure

A failure is a man who has blundered but is not able to cash in on the experience. -*Elbert Hubbard*

Fame/Corruption

Madame Curie was the only person I knew who was not corrupted by fame. -*Albert Einstein*

Fault

There are few things more painful than to recognize one's own faults in others. -*John Wells*

Fear

There are six basic fears: poverty, criticism, ill health, loss of love of someone, old age, and death. -*Napoleon Hill*

Feelings

Negative feelings "stuffed" alive never die. -*Joyce Meyer*

Fellowship

We desire a place where we are able to share our true feelings (authenticity); differences are respected (courtesy); we are encouraged to grow spiritually (mutuality); we spend time with people, getting to know them (hospitality); and we are supported in our purpose and are accepted, despite our weaknesses (unity). -*Pastor Rick Warren*

Fight/Size

What counts is not necessarily the size of the dog in the fight- it's the size of the fight in the dog. -*Dwight David Eisenhower*

Forgiveness

Forgive others because they don't deserve the power to turn you into a bitter, angry person. You're not hurting them by holding on to that resentment, but you're hurting yourself. *-Rabbi Harold Kushner*

The harder it is for you to forgive, the further you are from true love.

Forgiveness is essential, or you will stumble, and in many ways will stray from the course chosen for you. *-Rick Joyner*

Forgiving is never easy. There is a clear distinction between forgiveness and approval of the wrong that has been done. Forgiving does not mean caving in; it means ceasing to be a victim. *-Edward M. Hallowell, MD*

Only the brave know how to forgive. A coward never forgives. It is not in his nature. *-Robert Muller*

When you refuse to forgive, you have turned control of your emotional life over to the very person who has hurt you. Only by forgiving can you sever your emotional and psychological ties to the offending party, so they lose the power to hurt you. *-Hamilton Beazley, Author*

Freedom

A man's worst difficulties begin when he is able to do as he likes. *-Thomas Henry Huxley*

But what is freedom? Rightly understood, a universal license to be good. *-Hartley Coleridge*

Freedom without moral commitment is aimless and promptly self-destructive. *-John W. Gardner*

French Wit

Translations are like women: if true, rarely beautiful, and if beautiful, rarely true. *-Martin Fischer, Translator of Baltasar Grecian's works, 1601-58*

Friend

A friend is a person with whom I may be sincere. Before him I may think aloud. -*Emerson, 1841*

Confidence is the only bond of friendship. -*Publilius Syrus, 100 BC*

Real friends are those who when you've made a fool of yourself, don't feel you've done a permanent job.

Generalization

All generalizations are dangerous, even this one. -*Alexandre Dumas*

Generations

In a brief space, the generations of living beings are changed and like runners pass on the torches of life. -*Lucretius, 100 BC*

We think our fathers fools, so wise we grow; our wiser sons, no doubt, will think us so. -*Alexander Pope*

Genius

We wish genius and morality were affectionate companions, but it is a fact that they are often bitter enemies. They don't necessarily coalesce any more than oil and water do. -*Artemus Ward*

To do easily what is difficult for others is the mark of talent. To do what is impossible for talent is the mark of genius. -*Frederic Amiel*

Gentleman

A gentleman is one who thinks more of other people's feelings than of his own rights; and more of other people's rights than of his own feelings. -*Matthew Henry Buckham*

German

You can always tell a German but you can't tell them much. -*Bumper Sticker*

Gift

A man whose leg has been cut off does not value a present of shoes. -*Chuang Tzu, 400 BC*

I think the greatest gift you can give someone is an honest receiving of what that person has to offer. -*Fred Rogers*

The excellence of a gift lies in its appropriateness rather in its value. -*Charles Dudley Warner*

Glory

Glory is fleeting but obscurity is forever. -*Napoleon Bonaparte*

The nearest way to glory- a short cut, as it were- is to strive to be what you wish to be thought to be. -*Socrates, 400 BC*

Goal

Before you can score, you must first have a goal. -*Greek Proverb*

God

May the Father of all mercies scatter light, and not darkness, upon our paths, and make us all in our several vocations useful here, and in His own due time and way, everlastingly happy. -*George Washington*

Possessing God's power enables us to face life with enthusiasm; it gives us a deep inward peace because we are not afraid of tomorrow. There comes into our lives an inner joy that outward circumstances cannot reach. Because God is within us, and because God is love, there flows out from us a love for others that sweeps away all prejudice, jealousy, and hate. -*Charles L. Allen*

Golf

Playing golf is like chasing a quinine pill around a cow pasture. *-Winston Churchill*

In golf, as in life, thou shalt always follow through.

The most important shot in golf [as in life] is the next one, the one you can do something about. *-Michael K McIntyre, Plain dealer columnist*

Good/Evil

A wise man should do good: that is the only treasure that will not leave him. *-Buddha*

We cannot freely and wisely choose the right way for ourselves unless we know both good and evil. *-Helen Keller*

Conquer a man who never gives by gifts; subdue untruthful men by truthfulness; vanquish an angry man by gentleness, and overcome an evil man by goodness. *-Indian Proverb*

As I know more of mankind I expect less of them and am ready now to call a man a good man upon easier terms than I was formerly. *-Samuel Johnson*

Gossip

Bad news travels fast, but gossip always gets there first. *-Dan Childress*

He's my friend that speaks well of me behind my back. *-Thomas Fuller, 1640*

Whoever gossips to you will gossip about you. *-Spanish Proverb*

Grateful

Those who have the least are often the most grateful and therefore the most generous. *-Pastor Kelly Peters*

Gravity

It increases our weight, diminishes our height, lengthens our lives. It prevents us from whirling off the surface of a globe which spins, at the equator, at 1,000 miles an hour. It holds air to the earth, enabling us to breathe. It draws rain from the clouds, then pulls the water down through streams, lakes, and rivers to the ocean in a never-ending cycle on which all living things depend. Yet it can also cause death and destruction, bringing airplanes crashing to earth, toppling building during earthquakes. There is no other force in the universe remotely like the fantastic force of gravity. -*Ronald Schiller*

Greatness

No man is so tall that he need never stretch and none so small that he need never stoop. -*Danish Proverb*

Greed

Greed drives us to want more money than we need and the urge to get it by taking it from others. -*David Denby*

Grief

Grief can't be shared. Everyone carries it alone, his own burden, his own way. -*Anne Morrow Lindbergh*

Grief can take care of itself, but to get the full value of joy you must have somebody to divide it with. -*Mark Twain*

Grow

People grow from their weaknesses, not their strengths.

Guilt

Unconfessed guilt squeezes out spiritual power that can rid emotional, mental, and physical anguish- the consequences of sin. *-Editor*

Habit

I am what I am today because of the choices I mad yesterday. Habits are like cable. We weave strand of it everyday and soon it cannot be broken. *-Horace Mann*

The chains of habit are generally too small to be felt till they are too strong to be broken. *-Samuel Johnson*

Happiness

If you are happy, you can always learn to dance. *-Balinese Saying*

Happiness is like perfume; you can't give it away without getting a little on yourself.

Most people are as happy as they make up their minds to be. *-Lincoln*

It is the chiefest point of happiness that a man is willing to be what he is. *-Desiderius Erasmus*

No matter how dull, or how mean, or how wise a man is, he feels that happiness is his indisputable right. *-Helen Keller*

The greatest part of our happiness or misery depends on our dispositions and not on our circumstances. *-Martha Washington*

They say that money doesn't bring happiness, but it's nice to be able to find out for yourself.

Your happiness is your own responsibility.

What can be added to the happiness of a man who is in health, out of debt, and has a clear conscience? *-Adam Smith (1723-90)*

It's hard to be happy and miserable at the same time.

Happy

Just think how happy you would be if you lost everything you have right no—and then got it back again.

Hate

Hate is such an ugly emotion that it degrades the hater; hatred causes destruction; love causes construction. -*Marilyn Vos Savant*

Hate is like acid. It can damage the vessel in which it is stored as well as destroy the object on which it is poured. -*Ann Landers*

Help

Before you can find help in this world, you have to develop qualities that are respected by good people. -*Bill O'Reilly*

Honesty

Honesty doesn't come from out of nowhere. It is a product of your moral convictions. -*Dave Thomas*

No legacy is so rich as honesty. -*William Shakespeare*

Human Nature

In 20 years as a radio talk show host, I have dialogued with thousands of people, of both sexes and from virtually every religious, ethnic, and national background. Very early on, I realized that perhaps the major reason for political and other disagreements I had with callers was that they believed people are basically good, and I did not. I believe that we are born with tendencies toward both good end evil. Yes, babies are born innocent, but not good. -*Dennis Prager*

It is a common vice of human nature that everyone would rather hear evil than good about his neighbor.

Our real danger is our sentimental belief that human nature is naturally good. If human nature is good, we don't need either the wisdom of the Constitution or the Grace of God. -*Ricard S. Emrich*

Humility

Humility is to make a right estimate of one's self. -*Charles Haddon Spurgeon*

Humility means being modest rather than showy. Humble people are admired and respected by all. People want to be around them. They aren't braggers. They're quick to listen and slow to speak. They live their lives according to God's will rather than their won. -*Editor*

Humor

I once had a rose named after me, and I was very flattered. But I was not pleased to read the description in the catalogue: "No good in bed, but fine up against a wall." -*Eleanor Roosevelt*

You can observe a lot just by watching. -*Yogi Berra*

Humor is the great thing, the saving thing. The minute it crops up, all our irritations and resentments slip away, and a sunny spirit takes their place.

Short skirts have a tendency to make men polite. Have you ever seen a man get on a bus ahead of one? -*Mel Ferrer*

It ain't over till it's over. -*Yogi Berra*

You can fly but the cocoon has to go.

Hypocrisy

All are not saints that go to church. -*Proverb*

Ideas

A new idea is delicate. It can be killed by a sneer or a yawn; it can be stabbed to death by a quip and worried to death by a frown on the right man's brow. -*Charles Brower*

The thinker dies, but his thoughts are beyond the reach of destruction. Men are mortal, but ideas are immortal. -*Walter Lippmann*

Identity

Rain beats a leopard's skin, but it does not wash the spots. -*Ashanti Proverb*

We often think that what we say is who we really are, but we've got to understand that what we think on the inside is who we really are. -*Gail Ramsey*

If

If you believe people are born good, you will not stress character development when you raise children. If you believe people are born good, you will attribute evil to forces outside the individual. If you believe that people are basically good, God and religion are morally unnecessary, even harmful. Why would basically good people need a God or religion to provide moral standards? If you believe people are basically good, you, of course, believe that you are good- and therefore those who disagree with you must be bad, not merely wrong. -*Dennis Prager, Radio Talk Show Host*

Ignorance

Nothing is so good for an ignorant man as silence, and if he knew this he would no longer be ignorant. –*Sa'di, 1200*

Imagination

His imagination resembles the wings of an ostrich. It enables him to run, though not to soar. -*Lord Macaulay*

Individuality

Anybody who is any good is different from anybody else. *-Felix Furter Frank, Supreme Court Justice*

Men are born equal but they are also born different. *-Eric Fromm*

It is a common wonder of all men, how among so many millions of faces, there should be none alike. *-Thomas Browne*

A whole bushel of wheat is made up of single grains. *-Thomas Fuller, MD, 1640*

Ingratitude

A man is very apt to complain of the ingratitude of those who have risen far above him. *-Samuel Johnson*

Eaten bread is forgotten. *-Thomas Fuller, MD, 1640*

Inheritance

When it comes to divide an estate, the most polite men quarrel. *-Emerson, 1863*

Injustice

A poor man's field may produce abundant food, but injustice sweeps it away. *-Proverbs 13:23*

I feel as a horse must feel when the beautiful cup is given to the jockey. *-Edgar Degas*

Insincerity

A false friend and a shadow attend only while the sun shines. *-Benjamin Franklin*

Integrity

He has honor if he holds himself to an ideal of conduct though it is inconvenient, unprofitable, or dangerous to do so. -*Walter Lippmann*

Internet

The Internet is like a herd of performing elephants with diarrhea: massive, difficult to redirect, awe-inspiring; entertaining and a source of a mind-boggling amount of excrement when you least expect it. -*Gene Spofford*

Introspection

If we would use the power that God gives us to see ourselves as others see us, it would from many a blunder and foolish notion free us. -*Robert Burns*

Inventors

Inventors and men of genius have always been regarded as fools at the beginning (and very often at the end) of their careers. -*Dostoevsky*

Irrevocable

You can't unscramble eggs. -*American Proverb*

Isms

There are many isms today to perplex us, Nazism, Communism, Fascism, and so forth, but most of them will cancel each other out. There is only one ism which kills the soul, and that is Pessimism. -*Lord John Buchan Tweedsmuir*

Jealous

A jealous person is doubly unhappy over what he has, which is judged inferior, and over what he has not, which is judged superior. Such a person is doubly removed from knowing the true blessings of creation. -*Desmond Tutu*

Junk Food

The trouble with believers today is not that we do not take in good spiritual food; most of us do that. The problem is all of the junk that we take in (with our eyes and ears) along with the "good food." If physically I ate ninety percent bad food, and only ten percent good food, I would not have a healthy body. Likewise, in a given day, if I were to take in fifteen minutes of good, solid spiritual food and three hours of spiritual junk good, I would not wind up healthy on the spiritual level. -*Dr. James McKeever*

Joke

Know how to take them, but do not play them; let him who is piqued show no irritation toward him who piqued him. -*Baltasar Grecian*

Judging

We were called to be witnesses, not lawyers or judges.

Justice

Everyone loves justice in the affairs of another. -*Italian Proverb*

It is better to risk saving a guilty man than to condemn an innocent one. -*Voltaire*

It is impossible to be just if one is not generous. -*Joseph Roux*

Justice is always violent to the party offending, for every man is innocent in his own eyes. -*Daniel Defore*

Kindred

Everyone smiles in the same language.

Fish and visitors stink in three days. -*Benjamin Franklin*

Kindness

A kind word or smile can totally change your day. -*JoAnne Nimberger*

Ask any decent person what he thinks matters most in human conduct: five to one his answer will be "kindness." -*Lord Kenneth Clark*

An act of kindness benefits the person receiving it, the person performing it, and the person observing it. -*Editor*

No act of kindness, no matter how small, is ever wasted.

Knowing

The great trick in cards lies in knowing what to discard; the deuce of a suit that is trump is more valuable than the ace of a suit that was played. -*Baltasar Grecian*

Few sometimes may know when thousands err. -*Milton, 1667*

Knowledge/Wisdom

Knowledge comes by taking things apart. But wisdom comes by putting things together. -*John A. Morrison*

Knows

He that knows not and knows not that he knows not is a fool: shun him. He that knows not and knows that he knows not is a child: teach him. He that knows and knows not that he knows is asleep: wake him. He that knows and knows that he knows is a wise man: follow him. -*Arabic Proverb*

Laughter

The most completely lost of all days is that on which one has not laughed. -*Chamfort*

Law

Fifteen million laws have been passed to try to enforce the Golden Rule and the Ten Commandments.

Lawyers

Lawyers and painters can soon change white to black. *-Danish Proverb*

Wrong must not win by technicalities. *-Aeschylus, 458 BC*

Legacy

Leave a legacy; leave the world a better place. *-Editor*

Whatever else history may say about me when I'm gone, I hope it will record that I appealed to your best hopes, not your worst fears; to your confidence rather than your doubts. My dream is that you will travel the road ahead with liberty's lamp guiding your steps and opportunity's arm steadying your way. *-President Reagan*

Leadership

All good leaders have the gift of vision. First they imagine it, then they make it happen. *-Pastor Kelly Peters*

If you command wisely, you'll be obeyed cheerfully. *-Thomas Fuller, MD, 1640*

Leadership is a potent combination of strategy and character. But if you must be without one, be without the strategy. *-General H. Norman Schwarzkopf*

Humility rather than self-esteem is the key trait of successful leaders. *-Robert Hogan, Harvard Business Review*

Liar

The liar's punishment is not in the least that he is not believed but that he cannot believe anyone else. -*George Bernard Shaw*

Lie

A single lie destroys a whole reputation of integrity. -*Baltasar Grecian*

He who permits himself to tell a lie once, finds it much easier to do it a second and third time, till at length it becomes habitual; he tells lies without attending to it, and truth without the world's believing him. This falsehood of the tongue leads to that of the heart, and in time depraves all its good dispositions. -*Thomas Jefferson*

Nearly everyone will lie to you given the right circumstances. -*Bill Clinton*

Whoever has even once become notorious by base fraud, even if he speaks the truth, gains no belief. -*Phaedrus*

Limits

A bird can roost but on one branch. A mouse can drink no more than its fill from a river. -*Chinese Proverb*

Listening/Speaking

Everyone must be quick to listen, slow to speak, and slow to become angry. -*James 1:19*

From listening comes wisdom and speaking, repentance. -*Italian Proverb*

Love

Caring is the rock that love is built upon. -*Dave Thomas*

If you have love in your life, it can make up for a great many things you lack. If you don't have it, no matter what else there is, it's not enough. *-Sir James M. Barrie*

Love, not time, heals all wounds. *-Andy Rooney*

Love is patient, love is kind. It does not envy, it does not boast, it is not proud. It is not rude, it is not self-seeking, it is not easily angered, and it keeps no record of wrongs. Love does not delight in evil but rejoices with the truth. It always protects, always trusts, always hopes, and always perseveres. *-1 Corinthians 13:4-7*

Love is a fabric which never fades, no matter how often it is washed in the water of adversity and grief.

Love is the will to extend one's self for the purpose of nurturing one's own or another's spiritual growth. *-M. Scott Peck, MD and Author*

Many waters cannot quench love, rivers cannot wash it away. *-Song of Solomon 8:7*

Love cannot be learned in insulation. You have to be around people-irritating, imperfect, frustrating people. *-Pastor Rick Warren*

Love is the highest virtue. *-Martin Luther*

The root of the matter, if we want a stable world, is a very simple and old-fashioned thing, a thing so simple that I am almost ashamed to mention it for fear of the derisive smile with which the wise cynics will greet my words. The thing I mean is love, Christian love, or compassion. If you feel this, you have a motive for existence, a reason for courage, an imperative necessity for intellectual honesty. *-Bertrand Russell*

Loss

When you've experienced the loss through death of a spouse, child, or parent, it hurts terribly. And when people don't want to use their names or refer to the death, it's like losing that person all over again.

Loyalty

You cannot run with the hare and hunt with the hounds. *-Proverb*

Luxury

Luxury either comes of riches or makes them necessary; it corrupts at once, rich and poor, the rich by possession and the poor by covetousness. *-Rousseau*

Mad

"Mad" is a term we use to describe a man who is obsessed with one idea and nothing else. *-Ugo Betti*

Madman

The madman thinks the rest of the world crazy. *-Publilius, 100 BC*

Main

The main thing is to keep the main thing the main thing. *-Stephen R. Covey*

Man

Man is what he believes. *-Anton Chekhov*

Maturity

A mature person is one who does not think only in absolutes, who is able to be objective even when deeply stirred emotionally, who has learned that there is both good and bad in all people and in all things, and who walks humbly and deals charitably with the circumstances of life, knowing that in this world no one is all-knowing and therefore all of us need both love and charity. *-Eleanor Roosevelt*

I believe that the sign of maturity is accepting deferred gratification. *-Peggy Cahn*

Maturity is the capacity to endure uncertainty. *-John Finley*

Mass Media

Some television programs are so much chewing gum for the eyes. *-John Mason Brown*

When distant and unfamiliar and complex things are communicated to great masses of people, the truth suffers a considerable and often a radical distortion. The complex is made over into the simple, the hypothetical into the dogmatic, and the relative into an absolute. *-Walter Lippmann, 1955*

Measure

If there be any truer measure of a man than by what he does, it must be by what he gives. *-Robert South*

Meanness/Kindness

Choosing to react to someone's meanness with kindness helps the person extending the kindness most and may make the world a better place.

Medicine

If the Christian Scientists had some science an' th' doctors more Christianity, it wudden't make anny diff'rence which ye called in- if ye had a good nurse. *-Finley Peter Dunne*

Memory

The secret of memory is attention. If your attention is not in the right place when something goes by that you want to remember, you will not remember it no matter how good your memory is.

Men/Women

Most women have all other women as adversaries; most men have all other men as their allies. -*Gellett Burgess*

There was, I think, never any reason to believe in any innate superiority of the male, except his superior muscle. -*Bertrand Russell*

Mind

The human mind treats a new idea the way the body treats a strange protein; it rejects it. -*P.B. Medawar*

Mirror

The best mirror is an old friend. -*German Proverb*

The mirror usually reflects only the way others see us, the way we are expected to behave, forced to behave, hardly ever what we really are. -*Luigi Pirandello*

Moment

Love the moment and the energy of that moment will spread beyond all boundaries. -*Corita Kent*

Living in the moment reduces stress and helps us appreciate life more. -*David Spero, RN*

Money

If you have even a little money in the bank, spending money in your wallet or purse, and some spare change in a piggy bank or jar somewhere, you are wealthier than 92% of all people on earth. -*Dr. Philip M. Harter, Standord School of Medicine*

Money is like manure. If you spread it around, it does a lot of good. But if you pile it up in one place, it stinks like hell. -*Clint Murchison, Jr.*

Money cannot buy nor guarantee happiness; proof, ask some of those who have it. -*Editor*

Money often costs too much. -*Ralph Waldo Emerson*

When a feller says it ain't the money but the principle of the thing, it's the money. -*Abe Martin*

Mood

When you're in a good mood, bring up the past. When you're in a bad mood, stick to the present. And when you're not feeling emotional at all, it's time to talk about the future. -*Marilyn Vos Savant*

Morality

How is it that nobody has dreamed up any moral advances since Christ's teaching? -*Michael Green*

Morality is not taught, but caught, from the prevailing moral culture. -*Daniel Griswold, The Cato Institute*

The only immorality is to not do what one has to do when one has to do it. -*Jean Anouilh*

Whenever you are to do a thing, though it can never be known but to yourself, ask yourself how you would act were all the world looking at you, and act accordingly. -*Thomas Jefferson*

We have two kinds of morality side by side: one which we preach but do not practice, and another which we practice but seldom preach. -*Bertrand Russell*

Morals

Pope John Paul II accuses the media of poisoning morals, saying they often give a positive depiction of extramarital sex, contraception, abortion, and homosexuality that is harmful to society. He urges the media to promote traditional family life. 'All communication has a moral dimension. People grow or diminish in moral stature by the words which they speak and the messages which they choose to hear.' -*Associated Press*

Motives

We should often feel ashamed of our best actions if the world could see all of the motives which produced them. -*La Rochefoucauld*

Motivation

Too many of us are like wheelbarrows: useful only when pushed and too easily upset.

Movies/Education

There is only one thing that can kill the movies, and that is education. -*Will Rogers*

Mystery

I would rather live in a world where my life is surrounded by mystery than live in a world so small that my mind could comprehend it. -*Reverend Harry Emerson Fosdick*

Name

Honor and a good name are easily taken away, but not easily restored. -*Martin Luther*

Nature/Habit

Men's natures are alike; it is their habits that carry them apart. —*Confucius, 500 BC*

Narrow

It is with narrow-souled people as with narrow-necked bottles: the less they have in them, the more noise they make in pouring it out. *-Alexander Pope*

Minds that have nothing to confer find little to perceive. *-William Wordsworth*

Necessity

It is a hard nurse, but she raises strong children.

New

That which is true is not new, and that which is new is not true. *-Dr. Vernon McGee, Pastor*

News

What's one man's news is another man's troubles. *-Finley Peter Dunne*

New Morality

The new-morality concept of letting your feelings be your guide would be workable if human beings were merely animals, if they had no conscience or soul. But man is more than an animal and he debases himself when he lives on animalistic levels. *-Mary Jane Chambers*

Newspaper

Journalism is popular, but it is popular mainly as fiction. Life in one world and life seen in the newspaper is another. *-G.K. Chesterton, 1908*

The first duty of a newspaper is to be accurate. If accurate, it follows that it's fair. *-Herbert Bayard Swope, 1958*

None

None knows the weight of another's burdens. -*Thomas Fuller, MD, 1732*

Obedience

Learn to obey before you command. -*Solon, 700 BC*

Obedience is the only virtue that plants the other virtues in the heart and preserves them after they have been planted. -*Gregory the Great*

Obscurity

He is happiest of whom the world says least, good or bad. -*Thomas Jefferson, 1786*

It is better to be looked over than overlooked. -*Mae West, 1934*

Not a day passes over the earth, but men and women of no note do great deeds, speak great words, and suffer noble sorrows. -*Charles Reade, 1861*

Obstacles

Obstacles in the pathway of the weak become stepping stones in the pathway of the strong. -*Thomas Carlyle*

Occupied

Those who are much occupied with the care of the body usually give little care to the soul. -*Proverb*

Opposition

One fifth of the people are against everything all the time. -*Robert Kennedy*

Opportunity

Never miss an opportunity to make someone happy.

Pacifist

One ought not to return injustice, nor do evil to anybody in the world, no matter what one may have suffered from them. -*Socrates, 400 BC*

Pain

How much pain has cost us the evils which have never happened. -*Thomas Jefferson*

Patience

All commend patience, but none can endure to suffer. -*Thomas Fuller, MD, 1732*

Patience not only gets us through the circumstances of life, but transforms our lives and the lives of those around us. -*Marshall Beale*

Patience is a bitter plant but it has sweet fruit. -*German Proverb*

Whoever has no patience has no wisdom. –*Sa-di, 1200*

Peace

In this imperfect life…peace doesn't mean having no enemies. It means being ready to put up with ill-treatment. -*Thomas A. Kempis*
Just as procrastination is the thief of time, fear is the thief of peace.

Peace in your own soul first of all, then you can think about making peace with other people. -*Thomas A. Kempis*

Peace is not an absence of war; it is a virtue, a state of mind, a disposition for benevolence, confidence, justice. -*Benedict Spinoza*

People

People can be divided into three groups: Those who make things happen, those who watch things happen, and those who wonder what's happening.

The more we know about people who are different than we are, the less frightened we are of one another. -*Pastor Kelly Peters*

There are two kinds of people, the takers and the givers. The takers sometimes eat better, but the givers always sleep better. -*Danny Thomas, St. Jude Children's Research Hospital*

Perfection

The closest to perfection a person ever comes is when he fills out a job application form. -*Stanley J. Randall*

Could everything be done twice everything would be done better. -*German Proverb*

The farther a man knows himself to be from perfection, the nearer he is to it! -*Gerald Groote*

Performance

An acre of performance is worth a whole world of promise. -*Howell*

Permissible

Everything is permissible for me, but not everything is beneficial. -*St. Paul*

Perseverance

Perseverance is more prevailing than violence; and many things which cannot be overcome when they are together, yield themselves up when taken little by little. -*Plutarch, 100 AD*

Nothing of great value on life comes easily. -*Norman Vincent Peale*

There are only two creatures that can surmount the pyramids: the eagle and the snail. *-Eastern Proverb*

Trying times are no time to quit trying.

Persist

That which we persist in doing becomes easier, not that the nature of the task has changed, but our ability to do it has increased. *-Ralph Waldo Emerson*

Pettiness

Small minds are much distressed by little things. Great minds see them all but are not upset by them. *-La Rochefoucauld, 1665*

Pity

No man limps because another is hurt. *-Danish Proverb*

We all have enough strength to hear the misfortunes of others. *-La Rochefoucauld, 1665*

Plans

If you fail to plan, you plan to fail.

He who every morning plans the transactions of the day, and follows that plan, carries a thread that will guide him though the labyrinth of the most busy life. The orderly arrangement of his time is like a ray of light which darts itself through all his occupations. But where no plan is laid, where the disposal of time is surrendered merely to chance of incidents, all things lie huddled together in one chaos. *-Victor Hugo*

Pleasantness

Language specialists claim that the five sweetest phrases in English are: 'I love you,' 'Dinner is served,' 'All is forgiven,' 'Sleep until noon,' and 'Keep the change.' There are those who choose to add: 'You've lost weight.' -*L.M. Boyd*

Pleasure

Enjoying things which are pleasant, that is not evil; it is the reducing of our moral self to slavery by them that is. -*Thomas Carlyle, 1841*

Polish

Without cultivation every man is a clown and needs, no matter what his attributes, polish. -*Baltasar Grecian, 1600*

Popularity

A dish around which I see too many people doesn't tempt me. -*Julien Green, 1938*

Poverty

The poor man is not one who has little, but one who hankers after more. -*Seneca, 100 AD*

Power

Nearly all men can stand adversity, but if you want to test a man's character, give him power. -*Abraham Lincoln*

The measure of a man is what he does with power. -*Pittacus, 650*

Power intoxicates men. When a man is intoxicated by alcohol, he can recover, but when intoxicated by power, he seldom recovers. -*James F. Byrnes*

Praise

If my life is fruitless, it doesn't matter who praises me, and if my life is fruitful, it doesn't matter who criticizes me. -*John Bunyan*

Praise/Criticism

The trouble with most of us is that we would rather be ruined by praise than saved by criticism. -*Norman Vincent Peale*

Preachers

There are many preachers who don't hear themselves. -*German Proverb*

Pretense

Nothing is lasting that is feigned. -*English Proverb*

Pride

Pride leads to every other vice; it is the complete anti-God state of mind. -*C.S. Lewis*

Pride is the only disease known to man that makes everyone sick except the one who has it.

Pride is over-estimation of oneself by reason of self-love. -*Spinoza, 1677*

Pride is the mask of one's own faults. -*Hebrew Proverb*

Pride is tasteless, colorless, and sizeless; yet, it is the hardest thing to swallow. -*August B. Black*

Priorities

I am not bound to win, but I am bound to be true. I am not bound to succeed, but I am bound to live up to what light I have. I must stand with anybody that stands right; stand with him while he is right and part with him when he goes wrong. *-Abraham Lincoln*

Things which matter most must never be at the mercy of things which matter least. *-Goethe*

Prison

Prison will not work until we start sending a better class of people there. *-Laurence J. Peters*

Wherever anyone is against his will, that is to him a prison. *-Epictetus, 200 AD*

Problems

What concerns everyone can only be resolved by everyone. *-Friedrich Durrenmatt*

Profundity

Light boats sail swift, though greater hulks draw deep. *-Shakespeare, 1601*

Prophets

In Biblical days prophets were astir while the world was asleep; today the world is astir while church and synagogue are busy with trivialities. *-Abraham Joshua Heschel*

A prophet is not without honor except in his own country and in his own house. *-Matthew 13:57*

Prosperity/Adversity

Prosperity is a great teacher; adversity is greater. *-William Hazlitt, 1839*

Punishment

He only may chastise who loves. -*Rabindranath Tagore, "The Judge"*

Qualities

The qualities I most admire: a positive attitude, good work ethic, and honesty. -*Scott Cowan*

Rank

There may be as much nobility in being last as in being first, because the two positions are equally necessary in the world, the one to complement the other. -*Jose Ortega Y Gasset, 1914*

Reason

Reason deserves to be called a prophet; for in showing us the consequences and effects of our actions in the present, does it not tell us what the future will be. -*Schopenhauer, 1851*

'Tis in vain to speak reason where 'twill not be heard. -*Thomas Fuller, 1732*

Reality

There is no reality except the one contained within us. That is why so many people live such an unreal life. They take the images outside them for reality and never allow the world within to assert itself. -*Herman Mann*

Recompense

Recompense injury with justice, and recompense kindness with kindness. -*Confucius, 500 BC*

Refusal

Know how to refuse. Since you cannot accede to everything or to everybody, it becomes important to know how not to accede...Employ courtliness to fill the void of the denial, and let pleasing words disguise the failure of action. Yes and No are quickly spoken, but they demand long consideration. *-Baltasar Grecian*

Relationship

Good relationships have trust, respect, intimacy, passion, and commitment from both parties. *-David Coleman, Dating Doctor*

Relativity

In the eyes of the blind, the one eyed man is king. *-Michael Apostolius, 1500*

When a man sits with a pretty girl for an hour, it seems like a minute. But let him sit on a hot stove for a minute, and it's longer than any hour. That's relativity. *-Albert Einstein*

Retirement

Few men of action have been able to make a graceful exit at the appropriate time. *-Malcolm Muggeridge*

Responsible

Who is wise and understanding among you? Let him show it by his good life, by deeds done in the humility that comes from wisdom. *-James 3:13*

Results

The world isn't interested in the storms you encountered, but whether or not you brought in the ship. *-Raul Armesto*

Recycling

Recycling one aluminum can saves enough energy to keep a 100 watt bulb burning four hours or run your television three hours.

Right Concerns

The greatest concerns of men are these: to make him who is an enemy a friend, to make him who is wicked righteous, and to make him who is ignorant learned. *-Zend-Avesta*

Rumor

Rumor travels faster, but it don't stay put as long as the truth. *-Will Rogers*

Secrets

Love, pain, and money cannot be kept secret. They soon betray themselves. *-Spanish Proverb*

Seeing

Seeing ourselves as others see us wouldn't do much good. We wouldn't believe it anyway. *-M. Walthall Jackson*

Self Consciousness

No one will ever notice it on a galloping horse! *-Sue Kovach*

A man who is master of himself can end a sorrow as easily as he can invent a pleasure. *-Oscar Wilde, 1891*

He is a man whom it is impossible to please, because he is never pleased with himself. *-Goethe, 1774*

Self-Esteem

In 1973, psychologists everywhere were convinced that boosting self-esteem would help solve personal and social problems. A generation and many millions of dollars later, it turns out they have been mistaken. After all these years, I'm sorry to say, my recommendation is this: forget about self-esteem and concentrate more on self-control and self-discipline. *-Professor Baumeister, Florida State University*

Self-Improvement

Be what you are. This is the first step toward becoming better than you are. - *Julius and Augustus Hare*

Servants

Servants see interruptions as divine appointments for ministry and are happy for the opportunities to practice sowing. *-Pastor Rick Warren*

Service

The best cure for worry, depression, melancholy, brooding, is to go deliberately forth and try to lift the gloom of somebody else. *-Arnold Bennett*

In order to be of service to others we have to die to them; that is, we have to give up measuring our meaning and value with the yardstick of others…thus we become free to be compassionate. *-Henri Nouwen*

God determines your greatness by how many people you serve, not how many people serve you. *-Pastor Rick Warren*

Servitude

All spirits are enslaved which serve things evil. *-Shelley, 1818*

Men would rather be starving and free than fed in bonds. *-Pearl S. Buck*

Sexuality

Religions and moral values are the main reason why teenagers abstain from sex…The trick is to reinforce those values with sexuality education that stresses chastity as well as contraception and commitment. Such reinforcement would obviously be easier if popular culture glamorized character rather than instant gratification. *-Senator Hillary Rodham Clinton, January 2005*

Sharing

A whole bunch of candles can be lit from one without diminishing it.

There's no delight in owning anything unshared. -*Seneca, 100 AD*

Sight

Things seen are mightier than things heard. -*Alfred Lord Tennyson, 1864*

Our sight is the most perfect and most delightful of all our sense. It fills the mind with the largest variety of ideas, converses with its objects at the greatest distance, and continues the longest in action without being tried or satiated with its proper enjoyment. -*Joseph Addison, 1917*

Simplicity

Beauty of style and harmony and grace and good rhythm depend on simplicity. -*Plato, 400 BC*

The ability to simplify means to eliminate the unnecessary so that the necessary may speak. -*Hans Hofmann, 1967*

Sin

People are no longer sinful; they are only immature or underprivileged or frightened, or more particularly, sick. -*Phyllis McGinley, 1959*

Sin wouldn't be so attractive if the wages were paid immediately.

Sincerity

Man's noblest gift to man is his sincerity, for it embraces his integrity also. -*Henry David Thoreau*

Skepticism

Man's most valuable trait is a judicious sense of what not to believe. -*Euripides, 412 BC*

Smile

A smile costs nothing but creates much. It enriches those who receive without impoverishing those who give. It happens in a flash and the memory of it sometimes lasts forever. None are so rich they can get along without it and none so poor but are richer for its benefits. It creates happiness in the home, fosters good will in a business, and is the countersign of friends. It is rest to the weary, daylight to the discouraged, sunshine to the sad, and Nature's best antidote for trouble. Yet it cannot be bought, begged, borrowed, or stolen, for it is something that is no earthly good to anybody until it is given away. Nobody needs a smile so much as those who have none left to give. -*Editor*

Snobbery

Snobbery, being an aspiring failing, is sometimes the prophecy of better things. -*Charles Dudley Warner, 1873*

The worst cliques are those which consist of one man. -*George Bernard Shaw*

Solar System

This most beautiful system of the sun, planets, and comets could only proceed from the counsel and dominion of an intelligent and powerful being. -*Sir Isaac Newton*

Sophistication

Be wisely worldly, be not worldly wise. -*Francis Quarles, 1635*

Sorrow

Melancholy and remorse form the deep leaden keel which enables us to sail into the wind of reality. *-Cyril Connolly*

Sour Grapes

It is easy to despise what you cannot get. *-Aesop, 600 BC*

Sowers

It's what each of us sows, and how, that gives to us character and prestige. Seeds of kindness, goodwill, and human understanding, planted in fertile soil, spring up unto deathless friendships, big deeds of worth, and a memory that will not soon fade out. We are all sowers of seeds- and let us never forget it! *-George Matthew Adams*

Speaking

From listening comes wisdom and speaking, repentance. *-Italian Proverb*

Speech is a mirror of the soul: as a man speaks, so is he. *-Publilius Syrus, 100 BC*

Talking is like playing on the harp; there is as much in laying the hands on the strings to stop their vibrations as in twanging them to bring out their music. *-Oliver Yendell Holmes Sr., 1858*

The tongue is more to be feared than the sword. *-Japanese Proverb*

Talkers are no good doers. *-Shakespeare, 1592*

Specialist

A specialist is a person who knows very much about very little and continues to learn more and more about less and less until eventually he knows practically everything abut almost nothing at all.

Statistics

Statistics are like a bikini. What they reveal is suggestive, but what they conceal is vital. -*Aaron Levenstein*

Strength

Strong men can always afford to be gentile. Only the weak are intent on 'giving as good as they get.' -*Elbert Hubbard, 1927*

There are two ways of exerting one's strength: one is pushing down, the other is pulling up. -*Booker T. Washington*

Stress

Stress is a fact of life. It is the reaction of our bodies and minds to anything that upsets their regular balance. Studies show that it is the cause in up to 80% of all our medical complaints.
 Accept yourself as you are; it usually isn't that bad.
 Accustom yourself to unfairness; it is common around us.
 Allow more time to get where you're going; it usually takes longer.
 Be prepared to have to wait in line; it can cultivate patience.
 Complete important things first; it is usually the best way.
 Concern yourself with the present; it will take care of the future.
 Deal with the little problems; it prevents big ones.
 Discipline your children; it will benefit everyone.
 Do your best; it is good enough.
 Exercise often; it does even more good than most people realize.
 Expect 4 out of 5 stop lights to be red; it is a good time for prayer and introspection.
 Get outside yourself; it helps you the most.
 Live within your means; it allows you to be free.
 Refuse to talk negatively about others; it is counter-productive.
 Schedule fewer activities; it provides time for the unforeseen.
 Sprinkle your life with humor; it will benefit everyone.
 Take care of yourself; it includes a balanced diet and eight hours of sleep.
 View trying circumstances as character building opportunities; it results in the greatest good.

Watch less TV, especially 'news' programs; it is out to promote its own agenda.

Write things down; it is impossible to remember everything.

Stress has a direct bearing on our emotional, mental, and physical well being. Since we cannot eliminate stress, we need to do everything possible to minimize the negative consequences it generates. *-Editor*

Strutting

A man who struts in my presence hopes to find in my eyes an importance missing in his own. *-Ben Hecht*

Success

Eighty percent of success is showing up. *-Woody Allen*

In order to succeed, you must know what you are doing, like what you are doing, and believe in what you are doing. *-Will Rogers*

One of the most successful lessons in life is that success must continually be won and is never finally achieved. *-Charles Evans Hughes*

Success comes in cans. Failure comes in can'ts.

Behind every great man there is a great woman [and vice versa]. *-American Proverb*

Suffering

An hour of pain is as long as a day of pleasure. *-English Proverb*

A wounded deer leaps highest. *-Emily Dickinson, 1860*

Suitability

Send not for a hatchet to break open an egg with. *-Thomas Fuller, MD, 1732*

Superiority

There is nothing noble about being superior to some other man. The true nobility is in being superior to your previous self. *-Hindostani Proverb*

Superman

Three things make the superman, and they are the greatest gifts of divine generosity: a fertile mind, a deep understanding, and a cultivated taste. *-Baltasar Grecian*

Surrender

Everybody eventually surrenders to something or someone. *-Pastor Rick Warren*

Sympathy

Unto a broken heart no other one may go without the high prerogative itself hath suffered too. *-Emily Dickinson, 1862*

Tact

Silence is not always tact, and it is tact that is golden, not silence. *-Samuel Butler, 1902*

You never know till you try to reach them how accessible men are; but you must approach each man by the right door. *-Henry Ward Beecher, 1887*

Talent

There is hardly anybody good for everything, and there is scarcely anybody who is absolutely good for nothing. *-Lord Chesterfield, 1748*

Taste

Taste can be cultivated even as the intelligence: the better the appreciation, the greater the appetite, and when fulfilled, the greater the enjoyment. Good taste lends flavor to all of life. *-Baltasar Grecian*

Teaching

A teacher affects eternity; he can never tell where his influence stops. *-Henry Adams, 1907*

Technology

It is said that one machine can do the work of fifty ordinary men. No machine, however, can do the work of one extraordinary man. *-Tehyi Hsieh, 1948*

Temperament

He who is of a calm and happy nature will hardly feel the pressure of age, but to him who is of an opposite disposition; youth and age are equally a burden. *-Plato, 400 BC*

Thankful

Don't it always seem to go that you don't know what you've got til it's gone? *-A line from "Big Yellow Taxi" song*

Things

The best things in life aren't things- consider: faithfulness, gentleness, goodness, joy, kindness, love, patience, peace, and self-control.

Although I may not walk with kings, let me be big in little things. *-Edgar A. Guest*

The meaning of things lies not in the things themselves, but in our attitude toward them. *-Antoine de Saint-Exupery*

Thought

When a thought is too weak to be expressed simply it should be rejected. -*Vauvenargues, 1746*

Time

There is a time for everything and a season for every activity under heaven. -*Ecclesiastes 3:1*

Your time here is short, very short; take another look at the way in which you spend it. -*Thomas A. Kempis*

If you want to kill time why not try working it to death.

In youth the days are short and the years are long; in old age the years are short and the days are long. -*Panin*

Lives of great men all remind us we can make our lives sublime and, departing, leave behind us footprints on the sands of time. -*Henry Longfellow*

Tolerance

Tolerance is the positive and cordial effort to understand another's beliefs, practices, and habits without necessarily sharing or accepting them. -*Joshua Liebman*

Tradition

Continuity does not rule out fresh approaches to fresh situations. -*Dean Rusk, 1963*

Tragedy/Comedy

In tragedy every moment is eternity; in comedy, eternity is a moment. -*Christopher Fry*

Tragedies

Find a way to deal with the tragedies that will inevitably come your way.

Training

Training is everything; the peach was once a bitter almond; cauliflower is nothing but cabbage with a college education. -*Mark Twain*

Tranquility

Back of tranquility lies always conquered unhappiness. -*David Grayson*

Trifles

Even a single hair casts a shadow. -*Publilius Syrus, 100 BC*

Trust

It's a vice to trust all, and equally a vice to trust none. -*Seneca, 100 AD*

Truth

So long as we are able to distinguish any space whatever between the truth and us we remain outside it. -*Henri Amiel*

The truth will make you free, but first it will make you miserable. -*Tom DeMarco*

Truth always lags first, limping along on the sin of time. -*Baltasar Grecian*

Truth is what stands the test of experience. -*Albert Einstein, 1950*

There are three truths: my truth, your truth, and the truth. -*Chinese Proverb*

The truth is always the strongest argument. -*Sophocles, 435 BC*

Turmoil

To concede today may be the best way to succeed tomorrow; it takes little to muddy a spring, nor does it clear by being stirred, but by being left alone. There is no better remedy for turmoil than to let it take its course, for so it comes to rest of itself. *-Baltasar Grecian, 1600 BC*

Unconscious

Our unconscious is like a vast subterranean factory with intricate machinery that is never idle, where work goes on day and night from the time we are born until the moment of our death. *-Milton R. Sapirstein, 1955*

Understanding

Grieve not that men do not know you; grieve that you do not know men. *-Confucius, 500 BC*

Unique

There never were, since the creation of the world, two cases exactly parallel. *-Lord Chesterfield, 1748*

Unity

Let's agree to use all our energy in getting along with others. Help others with encouraging words; don't drag them down by finding fault. *-Romans 14:19*

Universe

Nothing puzzles me more than time and space; and yet nothing troubles me less. *-Charles Lamb, 1810*

Value

Everything is worth what its purchaser will pay for it. -*Publilius Syrus, 100 BC*

We cannot be sure that we have something worth living for unless we are ready to die for it. -*Eric Hoffer, 1951*

Vanity

A vain man may become proud and imagine himself pleasing to all when he is in reality a universal nuisance. -*Spinoza, 1677*

Few people are modest enough to be content to be estimated at their true worth. -*Vauvenaruges, 1746*

Every ass loves to hear himself bray. -*Thomas Fuller, 1732*

Vanity is so secure in the heart of man that everyone wants to be admired even I who write this, and you who read this. -*Blaise Pascal*

What renders other people's vanity insufferable is that it wounds our own. -*La Rochefoucauld, 1865*

Verbosity

Words are like leaves; and where they most abound, much fruit of sense beneath is rarely found. -*Alexander Pope*

Vices

Every vice has its excuse ready. -*Publilius Syrus, 100 BC*

We are more apt to catch the vices of others than their virtues, as disease is far more contagious than health. -*Charles Caleb Colton, 1825*

It is not possible to form any other notion of the origin of vice than as the absence of virtue. -*St. Gregory*

Most vices may be committed very genteelly: a man may debauch his friend's wife genteelly; he may cheat at cards genteelly. -*Samuel Johnson, 1775*

View

It's your point of view that decides what you see.

Vision

Hundreds of people can talk for one who can think, but thousands can think for one who can see. -*John Ruskin, 1843*

Virtue

Frequently noted virtues in the Bible: forgiveness, goodness, gratitude, honesty, kindness, thankfulness, and understanding. -*Editor*

If it be usual to be strongly impressed by things that are scarce, why are we so little impressed by virtue? -*La Bruyere, 1688*

The measure of any man's virtue is what he would do if he had neither the laws, nor public opinion, nor even his own prejudices to control him. -*William Hazlitt, 1823*

He is a truly virtuous man who wishes always to be open to the observations of honest men. -*La Rochefoucauld, 1665*

All virtue is loving right; all sin is loving wrong. -*Hubert van Zeller*

Wisdom is the highest virtue, and it has four other virtues: of which one is **Prudence**, another **Temperance**, the third **Fortitude**, the fourth **Justice**. -*Boethius*

Vocabulary

The difference between the right word and the almost right word is the difference between lightning and the lightning bug. -*Mark Twain*

Walking

When you stroll you never hurry back, because if you had anything to do, you wouldn't be strolling in the first place. -*Virginia Cary Hudson, 1962*

War

We often hear it said: 'If God existed there would be no wars.' But it would be truer to say: 'If God's laws were observed there would be no wars.' -*Yves Congar*

Waste

The inevitable result of waste is want. -*Benjamin E. Mays*

Wealth

It is only when the rich are sick that they fully feel the impotence of wealth. -*Charles Caleb Colton, 1825*

It requires a great deal of boldness and a great deal of caution to make a great fortune, and when you have got it, it requires ten times as much wit to keep it. -*Emerson, 1860*

Humanly speaking, it is only when the hair is white, when…life is almost over, that men begin to realize how hopelessly elusive is the happiness promised by wealth and fame. -*Joseph McSorley*

Wickedness

Wickedness is always easier than virtue, for it takes the short cut to everything. -*Samuel Johnson, 1773*

Win/Lose

We win or lose because of the choices we make. *-Phil Perrier*

Wisdom

The words of the wise are like goads [spurs], their collected sayings like firmly embedded nails- given by one shepherd [Scripture]. Be warned, my son, of anything in addition to them. *-Ecclesiastes 22:11*

The function of wisdom is to discriminate between good and evil. *-Cicero, 44 BC*

It is far easier to be wise for others than to be so for oneself. *-La Rochefoucauld*

Wise Saying

One of the greatest treasures is a collection of wise sayings and proverbs for sharpening the mind. *-P. Toynbee*

Woman

When a woman behaves like a man, why doesn't she behave like a nice man? *-Edith Evans*

Wonders

Wonders…to see, to hear, to touch, to taste, to feel, to smell, to laugh, and to love, and be loved.

Words

If someone were to pay you two cents for every kind word you have spoken about people and collect five cents for every unkind word, would you be rich or poor?

He can compress the most words into the smallest idea of any man I ever met. -*Abraham Lincoln*

Humanity now publishes as many words every week as it did in all human history up to 1800. -*The New York Times, 1993*

Words form the backbone of what we think. So, although it is possible to have thoughts without words, it's rarely possible to know what one thinks without bronzing it in words. Refine the words, and you refine the thoughts. -*Diane Acherman*

A thousand words will not leave so deep an impression as one deed. -*Henrik Ibsen*

Work

It doesn't seem like work when you spend time doing something you love. -*Dorene White, President and Owner of Cottonwood Furniture*

Work is more fun than fun. -*Noel Coward*

World

The most incomprehensible thing about the world is that it is comprehensible. -*Albert Einstein, 1955*

We read the world wrong and say that it deceives us. -*Rabindranath Tagore, 1916*

Worldliness

All the wisdom in the world and all human cleverness compared with the infinite wisdom of God is sheer and extreme ignorance. -*John of the Cross*

Worry/Faith

Worry looks around; faith looks up.

Worship

God prefers bad verses recited with a pure heart to the finest verses possible chanted by the wicked. -*Voltaire, 1764*

The world has a funny idea of religious worship. It does not worship in order to praise God but in order to entertain itself. Religious services have to be made attractive, have to show originality, have to be startling and unexpected. God does not delight in novelty, and if worship is not meant to delight God, then why worship? -*Hubert van Zeller*

Wronged

To be wronged is nothing unless you continue to remember it. –*Confucius, 500 BC*

Young/Old

All sorts of allowances are made for the illusions of youth; and none, or almost none, for the disenchantments of age. -*Robert Louis Stevenson, 1881*

The young man who has not wept is a savage, and the older man who will not laugh is a fool. -*George Santayana, 1925*

When a man is young he is so wild he is insufferable. When he is old he plays the saint and becomes insufferable again. -*Nikolai Gogol, 1482*

Young men think old men are fools; but old men know young men are fools. -*George Chapman, 1859*

The imagination of a boy is healthy, and the mature imagination of a man is healthy; but there is a space of life between, in which the soul is in a ferment, the character undecided, the way of life uncertain, the ambition thick sighted. -*John Keats, 1818*

Zeal

Whenever we find ourselves more inclined to persecute than to persuade, we may then be certain that our zeal has more of pride in it than of charity. - *Charles Caleb Colton, 1825*

10.
SPIRITUALITY MATTERS

Acceptance

Let us accept each day as the Lord sends it, living obediently and faithfully and not fearing what may come. We know that the glory ahead will obliterate the grim past. *-Ruth Bell Graham*

Accountable

Nothing in all creation is hidden from God's sight. Everything is uncovered and laid bare before the eyes of him to whom we must give account. *-Hebrews 4:13*

Adversity/Defeat

Adversity and defeat are more conducive to spiritual growth than prosperity and victory. *-John Steinbeck*

Adversity in the things of this world opens the door for spiritual salvation. *-A.J. Toynbee*

Appearance

While we look at outward appearances, the Lord looks at hearts (our inner disposition and character.) *-1 Samuel 16:7*

Anxiety

Self-centeredness is a terrible breeder of anxiety. Get your eyes off yourself; focus them upon God first, and then on others. *-Billy Graham*

Approved

Do your best to present yourself to God as one approved, a workman who does not need to be ashamed and who correctly handles the word of truth. -*2 Timothy 2:15*

Atheism

If God does not exist, everything is permissible. -*Fyodor Dostoevsky*

If I did not believe in God, I should still want my doctor, my lawyer, and my banker to do so. -*G.K. Chesterton*

The equal toleration of all religions…is the same thing as atheism. -*Pope Leo XIII*

Attitude

When you pray for anyone you tend to modify your personal attitude toward him. You lift the relationship thereby to a higher level. The best in the other person begins to flow out toward you as your best flows toward him.-*Norman Vincent Peal*

Belief/Unbelief

Since faith is never perfect, belief and unbelief are often mixed. I do believe; help me overcome my unbelief. -*Mark 9:24*

Bible

We shall not adjust our Bible to the age; by God's grace, we shall adjust the age to the Bible. -*C.H. Spurgeon*

A knowledge of the Bible is essential to a rich and meaningful life. -*Billy Graham*

Either the Bible will keep you away from sin, or sin will keep you away from the Bible! -*C.S. Lewis*

Men do not reject the Bible because it contradicts itself but because it contradicts them.

The Bible comforts the afflicted and afflicts the comfortable. *-Reverend Mark Degner*

The Bible tells us that the greatest treasure in life is not prestige, not power, not a possession; but the greatest treasure is love. *-Max Lucado*

The English Bible- a book which if everything else in our language should perish, would alone suffice to show the whole extent of its beauty and power. *-Thomas Babington Macaulay*

When you open your Bible God opens his mouth: when you close your Bible God closes his mouth.

Read the Bible—it will scare the hell out of you.

Big

Lord, keep me big enough to work with other people and let them get the credit.

Blessing

When we ask God's blessing, we're not asking for more of what we could get for ourselves but nothing more and nothing less than what God wants for us. *-Bruce Wilkinson*

Books

Other books were given for our information, the Bible was given for our transformation.

Brotherhood

It is easy enough to be friendly to one's friends. But to befriend the one who regards himself as your enemy is the quintessence of true religion. - *Mohandas Ghandi*

Building

Unless the Lord builds the house, its builders labor in vain. -*Psalm 127:1*

Change

Lord, when we are wrong, make us willing to change. And when we are right, make us easy to live with. -*Peter Marshall*

Charity

Give, and it will be given to you. A good measure, pressed down, shaken together and running over, will be poured into your lap. For the measure you use, it will be measured to you. -*Luke 6:38*

Chastity

The essence of chastity is not the suppression of lust, but the total orientation of one's life. -*Dietrich Bonhoeffer*

Christ

Living for Christ is a day-by-day experience. It is a continuous dependence upon the Spirit of God. It is believing in His faithfulness. -*Billy Graham*

The peace and joy that we have in Christ is not a guarantee for us against hardships, sufferings, and persecutions. -*Sami Dagher*

Christians

If Christians spent as much time praying as they do grumbling, they would soon have nothing to grumble about.

No man is a true Christian who does not think constantly of how he can lift his brother, how he can assist his friend, how he can enlighten mankind, how he can make virtue the rule of conduct in the circle in which he lives. -*Woodrow Wilson*

The Christian owes it to the world to be supernaturally joyful. -*A.W. Tozer, Theologian*

Christianity

All 123 of the first 123 colleges founded in America were founded by Christians for Christian purposes. The idea of the university was born in the bosom of the church. -*Dr. Paul Maier*

Christ has been the greatest benefactor to the human race the world has ever known. -*D. James Kennedy, Ph.D.*

Christianity is a thing of unspeakable joy, but it begins, not in joy, but in wretchedness. And it does no good to try to get to the joy by bypassing the wretchedness. -*C.S. Lewis*

Christianity is not a religion but a relationship of love expressed toward God and man. -*Sherwood Eliot Wirt, Editor*

Christianity has not been tried and found wanting; it has been found difficult and not tried. -*G.K. Chesterton*

If you have no joy in your religion, there's a leak in your Christianity. -*W.A. (Billy) Sunday*

No one is without Christianity, if we agree on what we mean by the word. It is every individual's individual code of behavior by means of which he makes himself a better human being than his nature wants to be than if he followed his nature only. -*William Faulkner*

Religion is based upon what we do, Christianity is based upon what Christ has done. -*Greg Albrecht*

The Catholic must adopt the decision handed down to him; the Protestant must learn to decide for himself. -*Rousseau*

The exclusive claims of Christianity: one God, one Savior, one Truth, one People, and one Way. -*The Bible*

The most prevalent failure of Christian love is the failure to express it. -*Reverend Paul E. Johnson*

Church

Church is not a haven for sinners; it's a hospital for sinners.

Going to church doesn't make you a Christian any more than going to McDonalds makes you a hamburger. -*Keith Green*

The church is not a gallery for the exhibition of eminent Christians, but a school for the education of imperfect ones. -*Henry Ward Beecher*

Cleverness

The height of cleverness is to be able to conceal it. -*La Rochefoucauld*

Comfort

Whatsoever I can desire or imagine for my comfort: I look for it not here, but hereafter. -*Thomas A. Kempis*

Coincidence

Coincidence is when God chooses to remain anonymous.

Citizen

Whatever makes men good Christians makes them good citizens. *-Daniel Webster*

Conduct

These are the things that you shall do: speak the truth to one another, render in your gates judgments that are true and make for peace, do not devise evil in your hearts against one another. *-Zechariah 8:16-17*

Confession

If we confess our sins, God will be faithful to His promises and forgive our sins. *-1 John 1:9*

Conscience

Conscience is the inner voice that warns us somebody may be looking. *-H.L. Mencken*

God never ordained you to have a conscience for others. Your conscience is for you, and for you alone. *- Henry Ward Beecher*

Keep a clear conscience so that those who speak maliciously against your good behavior in Christ may be ashamed of their slander. *-1 Peter 3:16*

Contentment

A great meal can make us feel content…for a few hours. A desired purchase causes contentment…until the novelty wears off. True contentment comes in serving the Lord: the God of yesterday, today and forever.

Conversion

Conversion is not a mere changing of habits, but a change of heart, a spiritual rebirth of man; that it is brought about by the power of God working through the Word. *-Martin Luther*

Created

Men are like trees: each one must put forth the leaf that is created in him. - *Henry Ward Beecher*

Creation

No philosophical theory which I have yet come across is a radical improvement on the words of Genesis, that "In the beginning God made Heaven and Earth." -*C.S. Lewis*

Darkness

If our spiritual darkness teaches us nothing more than that we cannot be sure of ourselves, that without the help of grace we are bound hand and foot, that God is our only hope, it has taught us all that we need to know. -*Hubert van Zeller*

Daily Needs

Give me neither poverty nor riches, but give me only my daily bread. - *Proverbs 30:8*

Death

Jesus has destroyed death and has brought life and immortality to light through the gospel. -*2 Timothy 1:10*

Debt

Jesus paid a debt that he did not owe, because we owed a debt we could not pay. -*Greg Albrecht*

Deeds

There aren't enough "good deeds" to get us into heaven. There aren't enough "bad deeds" to keep us out. -*Robin Swoboda-Wagner*

Defeat

We are never defeated unless we give up on God. -*Ronald Reagan*

Dependence

Dependence on people often leads to slavery, but dependence on God leads to freedom. When we know that God holds us safely- whatever happens- we don't have to fear anything or anyone but can walk through life with great confidence. -*Henri J.M. Nouwen*

Despair

To eat bread without hope is still slowly to starve to death. -*Pearl S. Buck*

Devil

The existence of the devil is so clearly taught in the Bible that to doubt it is to doubt the Bible itself. -*Archibald G. Brown*

You won't be able to say no to the devil unless you've said yes to Christ. -*Rick Warren, Pastor*

Disciple

Four habits for every disciple: time with God's word, prayer, tithing, and fellowship.

Discernment

The man without the Spirit does not accept the things that come from the Spirit of God, for they are foolishness to him, and he cannot understand them, because they are spiritually discerned. *-1 Corinthians 2:14*

Doubt

Never doubt in the dark what God told you in the light. *-V. Raymond Edman*

Encouragement

So do not fear, for I am with you; do not be dismayed, for I am your God. I will strengthen you and help you; I will uphold you with my righteous right hand. *-Isaiah 41:10*

Equal

In Jesus Christ we are all equal. For God's Spirit makes us one.

Eternal Life

For God so loved the world that he gave his one and only Son, that whoever believe in him shall not perish but have eternal life. *-John 3:16*

[Jesus said,] "I tell you the truth, whoever hears My word and believes Him who sent Me has eternal life and will not be condemned; he has crossed over from death to life." *-John 5:24*

So we fix our eyes not on what is seen, but on what is unseen. For what is seen is temporary, but what is unseen is eternal. *-2 Corinthians 4:18*

Eternity

Christians can rejoice in tribulation because they have eternity's values in view. When the pressures are on, they look beyond their present predicament to the glories of heaven. The thoughts of the future life with its prerogatives and joys help to make the trials of the present seem light and transient. -*Billy Graham*

For a small reward, a man will hurry away on a long journey; while for eternal life, many will hardly take a single step. -*Thomas A. Kempis*

For the wages of sin is death, but the gift of God is eternal life in Christ Jesus our Lord. -*Romans 6:23*

Hold tightly to what is eternal and loosely to what is temporal.

Just as the nine months you spent in your mother's womb were not an end in themselves but preparation for life, so this life is preparation for the next. -*Rick Warren*

Keep eternity in mind- to make the most of each day.

Only what we have wrought into our character during life can we take away with us. -*Alexander von Humboldt*

That day, which you fear as being the end of all things, is the birthday of your eternity. –*Seneca, 100 AD*

The eternal life is not the future life; it is life in harmony with the true order of things- life in God. -*Henri Amiel*

When we become so preoccupied with this life and lose the value of eternity, then we lose this life as well. -*C.S. Lewis*

Where are you going…eventually?

Evangelism

But you be watchful in all things, endure afflictions, do the work of an evangelist, fulfill your ministry. -*2 Timothy 4:5*

Don't judge each day by the harvest you reap, but by the seeds you plant. -*Robert Louis Stevenson*

God is in the people-saving business, and His method is to use His people. - *David Siegmann*

Kindness had converted more people than zeal, science, or eloquence. - *Mother Teresa*

The greatest mission field we face is not in some faraway land. It's barely across the street. The culture most lost to the gospel is our own- our children and our neighbors. *-Dwight Ozard*

Go into all the world and preach the good news (the Gospel) to all creation. – *Matthew 28:19*

Whoever believes and is baptized will be saved, but whoever does not believe will be condemned. *-Mark 16:15-16*

If he has faith, the believer cannot be restrained. He betrays himself. He breaks out. He confesses and teaches this gospel to the people at the risk of life itself. *-Martin Luther*

Evil

Evil enters like a needle and spreads like an oak tree. *-Ethiopian Proverb*

The man who does evil to another does evil to himself. *-Hesoid, 800 BC*

Evolution

What can be more foolish than to think that this rare fabric of heaven and earth could come by chance, when all the skill of science is not able to make an oyster. *-Jeremy Taylor*

Intermediate links? Geology assuredly does not reveal any such finely graduated organic change, and this is perhaps the most obvious and serious objection which can be urged against the theory of evolution. *-Charles Darwin*

Exalted

Be still and know that I am God. I will be exalted among the nations; I will be exalted in the earth! -*Psalm 46:10*

Excuses

The answer to all our problems of living is how we face them, not where we were born, not that we have had a poor environment, not that we had no chance of education. The answer is always within ourselves and our relationship with Christ. -*Albert E. Cliffe*

Faith

And without faith it is impossible to please God, because anyone who comes to him must believe that he exists and that he rewards those who earnestly seek him. -*Hebrews 11:6*

As he that fears (reveres) God fears nothing else, so, he that sees God sees everything else. -*John Donne*

Faith but itself, if it is not accompanied by action, is dead. -*James 2:17*

Faith consists in believing when it is beyond the power of reason to believe. It is not enough that thing be possible for it to be believed. -*Voltaire*

Faith helps people cope better with stress and personal problems. -*Sociologist Steven Barhan and Susan Greenwood of the University of Maine*

Faith in God may be an elective in our university of daily living. In the presence of death it assumes crucial significance. -*Sidney Greenberg*

Faith is being sure of what we hope for and certain of what we do not see. -*Hebrews 11:1*

God our Father has made all things depend on faith so that whoever has faith will have everything, and whoever does not have faith will have nothing. -*Martin Luther*

In God's faithfulness lies eternal security. -*Corrie Ten Boom*

Faith may be defined briefly as an illogical belief in the occurrence of the improbably. -*H.L. Mencken*

Faith means being grasped by a power that is greater than we are, a power that shakes us and turns us, and transforms and heals us. Surrender to this power of faith. -*Paul Tillich*

Faith is a matter of trusting God's promises. -*Editor*

Faith should rest on the solid rock of Scripture, rather than on the shifting sands of our experience. -*Julene Gernant Dumit*

God didn't ask me to be successful; He asked me to be faithful. -*Mother Teresa*

My most cherished possession I wish I could leave you is my faith in Jesus Christ, for with Him and nothing else you can be happy, but without Him and with all else you'll never be happy. -*Patrick Henry*

Never, never pin your whole faith on any human being: not if he is the best and wisest in the whole world. There are lots of nice things you can do with sand; but do not try building a house on it. -*C.S. Lewis*

Understanding is the reward of faith. Therefore, seek not to understand that thou mayest believe, but believe that though mayest understand. -*Saint Augustine*

You can keep a faith only as you can keep a plant, by rooting it into your life and making it grow there. -*Phillips Brooks*

You'll never achieve success in life without having faith in God. When you start to have this faith, positive things start to happen in your life. -*Dr. Robert Schuller*

Faithfulness

Faithfulness means continuing quietly with a job we have been given, in the situation where we have been placed; not yielding to the restless desire for change. It means tending the lamp quietly for God without wondering how much longer it has to go on. *-Evelyn Underhill*

Faith/Morals

You cannot separate faith and morals. It is our faith that forms the foundation for our morals. It is spiritually redeemed men and women who influence cities and nations for righteousness. *-Franklin Graham*

Fear

Fear knocked at the door. Faith answered. There was no one there. *-Martin Luther King Jr.*

Faithful people do not need to live in fear. *-J.G. Deitz*

Never be afraid to trust an unknown future to a known God. *-Corrie Ten Boom*

The remarkable thing about fearing (reverence) God is that when you fear God, you fear nothing else, whereas if you do not fear God, you fear everything else. *-Oswald Chambers*

Focus

If you look at the world you'll be distressed. If you look within you'll be depressed. But if you look at Christ you'll be at rest. (Your focus will determine your feelings.) *-Corrie Ten Boom*

Trust in the Lord with all your heart and lean not on your own understanding; in all your ways acknowledge Him and he will make your paths straight. *-Proverbs 3:5-6*

Forgiveness

Where is the foolish person who would think it in his power to commit more sin than God could forgive? *-Francis de Sales*

Fruit

The fruit of the Spirit is love, joy, peace, patience, kindness, goodness, faithfulness, gentleness, and self-control. *-Galatians 5:22*

Future

The future is as bright as the promises of God. *-William Carey*

Future/Past

The worst sinner has a future, even as the greatest saint has had a past. No one is so good or so bad as he imagines. *-Sarvepalli Radhakrishnan*

Gentleness

The Lord is consistently gentle with us. He stands beside us in the midst of trouble and tragedy, nursing us through it all. This is the same kind of encouragement the people around us need. *-Lloyd John Ogilvie*

The way in which Jesus presents Himself to us is the epitome of gentleness. As in the days when He walked in the flesh, our Lord does not force His way into your life. Since He desires a relationship of love and trust, He never attempts to coerce you, though He has the ability to do so. He seeks you, and offers Himself to you. Whether you recognize and welcome His approach is up to you. *-Peter Lord*

Gifts

Each one should use whatever gift he has received to serve others, faithfully administering to God's grace in its various forms. *-1 Peter 4:10*

We have different gifts, according to the grace given us. If a man's gift is prophesying, let him use it in proportion to his faith. If it is serving, let him serve; if it is teaching, let him teach; if it is encouraging, let him encourage; if it is contributing to the needs of others, let him give generously; if it is leadership, let him govern diligently; if it is showing mercy, let him do it cheerfully. -*Romans 12:6-8*

We rejoice with the gifts of hope, endurance, encouragement, peace and joy through the power of the Holy Spirit. -*Church Bulletin*

What you are is God's gift to you.

God

Do a good deed every day if you can, peace and joy will come if you accept God's plan! -*Marianne Highsmith Hill*

Don't put a question mark where God puts a period.

God does not promise us happy endings in a world where laws of nature and human cruelty take their daily toll; God's promise is not that we will be safe, but that we will never be alone. -*Rabbi Harold S. Kushner*

God doesn't call the qualified, he qualifies the called. -*Greg Albrecht*

God is looking for obedience, not just good intentions.

God is real, no matter how you feel. -*Rick Warren, Pastor*

God is too big to fit inside one religion. -*Dr. Paul Hinko*

God never asks about our ability or our inability- just our availability.

God promises a safe landing- not a calm passage.

I believe whatever God has in store for us will be unbelievably more joyous, more delightful, and more wonderful than what we now enjoy. -*Billy Graham*

If God is your Co-Pilot, switch seats.

In my most extreme fluctuations I have never been an atheist in the sense of denying the existence of God. -*Charles Darwin*

I tremble for my country when I reflect that God is just. -*Thomas Jefferson*

Looking at the earth from his vantage point (of the moon), looking at this kind of creation and to not believe in God, to me, is impossible. To see (earth) laid out like that only strengthens my beliefs. -*John Glenn*

No matter how good we are, God could love us no more, and no matter how bad we are, He could love us no less. His love is prompted by nothing we do. -*Mike Huckabee*

One on God's side is a majority. -*Wendell Phillips*

The best proof of God's existence is what follows when we deny it. -*William L. Sullivan*

The Lord is not slow in keeping his promise, as some understand slowness. He is patient with you, not wanting anyone to perish, but everyone to come to repentance. -*2 Peter 3:9*

We don't change God's message; His message changes us.

We have been born under a monarchy; to obey God is freedom. -*Seneca, 100 AD*

We know that all things work together for good to those who love God. -*Romans 8:28*

With God there is no mutual ground; one chooses to be Godly or worldly. -*Reverend Daniel Wegrzyn*

People will be lovers of themselves, lovers of money, boastful, proud, abusive, disobedient to their parents, ungrateful, unholy, without love, unforgiving, slanderous, without self-control, brutal, not lovers of good, treacherous, rash, conceited, lovers of pleasure rather than lovers of God. *-2 Timothy 3:2*

God/Money

No one can serve two masters. Either he will hate the one and love the other, or he will be devoted to the one and despise the other. You cannot serve both God and money. *-Matthew 6:24*

Goal

Forgetting what is behind and straining toward what is ahead, I press on toward the goal to win the prize. *-Philippians 3:13*

Goodness

Hate what is evil; cling to what is good. Be devoted to one another in brotherly love. *-Romans 12:9-10*

Grade

God does not grade "heaven entry" on a moral curve; He grades according to His own unchangeable standard. It remains the same forever. *-Mary Marr*

Grace

Grace keeps us from worrying because worry deals with the past, while grace deals with the present and the future. *-Joyce Meyer*

Greatest Commandment

Love the Lord your God with all your heart and with all your soul and with all your mind. This is the first and greatest commandment, and the second is like it. Love your neighbor as yourself. *-Matthew 22:37-39*

Guidance

Hang this question up in your house: "What would Jesus do?." For what Jesus would do, and how he would do it, may always stand as the best guide to us. -*C.H. Spurgeon*

I will instruct you and teach you in the way you should go; I will counsel you and watch over you, says the Lord. -*Psalm 32:8*

The Lord will guide you continually, and satisfy your soul in drought, and strengthen your bones; you shall be like a watered garden, and like a spring of water, whose waters do not fail. -*Isaiah 58:11*

Guilt

Religion has always known that lasting guilt can be a deadly poison. Buried or repressed guilt feelings don't just fade away. They stay there, festering. Religion teaches that the only way to deal with a guilt problem is to regret the offense, resolve not to repeat it, make amends if possible, seek forgiveness of the person you have wrong and then forget it. -*Reverend Norman Vincent Peal*

Happiness

Contrary to peer pressure and adversity, happiness and meaning in life come through relationships within ourselves, with others, with creation, and with God- not through stuff. -*Alternative for Simple Living*

Do you make others happy when you arrive...or when you depart? -*William Arthur Ward*

God designed the human machine to run on Himself. He is the fuel our spirits were designed to burn...God cannot give us happiness apart from Himself, because there is no such thing. -*C.S. Lewis*

Heaven

Aim at heaven and you will get earth thrown in. Aim at earth and you get neither. *-C.S. Lewis*

Heaven's gates are not as highly arched as prince's palaces; they that enter there must go upon their knees. *-John Webster*

He will wipe every tear from their eyes. There will be no more death or mourning or crying or pain, for the old order of things has passed away. *-Revelation 21:4*

[Jesus said,] "Let not your heart be troubled; you believe in God, believe also in Me. In my Father's house are many mansions; if it were not so, I would have told you. I go to prepare a place for you. And if I go and prepare a place for you, I will come again and receive you to Myself; that where I am, there you may be also." *-John 14:1-3*

You can experience something of what heaven is like when you experience God's presence here on earth. *-Pastor Kelly Peters*

Heaven/Hell

Absence from Christ is hell; but the presence of Jesus is heaven. *-C.H. Spurgeon*

Heaven or Hell cannot be forced on people. All have the freedom to choose the narrow road and serve God or, choose the broad road and serve the world and self. *-Editor*

Hell

God will not send us to hell; he will just honor our choice.

Hell-fire...is not literally physical fire. It is present pain of mind, spiritual torment which neither sleep nor time nor any distraction can alleviate. *-R.V.C. Bodley*

The national anthem of Hell is, "I did it my way." *-Peter Kreeft*

Help

If a friend is in trouble, don't annoy him by asking if there is anything you can do. Think up something appropriate and do it. *-Edgar Watson Howe*

Holy Spirit

Every time we say, "I believe in the Holy Spirit," we mean that we believe that there is a living God able and willing to enter human personality and change it. *-J.B. Phillips*

If you then, though you are evil, know how to give good gifts to your children, how much more will your father in heaven give the Holy Spirit to those who ask him. *-Luke 11:13*

Homosexuality

God loves homosexuals as much as anyone else. I think homosexuality is a sin, but no greater than idolatry and adultery. In my judgement, it's not that big. *-Billy Graham*

Honesty

The Lord abhors dishonest scales, but accurate weights are His delight. *-Proverbs 11:1*

Hope

Hope is a gift from God. It cannot be bought; it comes when we catch God's vision of the world. *-Pastor Kelly Peters*

May the God of hope fill you with all joy and peace as you trust in Him, that you may overflow with hope by the power of the Holy Spirit. *-Romans 15:13*

We can even rejoice in suffering, knowing that the eventual outcome is hope, which does not disappoint us. *-Fred Grundmann, Author*

Hospitality

Offer hospitality to one another without grumbling. Each one should use whatever gift he has received to serve others, faithfully administering God's grace in its various forms. -*1 Peter 4:9-10*

Human Condition

Thou hast created us for Thyself, and our heart is not quiet until it rest in Thee. -*St. Augustine*

Human Nature

Human nature is the same everywhere; the modes only are different. -*Lord Chesterfield*

Humility

Humility is not thinking less of yourself; it is thinking of yourself less. -*Rich Warren*

Humility is the first of the virtues- for other people. -*Oliver Wendell Holmes, Sr.*

It's hard to stumble when you're on your knees.

The first test of a truly great man is his humility. -*John Ruskin*

Young man, in the same way be submissive to those who are older. All of you, clothe yourselves with humility toward one another, because God opposes the proud but gives grace to the humble. -*1 Peter 5:5*

Hunger

Spiritual hunger is never satisfied by material food! -*Herbert W. Armstrong*

Idleness

If the Devil finds a man idle, he'll set him to work. -*James Kelly*

Immortality

Surely God would not have created such a being as man…to exist only for a day! No, man was made for immortality. -*Abraham Lincoln*

Inadequate

When you feel inadequate for the task, focus on the One who can do all things. -*Millie Dienert*

Individual

If this is God's world there are no unimportant people. -*George Thomas*

In God's eyes, every individual (prince or pauper) is viewed as being equal and that makes every single person equally valued. -*Editor*

Inside Out

The Lord works from the inside out. The world works from the outside in. The world would take people out of the slums. Christ takes the slums out of the people, and then they take themselves out of the slums. The world would mold men by changing the environment. Christ changes men, who then change their environment. The world would shape human behavior, but Christ can change human nature. -*Ezra Taft Benson*

Instruction

For everything that was written in the past was written to teach us, so that through endurance and the encouragement of the Scriptures we might have hope. -*Romans 15:4*

Intellect/Heart

Not one word is said in the whole of the New Testament about our Lord's intellect; only always about His heart. -*Alexander Whyte*

Jesus

As the centuries pass the evidence is accumulating that, measured by His effect on history, Jesus is the most influential life ever lived on this planet. -*Kenneth Scott Latourette*

Christians believe "The Passion of the Christ" represents the greatest act of sacrificial love in human history: Jesus dying on the cross for the sins of all humanity. -*David Briggs, Plain Dealer Religion Reporter*

For there is one God and one Mediator between God and men; the Man Christ Jesus. - *1 Timothy 2:5*

I am the resurrection and the life. He who believes in me will live, even though he dies; and whoever lives and believes in me will never die. -*John 11:25*

I am the vine, you are the branches. He who abides in Me, and I in him, bears much fruit; for without Me you can do nothing. -*John 15:5*

If you seek your Lord Jesus in all things you will truly find Him, but if you seek yourself you will find yourself, and that will be your own great loss. -*Thomas A. Kempis*

Jesus, a man who was completely innocent, offered himself as a sacrifice for the good of others, including his enemies, and became the ransom of the world. It was a perfect act. -*Mohandas K. Gandhi*

Take My yoke upon you and learn from Me, for I am gentle and humble of heart, and you will find rest for your souls. For My yoke is easy and My burden is light. -*Matthew 11:29-30*

Therefore everyone who hears these words of Mine and puts them into practice is like a wise man who built his house on the rock. The rain came down, the streams rose, and the winds blew and beat against that house; yet it did not fall, because it had its foundation on the rock. -*Matthew 7:24*

To those who hear and respond to His call, He offers the promise of grace, forgiveness, restoration, and a glorious eternity. -*Dr. James Dobson*

You only love Jesus as much as the person you love the least.

Joy

A gospel song says of joy, "The world didn't give it to me, and the world can't take it away." Real joy does not depend upon circumstances. Real joy is the exhilarating realization of the indwelling, eternal hope deep in our hearts because of Christ.

God cannot endure that unfestive, mirthless attitude of ours in which we eat our bread in sorrow, with pretentious, busy haste, or even with shame. Through our daily meals He is calling to rejoice, to keep holiday in the midst of our working day. -*Dietrich Bonhoeffer*

I delight greatly in the Lord; my soul rejoices in my God. -*Isaiah 61:10*

The opposite of joy is not sorrow. It is unbelief. -*Leslie Weatherhead*

There's nothing naive about joy. Joy doesn't pretend that life is always a spring day with daffodils blooming. Joy remembers the winter months, and knows they will come again. There are dark nights, and God will see us through them. -*Reverend Kelly Peters*

This is the day the Lord has made; we will rejoice and be glad in it. -*Psalm 118:24*

Though the fig tree does not bud and there are no grapes on the vines, though the olive crop fails and the fields produce no good, though there are no sheep in the pen and no cattle in the stalls, yet I will rejoice in the Lord, I will be joyful in God my Savior. -*Habakkuk 3:17-18*

Judging

He that is without sin among you, let him first cast a stone. -*Jesus*

Human beings judge one another by their external actions. God judges them by their moral choices. -*C.S. Lewis*

Let us be slow to judge and quick to forgive, show patience, empathy, and love. -*Jesus*

Judge/Love

If you judge people, you have no time to love them. -*Mother Teresa*

Judgment

Everyone must face God as savior or judge. Live today as you will wish you had lived when you stand before God.

For we must all appear before the judgement seat of Christ, that each one may receive what is due to him for the things done while in the body, whether good or bad. -*2 Corinthians 5:10*

For God will bring every deed into judgement, including every hidden thing, whether it is good or evil. -*Ecclesiastes 12:14*

On Judgement Day, God will not ask to what sect you belonged, but what manner of life you led. -*I.M. Kagan*

Justified

Therefore, since we have been justified through faith, we have peace with God through or Lord Jesus Christ.

Knowledge

Seek not to grow in knowledge chiefly for the sake of applause, and to enable you to dispute others; but seek it for the benefit of your souls. -*Jonathan Edwards*

Labor

No labor, however humble, dishonors a man. -*Talmud*

Laws

Just as there are physical laws that govern the physical universe, so are there spiritual laws that govern our relationship with God.

There is God's law which all equitable laws of man emerge and by which men must live if they are not to die in oppression, chaos, and despair. -*Cicero*

The entire law is summed up in a single command: Love your neighbor as yourself. -*Galatians 5:14*

Life

Christians can be joyful in hope, patient in affliction, and faithful in prayer. -*The Bible*

Humanity is made in the image and likeness of God, and the purpose of our life is to glorify God by expressing God in every aspect of our existence in our daily living. -*John White*

I have set before you life and death, blessings and curses. Now choose life so that you and your children may live. -*Deuteronomy 30:19*

No life is pleasing to God that is not useful to man.

Light

I [Jesus] have come into the world as a light so that no one who believes in me should stay in darkness. -*John 12:46*

Limitations

Those who trust in their wealth and boast in the multitude of their riches, none of them can by any means redeem his brother, nor give to God a ransom for him. -*Psalm 49:6-7*

Listening

If you listen to me [God], you will know what is right, just, and fair. You will know what you should do. -*Proverbs 2:9*

Living

How to live when you're uncertain about your future...You live in hope and confidence that God is present in the world, and you live as a sign of God's presence. -*Reverend Kelly Peters*

Loneliness

The soul hardly ever-realizes it, but whether he is a believer or not, his loneliness is really a homesickness for God. -*Hubert Van Zeller*

Lord

Though my father and mother forsake me, the Lord will receive me. -*Psalm 27:10*

Love

It only takes a spark to get a fire going, and soon all those around can warm up in its glowing. -*Kurt Kaiser, 1934*

Let us love one another, for love comes from God. Everyone who loves has been born of God and knows God. Whoever does not love does not know God, because God is love. -*1 John 4:7-8*

Love of man leads to the love of God. -*Indian Proverb*

Love is the will to extend one's self for the purpose of nurturing one's own or another's spiritual growth. -*M. Scott Peck*

Of course, love is designed to be reciprocated, but true love is not about how lovable the object is but rather the heart of the one loving. -*Robert McQuilkin, President of Columbus Bible College*

One word frees us of all the weight and pain of life: that word is love. -*Sophocles, 401 BC*

The love we give away is the only love we keep. -*Elbert Hubbard*

There is no fear in love, but perfect love drives out fear. -*1 John 4:18*

Lying

Woe unto them that call evil good, and good evil; that put darkness for light, and light for darkness; that put bitter for sweet, and sweet for bitter! -*Isaiah 5:20*

Lust

Lust is an appetite by which temporal goods are preferred to eternal goods. -*St. Augustine*

Majority

A man with God is always in the majority. -*John Knox*

Make

God can make a way where there seems to be no way!

Malice

Get rid of all bitterness, rage and anger, brawling and slander, along with every form of malice. Be kind and compassionate to one another, forgiving each other, just as in Christ God forgave you. *-Ephesians 4:31-32*

Man/God

Since man is made in God's image, every human being is worthy of honor and respect; he is neither to be murdered nor cursed. *-Genesis 1:26*

Mankind

So God created man in his own image, in the image of God he created him; male and female he created them. *-Genesis 1:27*

Maturity

A mature Christian has a healthy attitude toward self and others- neither martyring one's self in a frenzy of taking care of others, nor lapsing into a life of self-centeredness. *-Reverend Kelly Peters*

Meditation

When the time is not right, God says 'Slow'; when the request is not right, God says 'No'; When you are not right, God says 'Grow'; When everything is right, God says 'Go.'

Meekness

What is usually misunderstood concerning meekness is that to which this quality relates. Meekness is our attitude toward God, not man. It is vertical, not horizontal. *-Charles R. Hembree*

Mercy

And His mercy is on those who fear Him from generation to generation. -*Luke 1:50*

His mercy hath no relation to time, no limitation to time; it is not first, nor last, but eternal, everlasting. -*John Donne*

Pour not water on a drowning mouse. -*Thomas Fuller, M.D, 1640*

Message

We don't change the Message, the Message changes us.

Ministry

The tender ministry of the Holy Spirit is expressed so beautifully through the heart of a mother helping, caring, comforting, and coming alongside her children with endless expressions of kindness, generosity, and love. -*Roy Lessin*

Misfortune

If all misfortunes were laid in one common heap whence everyone must take an equal portion, most people would be content to take their own and depart. -*Socrates*

Money

Most of what we spend money on eventually becomes worthless. However, money used to promote the Lord's work has eternal value. God's word is proclaimed…lives are changed…souls are won.

Morality

Morality is everywhere the same because it comes from God. -*Voltaire 1764*

Motive

All a man's ways seem innocent to him but motives are weighed by the Lord. -*Proverbs 16:2*

God is more pleased by one work, however small, done secretly, without desire to be known, than a thousand done with the desire that people know of then. -*John of the Cross*

Mystery

Anybody who claims he thoroughly understands God is somebody to be aware of. -Dick *Feagler, Columnist*

Nature

Anyone can count the seeds in an apple, but only God can count the number of apples in a seed. -*Robert H. Schuller*

Nature is the art of God. -*Dante*

Obedience

Anyone who breaks one of the least of these commandments and teaches others to do the same will be called least in the kingdom of heaven, but whoever practices and teaches these commandments will be called great in the kingdom of heaven. -*Matthew 5:19*

As we walk in obedience to the Word of God, we are kept clean and free from the defiling things of this world.

Peter and the other apostles replied, 'We must obey God rather than men!' -*Acts 5:29*

True obedience is true liberty. -*Henry Ward Beecher*

When we one day stand before our Creator, we will be judged by our obedience to Him, not our obedience to the world. -*D. Marylyn Kuivinen*

Opinion

The notion that one opinion is as good as another will not work in any other area of human experience, why should it work in the area of faith? -*David E. Trueblood*

Optimism

If more people would look up when everything seems to be going wrong, they would find that their lives would begin to look up too.

Originality

What has been will be again, what has been done will be done again; there is nothing new under the sun. -*Ecclesiastes 1:9*

Original Sin

Original sin is the only rational solution of the undeniable fact of the deep, universal, and early manifested sinfulness of men in all ages, of every class, and in every part of the world. -*Charles Hodge*

Other Religions

The Bible offers no hope that sincere worshipers of other religions will be saved without personal faith in Jesus Christ. -*The Gospel of Jesus Christ*

Overawed

Do not be overawed when a man grows rich, when the splendor of his house increases; for he will take nothing with him when he dies, his splendor will not descent with him. -*Psalm 49:16-17*

Parable

Parables are earthly stories with heavenly meanings. -*Editor*

Patience

Patience is trusting in God's timing.

Past/Future

God never consults your past to determine your future.

Patronizing

Never look down on anybody unless you are helping him up. *-Jesse Louis Jackson*

Peace

As long as our mind is stayed on our dear selves, we will never have peace. *-Dwight L. Moody*

As water is restless until it reaches its level, so the soul has no peace until it rest in God. *-Sundar Singh*

No Jesus, no peace; know Jesus, know peace.

Peacemakers who sow in peace raise a harvest of righteousness. *-James 4:18*

Peer Pressure

See to it that no one takes you captive through hollow and deceptive philosophy, which depends on human tradition and the basic principles of this world rather than on Christ. *-Colossians 2:8*

People

There are two kinds of people: those who say to God, "Thy will be done" and those to whom God says, "All right then, have it your way." *-C.S. Lewis*

Persecution

Blessed are those who are persecuted for righteousness' sake, for theirs is the kingdom of heaven. -*Matthew 5:10*

Piety

One cannot weep for the entire world. It is beyond human strength. One must choose. -*Jean Anouilh*

Set your mind on things above, not on things on the earth. -*Colossians 3:2*

The best way to see divine light is to put out thy own candle. -*Thomas Fuller, M.D., 1732*

The strength of a man consists in finding out the way in which God is going and go in that way too. -*Henry Ward Beecher, 1887*

Perfection

The love of God never looks for perfection in created beings. It knows that it dwells with Him alone. As it never expects perfection, it is never disappointed. -*Francois Fenelon*

Plans

Commit to the Lord whatever you do, and your plans will succeed. -*Proverbs 16:3*

'For I know the plans I have for you,' says the Lord. 'They are plans for good and not for evil, to give you a future and a hope.' -*Jeremiah 29:11*

Pleasure

Worldly pleasure is anything that crowds Christ out of your life.

Poor/Rich

In the sigh of a God no man is poor, but him who is wanting in goodness; and no man is rich but him who abounds in virtues. -*Lactantius*

Popularity

Woe unto you, when all men shall speak well of you. -*Luke 6:26*

Poverty

For those of us with faith, it is enough to remember that we are called on by the Lord not to eradicate poverty, but to help our neighbor. -*Foster S. Friess*

Power

He gives power to the weak, and to those who have no might He increases strength. -*Isaiah 40:29*

Prayer

A man who is intimate with God will never be intimidated by men. -*Leonard Ravenhill*

A prayer may chance to rise from one whose heart lives in the grace of God. A prayer from any other is unheeded. -*Dante, 1300*

As a child of God, prayer is kind of like calling home everyday.

A sinning man will stop praying. A praying man will stop sinning. -*Leonard Ravenhill*

Be joyful always; pray continually; give thanks in all circumstances, for this is God's will for you in Christ Jesus. -*1 Thessalonians 5:16-18*

Disturb us, O Lord, when we are too pleased with ourselves, when our dreams have come true because we have dreamed too little, when we have arrived in safety because we've sailed too close to shore...Stir us, O Lord, this day, to dare more boldly, to venture on wider seas, where storms shall show us Your majesty, where losing sight of land we will find the stars. - *Pastor Degner*

Do not make prayer a monologue; make it a conversation.

Do not pray for easy lives. Pray to be stronger men. Do not pray for tasks equal to your powers. Pray for powers equal to your tasks! Then the doing of your work shall be no miracle, but you shall be a miracle. Every day you will wonder at yourself, at the richness of life that has come to you by the Grace of God. -*Philip Brooks*

God answers to knee mail.

Holy God, you are greater than anything we can imagine. Plant within us your vision for a better world, and then inspire us to work to make it a reality, and to share the vision with others. -*Pastor Kelly Peters*

I believe God gives three answers to prayer: Yes, no, and I have something better in mind. -*Pastor Arthur Caliandro*

I can always pray for someone when I don't have the strength to help him in some other way. -*Andy Rooney*

If the only prayer we say in our lifetime is 'Thank You,' that would be enough. - *Meister Eckhardt*

I have lived to thank God that all my prayers have not been answered. -*Jean Ingelow*

In prayer it is better to have a heart without words than words without a heart. -*John Bunyan*

Is prayer your steering wheel or your spare tire? -*Corrie Ten Boom*

It is well said that neglected prayer is the birth-place of all evil. -*C.H. Suprgeon*

It is impossible to pray correctly apart from knowing and believing the teachings of Christ. -*John 15:7*

It is not well for a man to pray cream and live skim milk. -*Henry Ward Beecher*

Just pray for a tough hide and a tender heart. -*Ruth Graham*

Lord, help me to spend more time listening to Your Word than I do listening to the world's word. Your Word uplifts and builds; the world destroys and discourages.

Lord, help us to learn that the rest of our lives will only fall into place if you are our most important priority.

Lord, let my life be a window for your light to shine through. -*Editor*

More things are wrought by prayer than this world dreams of. -*Alfred Lord Tennyson*

My words fly up, my thoughts remain below. Words without thoughts never to heaven go. -*Shakespeare, 1600*

One of the best ways to get on your feet is to first get on your knees.

Pray as if everything depended on divine action and labor as if it didn't. -*St. Ignatius*

Pray to God but continue to row to shore. -*Russian Proverb*

Prayer changes things? No! Prayer changes people, and people change things.

Prayer is asking for rain; faith is carrying the umbrella. -*John Mason*

Prayer gives the power to absorb hurts and misfortune and to turn disadvantages into advantages. -*Dr. Norman Vincent Peale*

Prayer is more than talking with God; it's spending time in His word, seeking to know His will. -*Editor*

Steps-In-Prayer: Confession- Praise- Thanksgiving- Intercession- Petition. -*Editor*

The devil smiles when we make plans. He laughs when we get too busy. But he trembles when we pray- especially when we pray together. -*Corrie Ten Boom*

There is no part of religion so neglected as private prayer. -*J.C. Ryle*

Those who pray constantly are able to overcome any difficult, to solve any problem, and to handle life creatively and victoriously. -*Dr. Norman Vincent Peale*

Until you are convinced that time spent in prayer is the best use of your time, you will not find time for prayer. -*Editor*

We must lay before Him what is in us, not what ought to be in us. -*C.S. Lewis*

We must remember that 'no' can be an answer to a prayer. -*Katie Pinson*

Where there is not faith and confidence in prayer, the prayer is dead. -*Martin Luther*

Who rises from prayer a better man, his prayer is answered. -*George Meredith, 1859*

Prepare

Having oil in your lamp is a way of saying that you are living in such a way that your faith is strong, your convictions clear, your relationship with God already established. -*Reverend Kelly Peters*

Pride/Humility

Pride builds walls between people; humility builds bridges. *-Pastor Rick Warren*

Pride precedes a disaster, and an arrogant attitude precedes a fall. *-Proverbs 16:18*

Problem

Every problem is a character building opportunity, and the more difficult it is, the greater the potential for building spiritual muscle and moral fiber. Your circumstances are temporary, but your character will last forever. *-Pastor Rick Warren*

Protection

I am a creature of God, and he has an undoubted right to do with me as seemeth good in his sight. I rejoice that I am in his hand- that he is everywhere present and can protect me in one place as well as in another. *-Ann Hasseltine Judson*

Protestant/Catholic

The temptation of Protestantism has always been to magnify freedom at the expense of unity. The temptation of Roman Catholicism, on the other hand, has been to magnify unity at the expense of freedom. *-Samuel McCrea Cavert*

Providence

God gives, but man must open his hand. *-German Proverb*

God gives milk but not the pail. *-English Proverb*

Whoever falls from God's right hand is caught unto his left. *-Edwin Markham*

The Passion

My ultimate hope is that this story's message of tremendous courage and sacrifice might inspire tolerance, love, and forgiveness. -*Mel Gibson*

Pure

O Lord, help me to be pure, but not yet. -*St. Augustine*

Purity

It is not an inactive virtue; it does not merely consists in committing certain sins. It means using your life in the way God wants, exercising constant restraint. -*Francis Devas*

Purpose

Neither past nor future generations can serve God's purpose in this generation. -*Pastor Rick Warren*

Purgatory

God has placed two ways before us in His Word: salvation by faith, damnation by unbelief. He does not mention purgatory at all. Nor is purgatory to be admitted, for it obscures the benefits and grace of Christ. -*Martin Luther*

Rank

The good Lord sees your heart, not the braid on your jacket. Before Him, we are all in our birthday suits, generals and common men alike. -*Thomas Mann*

Reap/Sow

The one who sows to please his sinful nature, from that nature will reap destruction; the one who sows to please the Spirit, from the Spirit will reap eternal life. -*Galatians 6:8*

Recompense

God gives each his due at the time allotted. -*Euripides, 413 BC*

Relationship

Any relationship involves times of closeness and times of distance, and in a relationship with God, no matter how intimate, the pendulum will swing from one side to the other. -*Philip Yancey*

Religion

Frequently, religion has met with hostility on college campuses. But when it takes many students three quadruple espressos and unknown quantities of Prozac to get through the day, it's evident they need something more. -*Naomie Schaefer Riley, Author*

In prosperity no altars smoke. -*Italian Proverb*

It may be that religion is dead, and if it is, we had better know it and set ourselves to try to discover other sources of moral strength before it's too late. -*Pearl Buck, 1847*

Nature teaches us to love our friends, but religion- our enemies. -*Thomas Fuller, M.D., 1732*

We have just religion enough to make us hate, but not enough to make us love one another. -*Jonathan Swift, 1711*

Repentance

All criminals turn preachers when they are under the gallows. -*Italian Proverb*

Repent [change], then, and turn to God, so that your sins may be wiped out, that times of refreshing may come from the Lord. -*Acts 3:19*

The Bible teaches plainly, that as we die, whether converted or unconverted, whether believers or unbelievers, whether godly or ungodly, so shall we rise again when the last trumpet sounds. There is no repentance in the grace: there is no conversion after the last breath is drawn. *-J.C. Ryle*

The repentance of man is accepted by God as virtue. *-Voltaire, 1764*

To repent is to stop doing wrong, turn away from sin and move in the direction that the Bible tells us is correct. *-Luis Palau, Pastor*

Reputation

Reputation is what men and women think of us; character is what God and angels know of us.

Rest

Look around you and be distress; look within you and be depressed; look at Jesus and be at rest. *-Corrie Ten Boom*

My presence will go with you, and I will give you rest. *-Exodus 33:14*

Come to me, all you who are weary and burden, and I will give you rest. *-Matthew 11:28*

Resurrection

So will it be with the resurrection of the dead. The body that is sown is perishable, it is raised imperishable. *-1 Corinthians 15:42*

Retribution

But men never violate the laws of God without suffering the consequence, sooner or later. *-Lydia M. Child*

Reverence

Let us hear the conclusion of the whole matter: Fear God, and keep his commandments; for this is the whole duty of man. -*Ecclesiastes 12:13*

Righteousness

All my righteousness comes from You, God. Thank you. Remind me never to rely on my own version of righteousness.

Will the road you're on get you to my place? -*God*

Sabbath

The day you realize that God is all there is, every day will be the Sabbath Day for you. -*Emmet Fox, Author*

Salvation

Salvation is not putting a man in Heaven, but putting Heaven into a man. -*Maltbie D. Babcock*

Surely God is my salvation; I will trust and not be afraid. The Lord, is my strength and my song; He has become my salvation. -*Isaiah 12:2*

Strait is the gate, and narrow is the way, which leadeth to life, and few there be that find it. -*Matthew 7:14*

Good works will never produce salvation, but salvation should produce good works.

I tell you, now is the time of God's favor, now is the day of salvation. -*2 Corinthians 6:2*

Saved

And everyone who calls on the name of the Lord will be saved. -*Romans 10:13*

For it is by grace you have been saved, through faith- and this not from yourselves, it is the gift of God- not by works, so that no one can boast. -*Ephesians 2:8*

Science

We have grasped the mystery of the atom and rejected the Sermon on the Mount. -*General Omar N. Bradley*

Second Birth

That which is born of the flesh is flesh, and that which is born of the Spirit is spirit. -*John 3:7*

Second Coming

So Christ was sacrificed once to take away the sins of many people; and He will appear a second time, not to bear sin, but to bring salvation to those who are waiting for Him. -*Hebrews 9:28*

Scripture

All Scripture is given by inspiration of God, and is profitable for doctrine, for reproof, for correction, for instruction in righteousness. -*2 Timothy 3:16*

Security

The eternal God is your refuge, and underneath are the everlasting arms. -*Deuteronomy 33:27*

Seeking God

You will seek me and find me when you seek me with all your heart. -*Jeremiah 29:13*

Self-Control

The best way to be self-controlled is to be Christ-controlled.

Self-Esteem

It is difficult to make a man miserable while he feels worthy of himself and claims kindred to the great God who made him. *-Abraham Lincoln*

Self-Improvement

For God did not give us a spirit of timidity, but a spirit of power, of love, and of self-discipline. *-2 Timothy 1:7*

Self-Worth

For we are God's workmanship, created in Christ Jesus to do good works, which God prepared in advance for us to do. *-Ephesians 2:10*

Separation

All the nations will be gathered before Him, and He will separate them one another, as a shepherd divides his sheep from the goats. *-Matthew 25:32*

Serenity

Grant me the serenity to accept things I cannot change; the courage to change things I can, and wisdom to know the difference. *-Reinhold Niebhur*

Sermon

I'd rather see a sermon than hear one any day; I'd rather one should walk with me than merely tell the way. *-Edgar A. Guest*

Servant

If you will remind yourself at the start of every day that you are God's servant, interruptions won't frustrate you as much because your agenda will be whatever God wants to bring unto your life. Servants see interruptions as divine appointments for ministry. *-Pastor Rick Warren*

The Lord redeems the soul of His servants, and none of those who trust in Him shall be condemned. *-Psalm 34:22*

Serving

Each one should use whatever gift he has received to serve others. *-1 Peter 4:10*

If serving the Lord seems undesirable to you, then choose for yourselves this day whom you will serve…But as for me and my household, we will serve the Lord. *-Joshua 24:15*

God is not unjust; He will not forget your work and the love you have shown Him as you have helped His people and continue to help them. *-Hebrews 6:10*

Service

All service ranks the same with God. *-Robert Browning*

As we serve God, let us never become troubled or anxious about what God will do for us. Life is so short if we suffer a little less or a little more, that is no great thing, when we keep our sight on the kingdom that will last forever. *-Francois Fenelon*

The Lord doesn't ask about your ability, only your availability; and, if you prove your dependability, the Lord will increase your capability

.

The service of the less gifted brother is as pure as that of the more gifted, and God accepts both with equal pleasure. *-A.W. Tozer, Theologian*

Shame

Where there's no shame before men, there's no fear of God. -*Yiddish Proverb*

Sin

Anyone, then, who knows the good he ought to do and doesn't do it, sins. -*James 4:17*

As Christians we know that Jesus took the punishment for our sins onto Himself and therefore God will not punish us for specific sins. However, we must remember that sin often has consequences that God does not remove. -*Fred Grundmann, Author*

Every thought, word, and deed contrary to God's Law is sin; that every human being is a sinner by birth; that all evil in the world is the consequence of man's sinning. -*Martin Luther*

He who conceals his sins does not prosper, but whoever confesses and renounces them finds mercy. -*Proverbs 28:13*

Jesus is the atoning sacrifice for our sins, and not only for ours but also for the sins of the whole world. -*1 John 2:2*

No matter how many new translations of the Bible come out, the people still sin the same way.

Sins cannot be undone, only forgiven. -*Igor Stravinsky*

Sin is disobedience of God. -*Pastor Charles Stanley*

The acts of the sinful nature are obvious: sexual immorality, impurity, and debauchery; idolatry and witchcraft; hatred, discord, jealousy, fits of rage, selfish ambition, dissensions, factions, and envy; drunkenness, orgies, and the like. I warn you, as I did before, that those who live like this will not inherit the kingdom of God. -*Galatians 5:19-21*

There is not a righteous man on earth who does what is right and never sins. -*Ecclesiastes 7:20*

Sin/Forgiveness

It can take less than a minute to commit a sin. It takes not as long to obtain God's forgiveness. Penitence and amendment should take a lifetime. -*Hubert Van Zeller*

Soul

A fair face may fade, but a beautiful soul lasts forever.

Each of us possesses a soul, but we do not prize our souls as creatures made in God's image deserve, and so we do not understand the great secrets they contain. -*St. Teresa*

The soul, like the body, lives by what it feeds on. -*J.G. Holland*

Solution/Problem

You're either part of the solution or part of the problem. -*Eldridge Cleaver*

Spiritual Issues

Whenever we use human methods and human strategies to address spiritual issues, the battle is no longer God's; it is ours and Satan will whip us every time. -*Pastor Tony Evans*

Stewardship

Each man should give what he has decided in his heart to give, not reluctantly or under compulsion, for God loves a cheerful giver. -*2 Corinthians 9:7*

Stress

Cast all your anxiety on Him because He cares for you. -*1 Peter 5:7*

Success

Commit to the Lord whatever you do, and your plans will succeed. -*Proverbs 16:3*

Secret to success: do unto others as you would have done unto you. -*Scott Cowan, CEO*

What definition did Jesus give of 'success'? He said that true success is to complete one's life. It is to attain eternal life; all else is failure. -*Toyohiko Kagawa*

Suffering

God will not look you over for medals, degrees, or diploma, but for scars. -*Elbert Hubbard*

Man is born broken. He lives by mending. The Grace of God is the glue. -*Eugene O'Neil, 1926*

The relish of good and evil depends in a great measure upon the opinion we have of them. -*Montaigne, 1580*

Who is going to harm you if you are eager to do good? But even if you should suffer for what is right, you are blessed. -*1 Peter 3:13-14*

Temptation

Every temptation is an opportunity to do good and grow spiritually; maturity takes time; we should never give up. -*Pastor Rick Warren*

No temptation has seized you except what is common to man. And God is faithful; he will not let you be tempted beyond what you can bear. But when you are tempted, he will also provide a way out so that you can stand up under it. -*1 Corinthians 10:13*

Thankful

Thanking God daily stimulates the constant flow of His goodness. -*Norman Vincent Peale*

We ought to give thanks for all fortune: if it is 'good,' because it is good, if 'bad,' because it works in us patience, humility, and the contempt of this world and the hope of our eternal country. -*C.S. Lewis*

Things God Hates

A proud look, a lying tongue, hands that shed innocent blood, a heart that devises wicked plans, feet that are swift in running to evil, a false witness who speaks lies, and one who sows discord among brethren. -*Proverbs 6:17*

Think

It is of very little account what people think of us, but it is of vast importance what God thinks of us. -*D.L. Moody*

Time

But, beloved, do not forget this one thing, that with the Lord one day is as a thousand years, and a thousand years is as one day. - *2 Peter 3:8*

If you picture time as a straight line along which we have to travel, then you must picture God as the whole page upon which that line is drawn. -*C.S. Lewis*

Make the very most of your time…-*Ephesians 5:16*

The Ten Commandments

The Ten Commandments can be divided into two groups. The first four tell us how to love God. The Remaining six tell us how to love our neighbor. 'And God spoke all these words saying':
1. You shall have no other gods before Me.

2. You shall not make for yourself an idol.
3. You shall not take the name of the Lord your God in vain.
4. Remember the Sabbath day by keeping it holy.
5. Honor your father and your mother.
6. You shall not murder
7. You shall not commit adultery.
8. You shall not steal.
9. You shall not give false testimony against your neighbor.
10. You shall not covet.

The Commandments have always served as a strong guide to control violent outbursts and keep order in the world.

God uses the Commandments to remove the confusion about right and wrong in today's relativistic culture, protect us from the consequences of our own moral weakness, and guide our thinking and action in every situation. -*Dr. Ron Mehl*

They're the Ten Commandments not the ten suggestions.

Tongue

With the tongue we praise our Lord and Father, and with it we curse men, who have been made in God's likeness. Out of the same mouth come praise and cursing. My brothers, this should not be. -*James 3:9-10*

Thoughts

Human thought, makes the world in its own image. -*Adam Clayton Powell, 1967*

You're never too young or too old to trust God and follow Him on a new adventure of service. -*Editor*

Treasure

Better is a little with the fear of the Lord, than great treasure with trouble. -*Proverbs 15:16*

Trials

Save me, O God! For the waters have come up to my neck. -*Psalm 69:1*

The righteous cry out, and the Lord hears them; he delivers them from all their troubles. -*Psalm 34:17*

Tribulation

For it's through life's tribulations our faith takes roots and grows; and when shaken by life's trials, God's strength He then bestows. -*Linda J. Stevenson*

God, who foresaw your tribulation, has specially armed you to go through it, not without pain but without stain. -*C.S. Lewis*

Triune God

There is one Person of the Father, another of the Son, and another of the Holy Spirit: three distinct persons in one divine being (the Holy Trinity), the glory equal, the majesty co-eternal. -*Athanasian Creed*

Trouble

In this world you will have trouble, but take heart! I have overcome the world. -*John 16:33*

The Lord is good, a refuge in times of trouble. He cares for those who trust in Him. -*Nahum 1:7*

Trust

I know God won't give me anything I can't handle. I just wish He didn't trust me so much. -*Mother Teresa*

Trust in the Lord will all your heart, and lean not on your own understanding. In all your ways acknowledge Him, and He shall direct your paths. -*Proverbs 3:5-6*

Trust in God, but tie your camel. -*Persian Proverb*

Truth

And you shall know the truth, and the truth shall make you free. -*John 8:30*

Jesus said, "I am the way and the truth and the life." -*John 14:6*

We need to recognize God's truth, no matter whose mouth it comes out of. -*Elizabeth Elliot*

God offers to every mind its choice between truth and repose. Take which you please; you can never have both. -*Ralph Waldo Emerson*

Turn

God can turn any difficulty into an opportunity.

Unbelief

The fool says in his heart, there is no God. -*Psalm 14:1*

The writers against religion, whilst they oppose every system, are wisely careful never to set up any of their own. -*Edmund Burke, 1756*

Unfairness

Yes, life is unfair. If you choose to live your life looking for unfairness and complaining about it, you'll live a bitter and unhappy life. If you choose instead to live aware of God's grace and even participating in it, you'll live a gracious life. -*Pastor Kelly Peters*

Upright

Those who walk uprightly enter into peace; they find rest as they lie in death. -*Isaiah 57:2*

Values

Christianity teaches that there are true basic values that will serve everyone under all circumstances at all times. -*Editor*

Validity

We must not try to determine the validity of the word of God by our experiences; we must determine the validity of our experiences by the word of God. -*Professor Howard G. Hendricks*

Victory

For whatever is born of God overcomes the world. And this is the victory that has overcome the world: our faith. -*1 John 5:4*

Waiting

What God does in us while we wait is as important as what it is we are waiting for...Waiting is not just something we have to do while we get what we want. It is part of the process of becoming what God wants us to be. -*John Ortberg*

Ways

Christians are called to actively respond by showing that they are people who do not live according to the ways of this world, but according to the ways of God. -*Reverend Kelly Peters*

Weakness

The spirit is willing, but the body is weak. -*Matthew 26:41*

Wealth

It is easier for a camel to go through the eye of a needle than for a rich man to enter the kingdom of God. -*Matthew 19:24*

Weeping

Weeping may endure for a night, but joy cometh in the morning. *-Psalm 30:5*

Will

The will of the world is never the will of God. *-William Hamilton*

Wisdom

Don't expect wisdom to come into your life like great chunks of rock on a conveyor belt. It isn't like that. It's not splashy and bold...nor is it dispensed like a prescription across a counter. Wisdom comes privately from God as a by-product of right decisions, godly reactions, and the application of spiritual principles to daily circumstances. Wisdom comes...not from trying to do great things for God...but more from being faithful to the small, obscure tasks few people ever see. *-Charles R. Swindoll, Pastor*

If any of you lacks wisdom, he should ask God, who gives generously to all without finding fault, and it will be given to him. *-James 1:5*

The fear [reverence] of the Lord, that is wisdom; and to depart from evil is understanding. *-Job 28:28*

Wise

The next best thing to being wise oneself is to live in a circle of those who are. *-C.S. Lewis*

Witness

Do you attract attention toward or away from God?

Enthusiasm for God is contagious; has anyone caught it from you?

Words

Let no corrupt word proceed out of your mouth, but what is good for necessary edification, that it may impart grace to the hearers. -*Ephesians 4:29*

The fewer the words, the better the prayer. -*Martin Luther*

Work

God is not unjust; He will not forget the work and the love you have shown Him as you have helped His people and continue to help them. -*Hebrews 6:10*

The pastor's wife is the unsung hero in the Lord's work. -*Pastor Gary Woodard*

Whatever you do, work at it with all your heart, as working for the Lord, not for men, since you know that you will receive an inheritance from the Lord as a reward. -*Colossians 3:23*

World/God

A feeble compromise between God and world will satisfy neither. God will reject you, and the world will drag you falling into its snares. -*Francois Fenelon*

Children need to be taught what it means for them to be in the world but not of it. That God's standards should influence the world and not the other way around. -*Editor*

For God did not send His Son into the world to condemn the world, but to save the world through Him. -*John 3:17*

You can please the world and not please God, or you can please God and not please the world. You can't do both. -*Pastor John Hagee*

See to it that no one takes you captive through hollow and deceptive philosophy, which depends on human tradition and the basic principles of this world rather than on Christ. *-Colossians 2:8*

Our Lord did not ask us to give up the things of earth, but to exchange them for better things. *-Fulton J. Sheen*

Worldly people harden under adversity; unworldly people, more ready to accept, become more flexible. The world does not like being shaped according to God's plan; the spirit does. *-Hubert Van Zeller*

You can in no manner be satisfied with temporal goods, for you were not created to find your rest in them. *-Thomas A. Kempis*

Worldliness

Do not love the world and what it offers. The world and its desires pass away, but the person who does the will of God lives forever. *-1 John 2:13,17*

Do not conform any longer to the pattern of this world. But be transformed by the renewing of your mind. *-Romans 12:2*

Worry

Never worry about anything. But in every situation let God know what you need, always asking Him with a thankful heart. And with God's peace, which is far beyond human understanding, will keep your hearts and minds safe, in union with Christ Jesus. *-Philippians 4:6-7*

Worship

He worships God who knows Him. *-Seneca, 100AD*

God is Spirit, and those who worship Him must worship in spirit and truth. *-John 4:24*

Jesus said, "It is written: worship the Lord your God and serve Him only." -*Luke 4:8*

The perfect church service would be one we were almost unaware of; our attention would have been on God. -*C.S. Lewis*

What is worship? Worship is the tenth leper turning back. -*Martin Luther*

When someone says, "Oh, I can worship God anywhere," the answer is, "Do you?" -*James A. Pike*

Zealous

First have a zealous regard for yourself and your own soul, and then you may more righteously and with better ordered charity have zeal for your neighbor's soul. -*Thomas A. Kempis*

INDEX